Sexist
Justice

Sexist Justice

by **Karen DeCrow**

Vintage Books
A Division of Random House
New York

FIRST VINTAGE BOOKS EDITION, February 1975

Copyright © 1974 by Karen DeCrow

All rights reserved under International and Pan-American Copyright Conventions. Published in the United States by Random House, Inc., New York, and simultaneously in Canada by Random House of Canada Limited, Toronto. Originally published by Random House, Inc., in 1974.

Library of Congress Cataloging in Publication Data

DeCrow, Karen.
Sexist justice.

Includes bibliographical references.
1. Women—Legal status, laws, etc.—United States.
2. Women—Legal status, laws, etc. I. Title.
[KF478.D4 1975]   346'.73'013   74–16440
ISBN 0–394–71359–1

Manufactured in the United States of America

*To Claudia Abt Lipschultz, who was my
dear sister before it was fashionable*

Acknowledgments

My thanks to the following persons, who helped me in the preparation of this book, by supplying me with case citations, ideas, or legal advice: Carolyn S. Bratt, Charlotte Adelman, Claudia Abt Lipschultz, David Diamond, Evelyn Sojda, Gene Boyer, J. William Hicks, Kay Doherty, Lillian Reiner, Marcia Boyd, Marguerite J. Fisher, Martin L. Fried, Nola Claire, Paula Franklin, Richard Abt, Shirley R. Bysiewicz, and Thomas J. Maroney.

Special thanks go to my mother, Juliette Abt Lipschultz, who works as my "clipping service," by going through countless newspapers and magazines each month, to find articles on women and the law.

I thank my editor, Toni Morrison, who, using the carrot theory rather than the stick theory, kept me happy the whole time I was writing this book. And, I am grateful to my copy editor, Cordelia Jason, and to Phyllis La-Vine, who helped me with my footnotes.

I thank Jeffrey Weitzman, who was my one fellow student in law school who never asked, "What's a thirty-one-year old woman doing here?" but, rather, treated me like a human being.

Lastly, I thank two friends—Joy and Howard Osofsky—without whom this book would never have been written. When I was sure I could never make it through law school, they, with affection, assured me that I could. So I enrolled.

Karen DeCrow
March 9, 1973

Contents

Sexist
Justice

Chapter One
Women and the Law:
A Study in Misogyny

Great cases like hard cases make bad law. For great cases are called great, not by reason of their real importance in shaping the law of the future, but because of some accident of immediate overwhelming interest which appeals to the feelings and distorts the judgment. These immediate interests exercise a kind of hydraulic pressure.

—*Northern Securities Co. v. United States,*
193 U.S. 197, 400–01 (1904)

꘎꘎꘎ This book is not a summary or a compendium of the laws on women. It is a feminist analysis of the laws, the legislators, the judges, the lawyers and the law professors that make up our legal system. Clearly, the "hydraulic pressure" at work in virtually all litigation involving women is the misogyny present in legal institutions, and in the men who create and run them.

Women have fared miserably under the law, not only in the decisions which went against us, but even in the cases that went "for" us; and we are deluding ourselves if we think that women can get justice in the courts. The record of court decisions, statutes, state constitutions, and legislative interpretations—all of these were written by men. And until they begin to be written by feminist women and feminist men, women will never achieve equity in our legal system.

Nor is it necessary to practice law for decades to be overwhelmed by this absence of equity, for it is obvious at the very beginning of legal training. So pervasive is sexism in legal education that the few women who do go through law school are invariably radicalized. If they are not, it is because they are convinced (by fellow students, professors, and the textbooks) that they are a special kind of woman—intelligent, probably not as intelligent as the men students, but clearly not of the same breed as the "regular" women in the United States.

I was the only woman in my class when I went to law school. I went at age thirty-one, with every conceivable roadblock in front of me—financial, conjugal, social and, most important, my own lack of self-confidence. During my interview, the dean asked me why I didn't have a baby. (The concern for women lawyers to also be mothers is very strong.) When Judge Nanette Dembitz, the first woman to run for the New York Court of Appeals, was interviewed by members of the Bar Association, she was asked how she could handle her "family responsibilities" while sitting on the bench in Albany, New York. (Judge Dembitz is fifty-nine years old and lives in New York City.)

There are now thirty-one women in the freshman class at my law school, which signifies not only a welcome increase in the number of women lawyers, but a surcease of the loneliness and isolation of any woman who aspires to enter the legal profession. While I was in school I tried to ignore much of the sexism around me —a self-preservative device, for I was afraid that if I mentioned any anti-woman bias I would be thought paranoid.

There *is* anti-woman bias in almost every case that deals with women. Obvious cases which prove this point are those which simply say that women can't vote, can't serve on juries, and can't tend bar in the state of X. Less obvious, but more important, are the cases that do not deal directly with sex discrimination, but with other matters entirely, in which women are plaintiffs or defendants. What the judge says about them, in passing, gives us the clue to what the jurisprudential world thinks of women.

Critical to a law student's legal understanding is a study of the comments and suggestions which follow each case in the book. As one might guess, the authors and editors of the casebooks are men, although one can assume that the editorial assistants working in the legal publishing houses are often women.

As I select examples from the casebooks, unless I am quoting directly, I am constantly forced to revise the language. References to "unchaste women," "adulterous women," "his mistress," "the mother's indiscretions," abound.

For example, in a textbook on *Trial Tactics and Methods*,[1] a seemingly sex-free subject area, the author goes into detail on how female witnesses burst into tears (which will only make the jury think you are a nasty man), and therefore the lawyer should be careful when questioning them. (Incidentally, in all legal textbooks it is assumed that the attorney is male, and that the secretaries in the office are female.) The men who conduct the New York bar review course, in addition to sprinkling the lectures liberally with jokes about large-breasted women, tell the future lawyers how to "handle" their secretaries. "If you want her to work overtime, buy her some nice perfume or something," they advise. Not surprisingly, Mr. Keeton, author of the trial tactics book, dedicated it "To Betty: who, substituting intuition for legal training, read the manuscript and caused me to rewrite every sentence she thought she did not understand. If you find the meaning of any passage obscure, seek the explanation of another with intuition."

In a section on whether you should cross-examine each witness separately, he discusses whether husbands and wives should both be examined.

> A wife may be forgiven for believing naïvely in her husband; she may even be applauded for doing so. Probably a jury would not conclude that your failure to cross-examine P's [plaintiff's] wife indicates that you acquiesce in the truth and accuracy of her testimony.[2]

Who are the writers of the opinions lauding the nobility, dignity, and grace of the deferring wife? They are men, and probably they are husbands. Although we like to think of our judges as objective, a review of judges' opinions in matters concerning women will show that people are what they are. President Nixon appointed judges who would vote as he expected them to, and they are doing just that. It is far better to remove the legal fiction of objectivity, and try to create balanced courts (as to sex, race, and economic class), than to appoint and elect all elderly, white, wealthy males—and then be surprised that they decide cases like elderly, white, wealthy males.

Glendon Schubert, a social scientist, has done many studies of judicial behavior. He concludes[3] that the U.S. Supreme Court does much more than decide cases— it makes policy. And not surprisingly, the attitudes previously held by each Justice cause him to vote in certain ways. The courts, therefore, behave like legislatures: the men who sit on them decide and vote according to their social, economic, and political beliefs.

The implications of this for issues relevant to the First and Fourth Amendment guarantees are enormous, but it is not the function of this book to explore them. What we do know, and should remember, is that the judges are male, and we have no evidence that they are liberated males. They received their sociopolitical training in a sexist country, and their legal training in sexist law schools. Therefore, it is an important function of women lawyers, and all women interested in justice, to help to educate these men to a brand of justice and equality which includes women.

Jerome Frank suggested that judges undergo psychoanalysis so that their biases would become apparent to them. Although a biased judge is predictable (and lawyers apparently feel more comfortable when case outcomes can be predicted), Frank thought that an unbiased judge would be more fair.

Before analyzing some cases, a few more words are in order about legal education, through which every lawyer and judge must go. A popular first-year property casebook explains "For, after all, land, like woman, was meant to be possessed."[4]

Ruth Bader Ginsburg notes that constitutional law is probably the most conspicuous area in which treatment of women by the law has been overlooked in the law schools.[5] "Standard casebooks deal with problems of classification and discrimination, relating principally to race, but also to alienage, condition of birth, and economic situation."

Two cases involving women are generally reported or extracted in historical context but not from the perspective at which contemporary feminists view them. *Muller v. Oregon*,[6] upholding state legislation limiting working hours for women after the Supreme Court had rejected a state attempt at hours limitation applicable to both sexes, is noted as one of a series marking the Supreme Court's retreat from substantive due process limitations on state economic regulation and as the occasion of the initiation of the Brandeis brief.

That *Muller* provided the legal basis for protective legislation for women, and is still used, sixty-four years later, to argue against the Equal Rights Amendment, is not mentioned by constitutional law professors—probably because they don't think about it. More important, and also not mentioned in the constitutional law texts, or by the teachers, is that *Muller* provided language which was seized upon to extend the doctrine of *sex as a basis for legislative classification.*

Professor Ginsburg discusses another landmark case which excludes women from the Equal Protection Clause.[7]

> *Goesaert v. Cleary,*[8] upholding a statute which kept bar ownership a male monopoly, is noted in the context of traditional equal protection standards and state restrictions on a business entry. Not even a note suggests the relationship of these decisions to the current controversy surrounding equal rights for women. Indeed, the proposed Equal Rights Amendment, although it has been in the congressional hopper for decades, is not mentioned.

When I was discussing the hiring of a woman tax law professor with one of my male law professors, he told me that a "woman law professor was a contradiction in terms." Law school hiring committees allegedly look for tax professors who are interested in policy, as well as those who can read and understand the Internal Revenue Code. However, one area of policy that is never discussed or thought about is the ramifications of the Code for women—wives, mothers, and especially working mothers.

If the judges, male and trained in male-oriented law schools, will not look fairly at women in court, perhaps women can fare better with the jury. Yet that, too, presents problems.

In the sixties, the U.S. Supreme Court was still allowing women to be absent from juries. An earlier case, in the thirties in Massachusetts,[9] outlined the issues. The defendant had complained that no women were on the lists from which the jurors were drawn. The Supreme Court of Massachusetts took eight pages to explain how originally jurors were drawn from people who voted, and how women did not have the vote when the state statute outlining jury selection procedures was passed.

It is clear beyond peradventure that the words of G.L. c. 234, paragraph 1 [the jury selection statute], when originally enacted could not by any possibility have included or been intended by the general court to include women among those liable to jury duty.[10]

G.L. c. 234, paragraph 1, had stated, "A person qualified to vote for representatives to the general court shall be liable to serve as a juror." The court then went into a lengthy discussion of the meaning of the word "person," trying to decide whether this included women. Reviewing many cases that covered many years, the court concluded that "person" has meant many things at many times—including a national bank, a corporation, a society, association, or partnership—but apparently not a woman. It quoted from a 1909 English case, which relied on Acts of Parliament of 1868 and 1881, wherein the university franchise was conferred upon "every person" whose name was on the register and on whom degrees had been conferred. At that time women were not admitted to graduation and could not receive degrees. In 1889, a further act was passed for the appointment of commissioners with extensive regulatory powers over universities. These commissioners adopted an ordinance enabling the universities to confer degrees on women for satisfactory academic accomplishments. The appellants, having received degrees upon graduation, contended that they had a right to vote. The court did not agree:[11]

> It proceeds upon the supposition that the word "person" in the act of 1868 did include women, though not then giving them the vote, so that at some later date an Act purporting to deal only with education might enable commissioners to admit them to the degree, and thereby also indirectly confer upon them the franchise. It would require a convincing demonstration to satisfy me that Parliament intended to effect a constitutional change so *momentous and farreaching by so furtive a process*. [emphasis mine] It is a dangerous assumption to suppose that the Legislature foresees every possible result that may ensue from the unguarded use of a single word, or that the language used in statutes is so precisely accurate that you can pick out from various Acts this and that expression and, skillfully piecing them together, lay a safe foundation for some remote inference.

What the judge, Lord Loreburn, is saying is that we lawyers cannot here do what we usually do—use the language from prior statutes and cases—to draw conclusions about present cases. The Lord discusses *Viscountess Rhondda's Claim*,[12] that an act of Parliament passed in 1919, providing that "A person shall not be disqualified by sex or marriage from the exercise of any public function," did not entitle a peeress of the United Kingdom in her own right to receive the writ of summons to Parliament.

Later in this chapter, we will see how the judges reacted to women who wanted the franchise. In *Welosky*, the judge had apparently accepted that abomination, but clearly could not see how voting rights led to the right to serve on a jury. He concluded that Ms. Welosky's rights had not been abridged, and that she had been judged by a jury "of her peers," even though no women were among them.[13]

> The Nineteenth Amendment to the federal Constitution conferred the suffrage upon an entirely new class of human beings. It did not extend the right to vote to members of an existing classification theretofore disqualified, but created a new class. It added to qualified voters those who did not fall within the meaning of the word "person" in the jury statutes . . . The change in the legal status of women wrought by the Nineteenth Amendment was radical, drastic and unprecedented. While it is to be given full effect in its field, it is not to be extended by implication. *It is unthinkable that those who first framed and selected the words for the statute now embodied in G.L. c. 234, had any design that it should ever include women within its scope.* [emphasis mine] . . . When they used the word "person" in connection with those qualified to vote for members of the more numerous branch of the general court, to describe those liable to jury service, no one contemplated the possibility of women becoming so qualified.

> . . . No intention to include women can be deduced from the omission of the word "male."

> . . . The conclusion is that, by the true construction of the statues of this commonwealth, in the light of relevant constitutional provisions, women are not eligible

to jury service and that the preparation of the jury lists from which the jury in the case at bar was drawn from men alone was right.

. . . The contention of the defendant is that, by reason of the exclusion of women from the jury list, she has been denied the equal protection of the laws contrary to the guaranty contained in the Fourteenth Amendment to the federal Constitution.

. . . We think that the defendant has not been deprived of the equal protection of the laws guaranteed to her under the Fourteenth Amendment to the federal Constitution.

For the reasons already stated, we are of the opinion that the defendant has had a trial by the judgment of her peers in conformity to the requirement of article 12 of the Declaration of Rights of the Constitution of this commonwealth. She has been tried by a jury selected according to the standing and valid laws of the commonwealth and according to the principles of the common law.

. . . Exceptions overruled.

Ms. Welosky was indeed tried by the principles of the common law. As Chief Justice Gray points out, in *Robinson's Case*:[14]

Whenever the legislature has intended to make a change in the legal rights or capacities of women, it has used words clearly manifesting its intent and the extent of the change intended. . . . In making innovations upon the long-established system of law on this subject, the legislature appears to have proceeded with great caution, one step at a time; and the whole course of legislation precludes the inference that any change in the legal rights or capacities of women is to be implied, which has not been clearly expressed.

One textbook where the *Welosky* case appears is Mishkin and Morris's highly regarded *On Law in Courts*.[15] This text is an introduction to judicial development of case and statute law, and is designed to help the law student "think like a lawyer." The *Welosky* case was used to illustrate the construction and application of statutes. Mishkin and Morris go through a long and carefully thought-out analysis of the statute, of the word "person," and of the importance of considering legislative intent. They never mention the content of the case—certainly an acceptable omission when illustrating form or structure, but certainly an unacceptable omission when you are trying to teach law students to think like lawyers, i.e., to seek justice. Specifically, what we learn here is that because the legislature never in their wildest dreams intended for women to be persons enough to serve on juries (even when trying other women), the court cannot reason from the voting amendment to a revision of the jury statute.

The first page of the Mishkin and Morris text contains a quote from Plato, *Laws*, Book I:

> Athenian Stranger: Your laws being wisely framed, one of the best of your laws is that which enjoins that none of the youth shall inquire which laws are wrong and which right, but all shall declare in unison, with one mouth and one voice, that all are rightly established.
>
> Well, there are no young people with us now; so we may be permitted by the law giver, old as we are, to discuss these matters among ourselves privately without offense.

Certainly, if women are ever to get justice in the courts, we will have to stop operating under not the legal method, but the mystical legal formalism which can be used to whatever ends the legal mind using it chooses.

The authors ask the students to "among other things, consider in what relevant sense women constitute 'an entirely new class of human beings.' Is this a statement of the view of the enacting legislature or of this court?"[16] The moral content in such speculation is similar to an artisan's doing a careful analysis of the best ways to make lampshades out of human skin. If we are to change the laws and their application to women, looking to *either* legislative intent or judicial reasoning will be disastrous, since neither the legislators nor the judges even approach feminist consciousness.

Mishkin and Morris advise the students:[17]

> The problem then becomes whether judicial construction of the statute should be confined within those meanings which its words can reasonably be made to bear.
>
> . . . Certainly the precise words of a statute are of prime importance. Those words are the subject of the formal votes of the legislature; those words must be approved in identical form by both houses of a bicameral legislature; and those words are approved by the Governor or President.
>
> . . . the majority of states held women eligible to serve as jurors.
> . . . This was true despite the fact that the relevant statutes at times used the word "men" (e.g., grand jury to consist of "fifteen good and lawful men").

Ruth Bader Ginsburg also notes the total lack of attention to content in the treatment of a consortium case, used in conflicts of laws textbooks.[18] The conflicts casebooks currently in use report or note a 1967 decision of the Oregon Supreme Court[19] as illustrative of a "true conflicts" case. The court wrestled with the problem of whether to apply forum law (the law of the place of the litigation), allowing a forum wife to collect for loss of consortium (the right to sexual services) or the law of the place of injury, which allowed such recovery to a husband but not to a wife.

Professor Ginsburg notes:[20]

> Oregon took a "restrained," if not "enlightened," view and deferred to the law of the state where the accident occurred. The court barely considered the possibility of a "no conflict" solution; if the sister state law, recognizing a right in the husband but not in the wife, had been put to the rational classification test of the fourteenth amendment's equal protection clause, the higher authority of the Constitution should have resolved the conflict.[21] Sauce for the gander should serve as sauce for the goose as well.

Jury cases are another good barometer as to where the courts are, vis-à-vis women. In 1916, the U.S. Supreme Court found no suspicion of denial of equal protection of the laws when only 10 of 10,000 jurors were women, and justified this because "Woman is still regarded as the center of home and family life."[22] In this, the famous *Hoyt v. Florida* case, the court required a woman but not a man to register affirmatively for jury service.

As Wilma Scott Heide, president of NOW, points out, with reference to the *Hoyt* decision:[23] "Stereotyped psychological conditioning momentarily aside, this is blatant sex discrimination."

Although *White v. Crook*[24] later declared that "jury service is a responsibility and a right that should be shared by all citizens, regardless of sex,"[25] women serve on the same grounds as men in only twenty-eight states.[26] The common law tradition was that juries were composed of men, except in certain situations involving a pregnant woman. Only recently have three states (Alabama, South Carolina, and Mississippi) changed their policies of totally excluding women from juries; only since 1957 has service on federal juries been equalized for men and women.[27]

In a 1970 decision,[28] a New York trial court rejected the challenge of a female plaintiff to a jury system with automatic exemptions for women. As a result of these exemptions, women constituted less than 20 percent of the available jury pool. (Whereas a man had to state some ground to be excused from jury service, a woman merely had to state, "I am a woman.") The judge advised the woman plaintiff that she was in the "wrong forum":

> Her lament should be addressed to the "Nineteenth Amendment State of Womanhood" which prefers cleaning and cooking, rearing of children and television soap operas, bridge and canasta, the beauty parlor and shopping, to becoming embroiled in plaintiff's problems.[29]

The same judge also inquired considerately, "What woman would want to expose herself to the peering eyes of women only?"

The right to serve on a jury seems to be linked, in the state statutes and in men's minds, to the right to vote. *The* case on the right to vote is that of Susan B. Anthony. She was tried for—nothing more, nothing less—being a woman.

As Sophy Burnham and Janet Knight[30] point out in

their recent article on the trial, women have been written out of history.

> The annals of political trials bring to mind many familiar names: Socrates, Jesus, Dreyfus, Bobby Seale, the Berrigans, Ellsberg. All are men. It is not as easy to conjure up many women for this list; not that they haven't existed, but that historians have never felt their efforts added much to the general development of "mankind." Joan of Arc and Anne Boleyn are occasionally cited, usually in a more general context, as martyrs or misguided unfortunates.

It was on November 1, 1872, that Susan B. Anthony registered, illegally, to vote. On November 5, she led a small group of women to the polls in Rochester, New York. They all voted. On November 18, Susan B. Anthony was arrested by a U.S. marshal. As she boarded the bus, she told the driver, "I am traveling at the expense of the government. This gentleman is escorting me to jail. Ask him for my fare."

The prosecutor at the trial, Richard Crowley, relied on the old circular reasoning of legislative intent. Susan B. Anthony was a woman, and therefore not entitled to vote. She, knowing that she was a woman and not entitled to vote, had voted anyway. Whatever her intention, good or bad, she was guilty. It was certainly not for the courts to interpret the Constitution. That was the job of Congress. At the trial, the prosecutor stated:[31]

> . . . and upon the fifth day of November, 1872, she voted for a Representative in the Congress of the United States . . . At that time she was a woman. I suppose there will be question about that!

Her attorney, Henry Selden, summarized the charges:

> The only alleged ground of illegality of the defendant's vote is that she is a woman. If the same act had been done by her brother under the same circumstances, the act would have been not only innocent, but honorable and laudable; but having been done by a woman, it is said to be a crime. The crime therefore consists not in the act done, but in the simple fact that the person doing it was a woman and not a man. I believe this is the first instance in which a woman has been arraigned in a criminal court, merely on account of her sex.

Just as "uppity" blacks are advised to "go back to Africa," *The Albany Law Journal*, a state trade paper, advised Susan B. Anthony that if she didn't like our laws she should "emigrate."

Ms. Anthony was not permitted to speak at her trial. At her sentencing, however, she was. Her speech is a most eloquent summary of the subjugation of women in, as the popular song says, "A Man's World."

> All of my prosecutors—from the eighth-ward corner grocery politician who entered the complaint, to the United States Marshal, Commissioner, District Attorney, District Judge, your Honor on the bench—not one is my peer, but each and all are my political sovereigns; and had your honor submitted my case to the jury, as was clearly your duty, even then should I have had just cause of protest, for not one of those men was my peer . . . Even my counsel, the Hon. Henry R. Selden, who has argued my cause so ably, so earnestly, so unanswerably before your Honor, is my political sovereign. Precisely as no disenfranchised person is entitled to sit upon a jury, and no woman is entitled to the franchise, so none but a regularly admitted lawyer is allowed to practice in the courts, and no woman can

gain admission to the bar—hence, jury, judge, counsel, must all be of the superior class.

Judge Hunt: The Court must insist—the prisoner has been tried according to the established forms of law.

S.B.A.: Yes, your Honor, but by forms of law all made by men, interpreted by men, in favor of men, and against women; and hence, your Honor's ordered verdict of guilty, against a United States citizen for the exercise of that citizen's right to vote simply because that citizen was a woman and not a man . . .

Judge Hunt: The prisoner will stand up. The sentence of the Court is that you pay a fine of one hundred dollars, and the costs of the prosecution.

S.B.A.: May it please your Honor, I shall never pay a dollar of your unjust penalty. All the stock in trade I possess is a ten-thousand dollar debt, incurred by publishing my paper—the *Revolution*—four years ago, the sole object of which was to educate all women to do precisely as I have done, rebel against your manmade unjust, unconstitutional forms of law, that tax, fine, imprison, and hang women, while they deny them the right of representation in the government; and I shall work on with might and main to pay every dollar of that honest debt, but not a penny shall go to this unjust claim. And I shall earnestly and persistently continue to urge all women to the practical recognition of the old revolutionary maxim, that resistance to tyranny is obedience to God.

Judge Hunt: Madam, the Court will not order you committed until the fine is paid.

The hundred-dollar fine was small, but by refusing to imprison Susan until she paid the fine—as was the usual practice—Judge Hunt prevented her from appealing the case to the Supreme Court on a writ of habeas corpus. (Habeas corpus means literally you "have the body." The sole function of the writ is to release a person from unlawful imprisonment.)

Had the case been appealed, it probably would have been won, since Susan was denied a trial by jury. She never paid the fine; the government never tried to collect.

Years later, Selden's trial assistant, John Van Voorhis, wrote:[32] "There never before was a trial in the country of one-half the importance as this of Miss Anthony's." And, many years later, in 1947, Gertrude Stein and Virgil Thomson wrote, in their song, "The Mother of Us All:"[33]

> Susan B. was right, she said she was right and she was right.

An 1874 U.S. Supreme Court case, *Minor v. Happersett*,[34] established clearly that women could not get the vote through the courts, but would have to go the painfully slow route through the legislatures. (Suffrage was not won until August 26, 1920.) *Minor* held that the right of suffrage had not been one of the privileges or immunities of citizenship before the adoption of the Fourteenth Amendment; therefore the amendment did not add these privileges and immunities. The Fourteenth Amendment simply furnished additional guaranty for the protection of such rights as the citizen already had.

It is important to understand what sections of the Constitution this controversy centered about. The Fourteenth Amendment, Section 1, states that "All persons born or naturalized in the United States, and subject to the jurisdiction thereof, are citizens of the United States, and of the State wherein they reside. No State shall make or enforce any law which shall abridge the privileges or immunities of citizens of the United States." This section extended the privileges and immunities of citizens of this country from the original conceptualization in Article IV, Section 2, of the Constitution.

The Fifteenth Amendment, Section 1, states that "The right of citizens of the United States to vote shall not be denied or abridged by the United States or by any State on account of race, color, or previous condition of servitude."

Reading those two sections together, many women in the early suffrage movement dared to hope that they would be included among the "persons" who should not have their privileges and immunities denied. However, *Minor* made it very clear that the Fourteenth Amendment gave no new rights; it simply strengthened the rights which (male) persons already had. Neither the Constitution nor the Fourteenth Amendment made all citizens voters. A provision in a state constitution which confined the right of voting to "male" citizens of the United States, was "no violation of the Federal Constitution. In such a State, women have no right to vote."[35]

On October 15, 1872, Virginia Minor had tried to register to vote in the November elections in the state of Missouri. Her husband was her lawyer, and argued that the elective franchise was the greatest privilege and immunity. The Court wrote a long essay on citizenship, taking six pages to prove that women are indeed citizens. Voting requirements, however, the Court left to the states. (In various states, at that time, one needed money, or property, or a certain residency requirement, etc.)

. . . On this condition [varied requirements] of the law in respect to suffrage in the several States it cannot for a moment be doubted that if it had been intended to make all citizens of the United States voters, the framers of the Constitution would not have left it to implication.

. . . No new State has ever been admitted to the Union which has conferred the right of suffrage upon women, and this has never been considered a valid objection to her [the State's] admission.

Notice the best legal minds of the nineteenth century at work on Catch-22: If the fathers of our country had intended for women to vote, they would have said so in the Constitution. As new states get admitted to the Union, not a single one has ever allowed its women citizens to vote. This omission has not been considered fatal to admission. *Therefore*, we can't see that this is a valid constitutional issue.

One state—New Jersey—had given women the franchise, but in 1807 withdrew the right. The original suffrage statute of New Jersey defined as voters: "All inhabitants . . . of full age who are worth fifty pounds, proclamation-money, clear estate in the same, and have resided in the county in which they claim a vote for twelve months immediately preceding the election."

. . . On the contrary, . . . the right of suffrage was withdrawn from women as early as 1807 in the State of New Jersey without any attempt to obtain the interference of the United States to prevent it. Since then the governments of the insurgent States have been reorganized under a requirement that before their representatives could be admitted to seats in Congress they must have adopted new constitutions, republican in form. In no one of these constitutions was suffrage conferred upon women, and yet the States have all been restored to their original position as States in the Union.

. . . Our province is to decide what the law is, not to decide what it should be.

. . . The constitutions and laws of the several States which commit that important trust [the right to vote] to men alone are not necessarily void.[36]

So, the Court held that possession of citizenship did not confer the right to vote. *Minor* was the women's *Plessy v. Ferguson.*[37] This famous, now supposedly overruled case, declared the "separate but equal" doctrine.

An 1890 Louisiana statute required that all railway passenger coaches in the state have "equal but separate accommodations for the white, and colored races" and that seating be racially segregated. Mr. Plessy, alleging that he "was 7/8 Caucasian and 1/8 African blood; that the mixture of colored blood was not discernible in him; and that he was entitled to every right . . . of the white race," was arrested for refusing to vacate a seat in a coach where white passengers were accommodated. His attack on the statute's constitutionality was denied by Louisiana's supreme court.

The Supreme Court upheld the Louisiana court. Mr. Justice Brown, speaking for the Court, held:[38]

Laws permitting, and even requiring, their separation, in places where they are liable to be brought into contact . . . have been generally, if not universally, recognized as within the competency of the state legislatures in the exercise of their police power. The most common instance of this is connected with the establishment of separate schools for white and colored children, which have been held to be a valid exercise of the legislative power even by courts of states where the political rights of the colored race have been longest and most earnestly enforced.

Brown quotes from a Massachusetts case which provided for racially segregated schools.[39]

> The great principle advanced by the learned and eloquent advocate for the plaintiff (Charles Sumner), is that, by the constitution and laws of Massachusetts, all persons, without distinction of age or sex, birth or color, origin or condition, are equal before the law. . . . But, when this great principle comes to be applied to the actual and various conditions of persons in society, it will not warrant the assertion that men and women are legally clothed with the same civil and political powers, and that children and adults are legally to have the same functions and be subject to the same treatment; but only that the rights of all, as they are settled and regulated by law, are equally entitled to the paternal consideration and protection for their maintenance and security.

Justice Brown also cites the laws on miscegenation:[40]

> Laws forbidding the intermarriage of the two races may be said in a *technical sense* [emphasis mine] to interfere with the freedom of contract, and yet have been universally recognized as within the police power of the state.

Incredibly, the *Plessy* case holds:

> We consider the underlying fallacy of the plaintiff's argument to consist in the assumption that the enforced separation of the two races stamps the colored race with a badge of inferiority. If this be so, it is not by reason of anything found in the act, but solely because the colored race chooses to put the construction upon it.

... Legislation is powerless to eradicate racial instincts, or to abolish distinctions based upon physical differences, and the attempt to do so can only result in accentuating the differences of the present situation. ... . If one race be inferior to the other socially, the Constitution of the United States cannot put them upon the same plane.[41]

Mr. Justice Harlan dissented.

Every one knows that the statute in question had its origin in the purpose, not so much to exclude white persons from railroad cars occupied by blacks, as to exclude colored people from coaches occupied by or assigned to white persons.

Perhaps a truer picture of where black people really stood can be gleaned from their "friends," not their enemies. Justice Harlan, arguing for integrated railroad coaches, continues:[42]

The white race deems itself to be the dominant race in this country. And so it is, in prestige, in achievements, in education, in wealth, and in power. So, I doubt not, it will continue to be for all time, if it remains true to its great heritage, and holds fast to the principles of constitutional liberty. ... *There is no caste here.* (emphasis mine)

One distinction between cases on race discrimination and those on sex discrimination is that white male judges can at least imagine that the legal status of black persons will make them angry; in Justice Harlan's dissent to *Plessy* he discusses how such decisions will provoke race hatred. That women will "turn on their masters" is never even assumed in the cases.

At the 1972 Democratic National Convention, during the South Carolina challenge, the "divide and conquer" technique was used. White women were pitted against black men—by white men—each group told that the other was trying to "get their seats." This sexist-racist maneuver should never work: all blacks and all women in the country should read *Plessy* and *Minor*—and realize where the real war is.

What do Mr. Plessy and Ms. Minor have in common?

Both courts stated plainly that state legislatures can *constitutionally* decree totally unequal treatment.

Both courts used circular logic to hold that because horror A was allowed to go on, therefore horror B was constitutionally permissible. For blacks, because laws against intermarriage and integrated schools were allowed to stand, therefore, Mr. Plessy had to sit in his separate railroad coach. For women, because no states permit women to vote, and because states had even been readmitted to the Union which did not allow women to vote, therefore, Ms. Minor could not vote.

We'll take care of you, say both courts. The paternalistic, "protective" attitude runs through all cases on race or sex.

> Their training had left them mere children, and as such they needed the protection which a wise government extends to those who are unable to protect themselves.[43]

Try to guess whether that quote comes from a Supreme Court case on women or blacks.

Both courts tell the plaintiffs to be happy with their status. How do you know we set up separate railroad cars to keep blacks out? Maybe we set them up to keep the whites out of your cars. Why do you want to sit on a jury when your province is in your blissful home with your sweet children?

What Mr. Plessy and Ms. Minor have in common is that a Supreme Court of white men did not perceive them as human beings.

Chapter Two
The Fourteenth
Amendment: Promoting
Whose General Welfare?

. . . nor [shall any State] deny to any person within its jurisdiction the equal protection of the laws . . .

The Constitution of the United States, Amendment XIV, Section I

❀❀❀ We sat in a large auditorium, almost two hundred of us. There were four women in the course on Constitutional Law, all extremely silent. Our professor was discussing cases illustrating the right to redress of grievances, using as examples the black civil rights marches. He reviewed the sit-in cases, and the standards which the Court had drawn when balancing constitutional rights against the rights of municipalities to keep the peace. He then spent about ten minutes making fun of the women's sit-ins and marches. At that time I was personally involved in challenging the New York public accommodations statute, which had not included the term "sex" until the women from NOW challenged it legally and politically.

Since first-year law students are terrified of looking like fools, I didn't speak in class, but went up to him afterwards. My memory of the incident is that I haltingly told him that I didn't think constitutional law professors should *teach* violation of the Fourteenth Amendment Equal Protection Clause. His recollection of the incident, which he mentioned three years later, was that I had been quite aggressive and had upset him. It was, however, the first in a series of many consciousness-raising episodes between me and the all-male faculty.

Although many persons who go to law school are primarily interested in corporate and commercial law, there are those who spend three years studying instead the various means of insuring human rights. Two sections of the Constitution which are absolutely essential to an understanding of the just relationship between people and their government are the Equal Protection Clause and the Due Process Clause. This chapter deals primarily with the Equal Protection Clause, but a word is necessary about due process.

The Fifth Amendment contains the clause ". . . nor [shall he] be deprived of life, liberty, or property, without due process of law." This amendment, which applied to the federal government, was made applicable to the states by the Fourteenth Amendment. In lay terms, this clause guarantees that one should be able to live life, speak freely, earn a living, control one's own person and property. And, should the government wish to usurp any of these rights, it must use just means to do so.

What does this mean? You are entitled to know the charges against you—so you can rebut them. You are entitled to a jury of your peers—so you will not be judged prejudicially. You are entitled to cross-examine your accusers—so you can find out if their data is valid. And you are entitled to be *represented by counsel*— because only counsel can figure out the incredible complexities of the court system.

At almost the same time that Susan B. Anthony was

being denied the right to vote, the U.S. Supreme Court
ruled in an important case that although women are
entitled to the right to counsel, it must be male counsel.
The Supreme Court of Illinois refused to grant to Myra
Bradwell a license to practice law in the courts of that
state, on the ground that females are not eligible under
the laws of Illinois. The U.S. Supreme Court held that
such a decision violates *no provision* of the federal Constitution.[1]

> The power of a state to prescribe the qualifications for
> admission to the bar of its own courts is unaffected by
> the 14th amendment, and this court cannot inquire into
> the reasonableness or propriety of the rules it may
> prescribe.

Myra Bradwell, residing in the state of Illinois, made
application to the judges of the Supreme Court of Illinois for a license to practice law. She showed good
character and that she had met the requisite qualifications.

On her application's first coming before the Court,
the license was refused, and it was stated as sufficient
reason that under the decisions of the Supreme Court
of Illinois, the applicant ". . . as a married woman
would be bound neither by her express contracts nor by
those implied contracts which it is the policy of the law
to create between attorney and client."

In other words, the legal disability that prevented a
married woman from entering into contracts could be
used to prevent her from practicing law.

> . . . it [the Court] should not admit any persons or class
> of persons who are not intended by the legislature to be
> admitted . . .

Whether, in the existing social relations between men and women, it would promote the proper administration of justice, and the general well-being of society, to permit women to engage in the trial of cases at the bar, is a question opening a wide field of discussion, upon which it is not necessary for us to enter. It is sufficient to say that, in our opinion, the other implied limitations upon our power, . . . must operate to prevent our admitting women to the office of attorney at law. If we were to admit them, we should be exercising the authority conferred upon us in a manner which, we are fully satisfied, was never contemplated by the legislature.

Once again, the Court reasons that injustice in one area justifies injustice in another.[2]

It is also to be remembered that women attorneys at law were unknown in England, and a proposition that a woman should enter the courts of Westminster Hall in that capacity, or as a barrister, would have created hardly less astonishment than one that she should ascend the bench of bishops, or be elected to a seat in the House of Commons.

. . . That God designed the sexes to occupy different spheres of action, and that it belonged to men to make, apply, and execute the laws, was regarded as an almost axiomatic truth. In view of these facts, we are certainly warranted in saying that when the legislature gave to this court the power of granting licenses to practice law, it was not with the slightest expectation that this privilege would be extended to women.

Ms. Bradwell, in fighting for her rights under laws made prior to the reign of James I, was represented by a male lawyer, Matthew Hale Carpenter. He drew

black-white analogies, argued privileges and immuni-
ites, but conceded "that the right to vote is not one of
these privileges."

Carpenter argued:[3]

> . . . a state legislature could not, in enumerating the
> qualifications [for bar admission] require the candidate
> to be a white citizen . . . yet no sound mind can draw
> a distinction between such an act and a custom, usage,
> or law of a state, which denies which privilege to all
> female citizens, without regard to age, character, or
> learning.

> . . . all the privileges and immunities which I vindicate
> to a colored citizen, I vindicate to our mothers, our
> sisters, and our daughters. The inequalities of sex will
> undoubtedly have their influence, and be considered by
> every client desiring to employ counsel.

Carpenter's analysis of hiring practices sounds familiar—rather like the law-firm rhetoric which keeps
women lawyers in the back room doing research.

> There may be cases in which a client's rights can only
> be rescued by an exercise of the rough qualities pos-
> sessed by men. There are many cases in which the silver
> voice of a woman would accomplish more than the
> severity and sternness of men could achieve.

The Court held that being a lawyer had nothing to do
with the privileges and immunities of being a citizen.

> . . . Certainly many prominent and distinguished law-
> yers have been admitted to practice, both in the State
> and Federal courts, who were not citizens of the United
> States or of any State.

... Being contrary to the rules of the common law and the usages of Westminster Hall from time immemorial, it would not be supposed that the legislature had intended to adopt any different rule.

Carpenter had argued the Equal Protection Clause of the Fourteenth Amendment. The Court rejected his plea.[4]

The 14th Amendment claim assumes that it is one of the privileges and immunities of women as citizens to engage in any and every profession, occupation, or employment in civil life.

... the civil law, as well as nature herself, has always recognized a wide difference in the respective spheres and destinies of man and woman. Man is, or should be, woman's protector and defender. The natural and proper timidity and delicacy which belongs to the female sex evidently unfits it for many of the occupations of civil life. The constitution of family organization, which is founded in the divine ordinance, as well as in the nature of things, indicates the domestic sphere as that which properly belongs to the domain and functions of womanhood. The harmony, not to say, identity, of interests and views which belong, or should belong, to the family institution is repugnant to the idea of a woman adopting a distinct and independent career from that of her husband.

The decision brings to mind Judge Nanette Dembitz's being asked about her family responsibility (this in 1972). The Court concludes:[5]

... The paramount mission of woman is to fulfill the noble and benign offices of wife and mother. This is the law of the creator.

. . . in view of the peculiar characteristics, destiny, and mission of woman, it is within the province of the legislature to ordain what offices, positions, and callings shall be filled and discharged by woman, and shall receive the benefit of those energies and responsibilities, and that decision and firmness which are presumed to predominate in the sterner sex.

After the Supreme Court ruled against her, Ms. Bradwell stated she would never try again to gain admission to the bar.[6] Soon after the Supreme Court decision she succeeded in getting the state legislature to pass a law that no profession could be forbidden to anyone because of sex. Years later, without any request by her except her original application to the bar which had been previously denied, the State Supreme Court admitted her. She was also admitted to the Supreme Court bar. Apparently she never actually practiced, although the work she did was closely related to the law.

Myra Bradwell had wanted to go to college, but was unable to do so because of the lack of higher education for women in the mid-nineteenth century. She had become a teacher. Married to a lawyer, she decided to study law in order to help her husband, rather than with any intention of becoming a lawyer herself. Later, she decided she too wanted to practice.

She founded the *Chicago Legal News*, of which she was both editor and business manager, a then unique position for a woman.[7] She drafted and urged the Illinois state legislature to pass a law establishing a married woman's right to her own earnings. Fortunately, for Ms. Bradwell and other Illinois women, the first case under the new law was one designed to arouse public sympathy. It concerned a Chicago scrubwoman who worked to support herself, but whose pay was taken by the saloon keeper to whom her husband owed money.

Ms. Bradwell also won passage of laws guaranteeing to a widow a share in her husband's estate and giving to widowers the same interest which widows had in a dead spouse's property.

Her daughter became a lawyer. And so did a handful of women in the hundred years that followed. Most of the state legislatures changed their laws, thereby admitting women to the bar. An example is the Wisconsin state legislature, which changed its law, following the _Goodell_[8] case, which held:

> We are satisfied that the applicant possesses all the requisite qualifications as to learning, ability, and moral character to entitle her to admission, no objection existing thereto except that founded upon her sex alone. Under the circumstances, a majority think that objection must be disregarded. Miss Goodell will therefore be admitted to practice in this court upon signing the roll and taking the prescribed oath.

In spite of these advances, it is my contention that women clients are denied _due process of the law_ in many ways, not the least of which is the fact that women are represented in the courts almost exclusively by male counsel. Even though the bar now admits women, only 2.8 percent of the attorneys in this country are female. The reasons are not subtle. Just as Ms. Bradwell first became interested in law only to better assist and understand her husband, most women today still (despite the women's liberation movement) do not think in terms of independent careers. As Carolyn Bird points out:[9]

> Women are still expected to work for men, to make life "sweet and agreeable" for them at home and now at

work, but their chores have changed with the needs of men, and they have more choices because men need them in many more ways. Most women frankly say they are working for money because that is what their families need most, but a woman may also work to make herself a more stimulating companion ("I charge her job to mental hygiene," a millionaire told us), to keep out of her children's hair, to clean up local politics as she would clean up a messy house, and to take care of the unfortunate. But never for herself first. Never for personal power or prestige.

This attitude is a New Masculinism. It recognizes many motives. It does not prescribe specific feminine duties. It does not define a specific woman's "place." It charges her instead with the duty of finding the task the men around her need done from moment to moment. The nature of the task doesn't matter. She may shoot a gun or drive a truck or serve out a husband's unexpired term in the legislature—providing only that she does it in the name of somebody else and not for the greater glory of herself.

More women are going to law school, but not enough more. The 8,680 women studying law in 1971 constituted 9.3 percent of the total number of law students— an increase from 3.6 percent in 1960.[10] Contrary to the popular stereotype, one study of women law graduates over a period of seventeen years showed that 84 percent remained in the profession, more than half of them in private practice. On the other hand, less than 12 percent of them were making more than $20,000, as compared to 50 percent of the men.

A percentage of 2.8 is extremely low, either when compared to other capitalist countries (in West Germany, 33 percent of the lawyers are women) or to Communist countries (in Russia, 36 percent of the lawyers are women). In addition, the American Bar Association has never had a woman as president, and there are no women on the A.B.A. board of governors.

In March 1971, the New York Bar Association scheduled a panel discussion on the topic "Has Women's Lib Liberated Anybody?" Women lawyers and law students protested the flippant and sexist programming, which was only the tip of the iceberg with regard to the horrors of the treatment of women by the bar. In addition to going on record as opposing the Equal Rights Amendment, the association has never gone on record as protesting discrimination against women in the legal profession.

It is relevant at this point to mention that male lawyers, law professors, and judges enjoy speaking to women's groups and clubs. Law schools all have Law Wives Clubs (composed of young women who are often raising children and working at low-paying jobs at the same time to put their husbands through school). Law professors speak to the wives, explaining how difficult is the job of law student and detailing how they (the women) should do everything in their power to make life comfortable and unstressful for their men.

These same professionals are less kindly and tolerant when it comes to women who aspire to be their peers. A statement from New York women lawyers to the New York Bar Association[11] summarized the situation of women lawyers, or more accurately, some reasons for the lack of women lawyers:

The New York Bar Association (probably one of the most "forward-thinking" bar associations in the country), in its 102-year history has had 45 presidents, 13 secretaries, 15 treasurers, 96 chairmen—none of them women. There are no women lawyers among their present officers; 46 of the committees have no women members at all, including critical committees such as the Judiciary, Judicial Selection and Tenure, Criminal Courts, Penology, Recruitment of Young Lawyers, Grievances Against Association Members, and Tax Problems in the Profession.

Discrimination against women in the legal profession includes extremely biased treatment of women by legal employers. One female law school graduate reported this interview: The partner of the firm who was interviewing her said he was uncomfortable talking to a woman interviewee, although of course he liked women and did not object to them in the profession. He said he didn't know what kinds of questions to ask her. She replied that he should ask her the same kinds of questions which men who apply for the job are asked. He said that when he interviewed men he talked to them about hunting and fishing.

The New York Bar Association has also failed to complain about discriminatory and offensive treatment of women attorneys by judges in the courts. (An unwavering habit of judges, when confronted by a woman lawyer, is to think she is her own secretary.) The New York women lawyers also found discriminatory hiring practices by private law firms, by government offices, and by judges seeking law clerks. They protested also the irrational rules which prevail in nearly every private dining club and university club in New York City—rules which allow them access to the club, but bar them from membership, deny them use of sports facilities, and segregate them into separate dining areas. (The Century Club in Syracuse, New York, has a strange rule which allows women and men to eat in the same dining room; but women cannot enter by the front door —they must use a back door.)

Until 1971, women sat separately when taking the

New York bar exam. The "rationale" given for this was that the presence of women would so excite the men taking the exam that they would be distracted from writing their answers.

Some California lawyers did, however, go on a sex tour.[12] Accompanied by doctors, the men were testing the "theory" that sexual repression in societies leads to aggression and wars. They were led through some European "sex centers" by Dr. William Bryan, director of the American Institute of Hypnosis, and obtained college credit for the trip from the Thomas A. Edison College of Palm Beach, California. Their studies included talking with the Bluebell chorus girls backstage at the Paris Lido, visiting brothels in Hamburg, visiting pornography shops in Denmark, and stripping off their clothes at the Ile de Levant nudist colony on the French Riviera.

It was also on a trip to Europe that the American women's movement began. Lucretia Mott and Elizabeth Cady Stanton, who had been activists in the abolitionist movement in this country, attended a world-wide abolitionist conference in England. When they arrived, they were told that they could not be seated because they were women. That information proved a great consciousness-raiser to them: they walked for hours in the parks of London discussing the necessity for a women's movement. They saw clearly the relationship between liberation for blacks and for women; they saw they were in a similar position to the slaves they had gone all the way across the ocean to help.

At that time, the Fourteenth Amendment had already been added to the Constitution (it was ratified in 1868). But neither it, nor the body of the Constitution itself, nor the Declaration of Independence, could assure women their independence or their equal treatment.

These documents were, then as now, interpreted by men.

Abigail Adams had warned her husband John of the danger of disregarding women's rights.[13]

> Remember: all men would be tyrants if they could . . . If attention is not paid to the ladies, we shall foment a rebellion and will not hold ourselves bound by any laws in which we have no voice or representation.

Except in rare women's movement demonstrations, no one has ever mentioned the inequity of taxation without representation. We have indeed held ourselves bound by the laws, but the laws have not freed us from bondage. The Equal Protection Clause gave us neither the right to vote, nor the right to practice law, nor the right to serve on juries.

Until 1971, the Supreme Court had never decreed that women are "persons" under the law and entitled to its equal protection. As recently as 1968, the Court refused to review two cases involving women's rights that had been appealed under the due process clause of the Fourteenth Amendment, which refers to (apparently male) "persons."[14]

What is a female citizen to think of law and order when she knows that the Fourteenth Amendment Equal Protection Clause prohibits any state action which denies equal protection of the law—and she lives in Texas, where a husband who murders his wife's lover can claim justification for his crime "of passion"—but a wife who kills her husband's lover has no similar defense? What were female citizens of Connecticut and Pennsylvania to think of justice and constitutional protection when, as recently as 1968, the laws of these two states decreed that any woman convicted of a crime must be given the maximum penalty, while a man convicted of the same crime could get the minimum? (In several states, the punishments for some crimes are not only different, but of greater or lesser degree, depending on the sex of the criminal.)

The argument is often made that whereas women do not indeed have equal rights in our country, we do not have equal obligations either. This supposedly balances the scales. Nothing could be further from the truth. In fact, it can be argued that our being excused from obligations is really an additional denial of rights.

For example, in twenty-two states and the District of Columbia, women may be excused from jury service on grounds not available to men. Of these, eleven states permit a woman to be excused solely on the ground that she is a woman. This not only creates an unjust jury pool for women defendants, it may create an unjust jury pool for men defendants. Since women are not imbued with the cult of bravado and toughness, they may react in a manner more sympathetic to a male defendant. I am not here stating that women will necessarily be kinder to a person charged with a crime; I am stating that women do not, cannot, identify with the revenge-is-mine-let's-kill-the-scoundrel ethos of the Western film. Exclusion of women from juries is also unfair to the potential jurors themselves: they are denied a voice in the democratic process. In much the same way that women have been "excused" from running for political office—their work in the kitchen and the nursery is "so important" they should not be forced into the political arena—they have been excused from jury duty. The total psychological effect upon the woman involved can only be the message, not that she is so important at home, but rather that her proper world is the private one, and that the public world can do very well without her.

Ten states, the District of Columbia, and Puerto Rico permit women to claim an exemption from jury service because of child care or family responsibilities. How much fairer it would be to allow such exemptions to both men and women. Perhaps a mother would prefer to spend the month on a jury, and let father stay at home with the children. Rhode Island provides that women be included for jury service only when courthouse facilities permit. And, in Louisiana, a woman must preregister in order to be considered eligible for jury service.

Another "protection" of women has been to deny them the right to serve on parole boards which decide the fate of women offenders in prisons. Again, this is unfair to the women prisoners and unfair to the potential female parole board members—who are denied an effective voice in determining the nature and level of law and order in the community.

During the four decades that women and men have been working to get the Equal Rights Amendment ratified, one argument against its passage has always been "We have the Equal Protection Clause of the Fourteenth Amendment." Although on November 22, 1971, the Equal Protection Clause was finally extended to women in the *Reed*[15] case, it was there applied in a very limited fashion. For an understanding of why the Equal Protection Clause has not worked for women, it is necessary not only to understand that the Supreme Court Justices have always been men, who would naturally incorporate most of the ideas of their social and economic milieu, but also to be familiar with the politics of *burden of proof*.

When a court looks to see whether equal protection has been violated, it first must find that there are two classes of persons, and that they are being treated differently. For example, people with blue eyes are not permitted to enter the school auditorium, whereas people with brown eyes are. Secondly, the court must examine the reasons for the differing treatment. Two standards have been developed by the courts to determine whether laws differentiating between classes of persons violate constitutional guarantees of equal protection of the laws. One such standard is that the law is valid if the class distinction is based upon some *reasonable* ground. Here the defendant must only show that he had a reason to make the distinction. Hundreds of cases have been lost to plaintiffs on the basis of the reasonableness test, merely because the agency thought the differentiating procedure *easier*—and the court bought the argument. (The court did not accept that reasoning in the *Reed* case.)

The other standard is that the class distinction is constitutional only if it is shown that the government has a *compelling interest* in making the class distinction. It is relevant to reiterate here that the Fourteenth Amendment applies only to *state action*. Purely private action cannot be regulated under the Fourteenth Amendment Equal Protection Clause. There are, however, dozens of cases coming down every month which are reshaping (and broadening) the concept of state action. Obviously, it is a much easier burden for any defendant to show that the behavior was reasonable, than that he had a compelling state interest in doing so.

Mary Eastwood has written a brilliant analysis[16] of the two tests, and how they are applied to women. She shows that the reasonableness test has generally been applied with respect to laws treating women as inferiors or restricting their liberties. The stricter compelling state interest test has been applied with respect to racial classifications and situations involving fundamental constitutionally protected liberties (such as First Amendment rights of free speech and freedom of religion).[17] The additional distinction between the two standards is that the burden is upon *the person* challenging a law to show that it is unreasonable; the burden is upon *the state* to show that it has a compelling interest.

Eastwood explains:[18]

> The more lax reasonableness standard applied by the courts in equal protection cases is that the classification must be based on "some difference which bears a just and proper relation to the attempted classification— and not a mere arbitrary selection."[19] Under the stricter standard, the mere showing of some rational basis for the classification is not sufficient to support its constitutionality. Racial classifications are subject to the stricter test since "all legal restrictions which curtail the civil rights of a single racial group are immediately suspect and . . . courts must subject them to the most rigid scrutiny."[20] Thus, in holding unconstitutional Virginia's anti-miscegenation law, the Supreme Court found "no legitimate overriding purpose independent of invidious racial discrimination" to justify the classification.[21] The showing of an overriding and compelling state interest is also required where the law affects fundamental individual liberties, such as freedom of religion,[22] freedom of association,[23] and the right to travel,[24] to vote,[25] to have offspring,[26] and to assert familial relationship.[27]

The legitimacy of sex differentiation, for the purposes of Fourteenth Amendment equal protection, was, as we have seen, established in the nineteenth century for pur-

poses of denying women the vote, the right to be lawyers, and the right to sit on juries. A major decision in
1908, *Muller v. Oregon*,[28] provided the legal basis for
protective legislation. More important, it contained language which is still being used to extend the doctrine of
sex as a basis for legislative classification to unrelated
subjects.

Although many women workers were delighted by
the holding in *Muller*, since working conditions were so
inhumane at the turn of the century, the feminists were
horrified. They agreed, of course, that working conditions for everyone, *male and female*, had to be improved. But they saw the legal and judicial results which
would be inevitable once sex was established as a reasonable classification for differentiation. So significant
is the holding in *Muller*, and so narrow has been the
view of those who cannot see the value of pushing for
fine working conditions for all workers, regardless of
sex, that some union representatives (in decreasing
numbers, fortunately) are still fighting the Equal Rights
Amendment, on grounds that it will obviate the protective laws. A recent argument from a Connecticut labor
leader, for example: Connecticut now has a law which
requires that a chair be provided for every woman who
works at certain kinds of factory work. This is a good
law, because the work is physically exhausting, dirty,
and noisy.

Clearly, working at a difficult and dirty task should
equally qualify men and women for a chair. But the
Muller language, and the *Muller* level of consciousness
still prevails. The Court stated:[29]

That woman's physical structure and the performance
of maternal functions place her at a disadvantage in the
struggle for subsistence is obvious. This is especially

true when the burdens of motherhood are upon her. Even when they are not, by abundant testimony of the medical fraternity, continuance for a long time on her feet at work, repeating this from day to day, tends to injurious effects upon the body, and as healthy mothers are essential to vigorous offspring, the physical well-being of woman becomes an object of public interest and care in order to preserve the strength and vigor of the race.

Still again, history discloses the fact that woman has always been dependent upon man. He established his control at the outset by superior physical strength, and this control in various forms, with diminishing intensity, has continued to the present . . .

Though limitations upon personal and contractual rights may be removed by legislation, there is that in her disposition and habits of life which will operate against a full assertion of those rights. She will still be where some legislation to protect her seems necessary to secure a real equality of rights . . .

Differentiated by these matters from the other sex, she is properly placed in a class by herself, and legislation designed for her protection may be sustained, even when like legislation is not necessary for men and could not be sustained. It is impossible to close one's eyes to the fact that she still looks to her brother and depends upon him.

. . . that her physical structure and a proper discharge of her maternal functions—having in view not merely her own health, but the well-being of the race—justify legislation to protect her from the greed as well as the passion of man.

. . . The two sexes differ in structure of the body, in the functions to be performed by each, in the amount of physical strength, in the capacity for long-continued labor, particularly when done standing, in influence of vigorous health upon the future well-being of the race, the self-reliance which enables one to assert full rights, and in the capacity to maintain the struggle for subsistence. This difference justifies a difference in legislation and upholds that which is designed to compensate for some of the burdens which rest upon her.

As Jo Freeman points out:[30] "With this precedent, the drive for protective legislation became distorted into a push for laws that applied to women only—on the principle that half a loaf was better than none. While this policy was also favored by male labor leaders who saw the 'protection' of women only as a way to limit competition, it is safe to say that the Supreme Court contributed significantly to the proliferation of state protective laws for women only."

The *Muller* language has been cited in excluding women from juries,[31] in permitting different treatment for men and women in licensing occupations,[32] and in keeping women out of state-supported colleges.[33] The idea of woman as earth mother is hardly new: centuries before *Muller*, women, whether or not they were mothers, were being defined in that capacity. The *Muller* language—we must keep women safe because they are the vessels for our children, and an unhealthy vessel cannot bring forth a healthy child—was also used in the first Title VII case involving sex discrimination to go to the Supreme Court. Ida Phillips[34] had charged that the Martin Marietta Corporation of Orlando, Florida, violated the 1964 Civil Rights Act by refusing to hire her because she was the mother of small children. The relevant section of the law reads:[35]

It shall be an unlawful employment practice for an employer to fail or refuse to hire or to discharge any individual or otherwise to discriminate against any individual with respect to his compensation, terms, conditions, or privileges or employment, because of such individual's race, color, religion, sex or national origin.

On January 25, 1971, the Court ruled that a woman cannot automatically be denied a job because she has preschool children. In a unanimous, unsigned decision, the Court ordered a lower court to reconsider the case of Ms. Phillips. She had contended that she was the victim of sex discrimination because the company did employ men with preschool children.

A U.S. District Judge in Orlando had awarded the company a summary judgment. His finding was upheld by the Fifth U.S. Circuit Court of Appeals (New Orleans). U.S. District Court Judge George C. Young of Orlando ruled that Ida Phillips was not refused a job because she was a woman (which is prohibited by Title VII of the Civil Rights Act), but because she was a woman with children, which he said was not prohibited.

Though the U.S. Supreme Court ruled for Ida Phillips, unfortunately the decision still holds out the possibility that mothers with small children can be denied employment—if a company can prove that not having children "is a bona fide occupational qualification reasonably necessary to the normal operation of that particular business or enterprise."[36]

It was Justice Thurgood Marshall who, in a concurring opinion, said he did not believe that Martin Marietta could establish a bona fide occupational qualification by showing that women with children have family responsibilities that would interfere with their work. Marshall questioned such an interpretation:[37]

> I fear that in this case . . . the Court has fallen into the trap of assuming that the (Civil Rights) Act permits ancient canards about the proper role of women to be a basis for discrimination. Congress sought just the opposite.

Marshall was being kind to Congress. The reason why "sex" is included in Title VII at all is that a group of Southern Senators, in a panic about a federal law about to be passed which prohibited race discrimination, stuck in "the women's rights" part, hoping that would make the whole bill ridiculous. To their amazement and surprise, the bill passed, and they then had to confront the law against both race and sex discrimination.

The *Phillips* opinion had discussed how parenthood is demonstrably more relevant to job performance for a woman than for a man. It is significant that although Ida Phillips is white, her case was handled by the NAACP Legal Defense Fund. Jack Greenberg, of the Defense Fund, said[38] the decision was particularly important for black women, "who constitute the most depressed part of the labor force."

The "sex-plus" or "race-plus" categorization constitutes a subtle (and unconstitutional) way to circumvent the laws on discrimination. Over 25 percent of all mothers with children under six are in the labor force. Eighty-five percent of them work for economic reasons. Over half a million are widowed, divorced, or separated. Their incomes are vitally necessary to their own support and that of their children.

Although *Phillips* was argued under Title VII, not under the Equal Protection Clause, it is relevant that in the sixty-three years separating *Muller* and *Phillips*, there was little, if any, change in the idea that sex is a viable classification—*because of motherhood.*

The Appeals Court discussed the intent of Congress in *Phillips:*[39]

> (It was *not* the intent of Congress) to exclude absolutely any consideration of the differences between the normal relationships of working fathers and working mothers to their pre-school-age children, and to require that an employer treat the two exactly alike in the administration of its general hiring policies . . . The *common experience of Congressmen* [emphasis mine] is surely not so far removed from that of mankind in general as to warrant our attributing to them such an irrational purpose in the formulation of this statute.

Human Rights for Women, a women's civil rights and legal defense association, filed an amicus curiae brief in the *Phillips* case. It points out[40] the glaring omission of any attack on "sex-plus" theories in the briefs of either Ms. Phillips' lawyers or the United States (the federal government filed an amicus brief).

> This case involves important issues of interpretation of Title VII of the Civil Rights Act of 1964, which is designed to protect women against discrimination in employment because of sex. It is the first Title VII case involving sex discrimination to be considered on the merits by this Court. Neither the petition for writ of certiorari filed by counsel for Ida Phillips nor the supporting brief of the United States as *amicus curiae* on petition for writ of certiorari argues, as does the attached HRW *amicus* brief, that the "sex plus" theory of the Fifth Circuit in this case is wrong because under Title VII "sex" cannot be even one element in employment consideration. The Ida Phillips petition argues

that sex plus the additional element (parent of pre-school-age children) has not been shown to be a "bona fide occupational qualification," while the United States' supporting brief argues that the employer has not shown that its rule against the combination of sex and pre-school-age children is a "business necessity." These represent two different analyses of the issue in this case, both of which, we submit, are misleading.

We saw how, in the *Bradwell* case, her lawyer argued that she should be permitted to practice law in Illinois, but he assured the Court that he did not think the privileges and immunities section of the Constitution would guarantee women the right to vote! Here, we see Ida Phillips' lawyers not doing away with the potentially disastrous concept of "sex plus." Perhaps even the friends of women are not doing as much to help us as they should be—not from malice, not out of negligence, but from a lack of feminist consciousness about what constitutional equality really means.

In the next chapter, we will explore some additional cases where the Fourteenth Amendment was extended to women, and then, viewing the kinds of laws that have been and are still considered permissible under the Fourteenth Amendment, suggest the necessity for a constitutional mandate. Perhaps only the Equal Rights Amendment can prevent us from being viewed as that special species of baby machine that even the most brilliant jurists have in their vocabularies—and in their heads.

Chapter Three
The Federal Government:
Women Are to March
with the Baggage

You are to provide provision on the South Branch for 70 men; No Forage is to be issued at Ft. Cumberland, but to the public horses . . . You are to issue to the Officers at Ft. Cumberland a sufficient allowance of tallow monthly . . . Three women are to be allowed each Company and provisions drawn for them; on condition of their behaving well, and washing for the men; No more women will be allowed to draw provisions.

—*Instructions for Commissary,* JAN. 10, 1756

General instructions for all Captains. On supplies: You are to take care that only one pound of flour, and the like quantity of meat, be delivered to each man per day, and that no more women draw provisions, than in proportion as to 100 men.

—JULY 29, 1757

All baggage Waggons . . . are to move this afternoon towards Boone-Town. Women are to march with the baggage.

—*General Orders, Morristown,* JULY 10, 1777

(*From* The Writings of George Washington)

✂✂✂ Since judges are either elected or appointed, the political process is vitally interconnected with the justice that women get in the courts. But additionally, and perhaps more importantly, the climate which is created—determined primarily by the executive branch of government—affects greatly the kind of justice which is meted out.

The federal government, therefore, is not only a giant employer of women and men, it is an image-maker.

Members of Federally Employed Women think it is more than a coincidence that 80 percent of the one million women who work for the federal government are concentrated in the lowest six grades of Civil Service.[1] Although one-third of all federal government workers are women, less than one percent of them have any authority to make decisions.

Discrimination in government employment is subtle, just as in private industry. Women are called administrative assistants, men are called administrative officers. And paid $4,000 a year more.

And as to female attorneys—no federal agency has ever had a woman as general counsel. No state has a woman as attorney general. The ninety-three district attorneys in the federal service are all men.[2]

Government, including the military, employs more than 15,000,000 people—more than 20 percent of the labor force.[3] More important than the actual numbers suggest, government is often looked to by private employers as a model, in relation to employment practices. And a very poor model it is.

Are women who work for the government entitled to equal opportunities in hiring, training, and promotion under Title VII of the Civil Rights Act of 1964? Perhaps the attitude toward women is best shown by the federal government in its treatment of poor women. In New York, Wisconsin, and other states, the law requires that a woman applicant for Aid to Families with Dependent Children (AFDC) must declare her willingness to file criminal nonsupport charges against the father in order to be eligible for benefits.

The Supreme Court recently[4] ordered three federal judges to reconsider their June 1972 decision to toss out a state welfare regulation requiring welfare mothers to begin legal action in the search for so-called deserting fathers. The three-judge court had ruled that welfare departments could not cut off assistance to a welfare mother if she refused to initiate or continue prosecution of a nonsupport suit against her missing spouse.

In a very real sense, any discussion of poverty law is a discussion of women's law. In my poverty law class, for example, the professor was surprised to find a chapter on sex discrimination in employment in the poverty law textbook. Even after it was explained to him that over 80 percent of the Americans who live below the poverty line are women and their children, and that one of the reasons for this is women's low wages—he still didn't understand. (He also told the next year's class that he didn't see why sex discrimination was in the book.)

Many families headed by a woman are poor even though the woman works. The reason for this, obviously, is that women earn about 60 percent of what men do, for the same work, and in addition are not allowed into many of the more lucrative fields. Among families headed by a woman who worked in 1968, 45 percent of those of minority races and 16 percent of the whites lived in poverty. In contrast, among families headed by a man who worked in 1968, only 16 percent of the minority families and 4 percent of the white families were poor.[5]

Not only do women earn less money, and find it more difficult to find employment, they have the primary responsibility for children. This is part of the historical value system; the difference between the *social* role of the suburban housewife and the welfare mother is that the suburban housewife has more money.

The only mothers who are "supposed to work," according to the social mores, are women on welfare. In a Virginia case,[6] however, a challenge by mothers to the welfare work program succeeded. The plaintiffs, four mothers, received welfare aid under the Aid to Families with Dependent Children program. The state required that such recipients accept work under certain conditions, including the provision of what the state considered to be adequate child care. The state terminated the welfare grant for one of the plaintiffs and her daughter because she would not accept a live-in job at twenty dollars a week caring for five children and an invalid, and also doing much of their housekeeping. Her own child was to be taken care of by her on the job or by the child's grandmother, who had seven children at home herself. It was claimed that state regulations denied due process and equal protection and were inconsistent with federal welfare law, which was also claimed to preempt this area. A single-judge court did not reach the constitutional issues, but held the work rule invalid because of its conflict with the procedural and services safeguards mandated by federal legislation for work programs, the Department of Labor's Work Incentive Program (WIN) and with the philosophy that those such as the mothers here, who could not be mandatorily referred to WIN, also could not be forced to work by the state.

The WIN program itself is under legal attack for being discriminatory, as it creates a preferential classification based on sex.[7] A Washington resident, Michele O'Donnell, complained because when she applied for the WIN program she was told men were given priority, and she was not referred. The Equal Employment Opportunities Commission (EEOC) investigation found that the guidelines (of the U.S. Department of Labor) are, or may be, discriminatory against mothers, but that the State of Washington was not following them, and that 85 percent of the WIN enrollees were female. Ms. O'Donnell appealed, furnishing evidence that the state did follow the discriminatory guidelines, that she was not referred for that reason, and that the high proportion of women in WIN reflected the fact that there were many more women than men on welfare, rather than proving WIN was not discriminatory.

Thorn v. Richardson[8] is a lawsuit alleging that the Department of Labor guidelines for eligibility for the WIN program are discriminatory and are followed in violation of the Fifth and Fourteenth amendments, thus creating a preferential classification based on sex. The guidelines set up the following priorities: (1) unemployed fathers; (2) mothers in a work program who volunteer; (3) teenagers; (4) mothers who volunteer, are not in a work program, and have no preschool children; (5) others.

A District of Columbia court found[9] that a mother and her children are not entitled to welfare benefits when the father who refuses to support the family returns to the home against the mother's will. Mary Elizabeth Trull and her children received welfare payments after she separated from her husband because of his drinking and violent behavior. He later returned to the home against her will and continued to refuse to support the family. She was unable to make him leave although she went to the police, the district attorney, and Legal Aid. The welfare department ended benefits for the mother and the children, because its regulations provided that children with two employable parents in the home were not "dependent." The court upheld this determination, rejecting a claim of denial of equal protection, and finding that the father's presence in the home would make the children ineligible until he left.

A New Jersey court, however, rendered a welfare opinion unusual in its recognition of the plight of welfare mothers.[10] It held that the welfare department must provide the full grant when support payments have been delinquent once, without waiting the (customary) three months for late payment. The plaintiffs were welfare recipients who were also persons to whom court-ordered support payments, usually from deserting fathers, were to be paid. They complained that the combination of the uncertainty of these payments, plus the refusal of the welfare department to admit that this uncertainty existed, left them without money to live on. It was not until such payments had been delinquent for at least three consecutive months that the welfare department would order the fathers to make such payments directly to it, and would itself immediately pay to the mother the full amount it calculated the family needed, rather than making her wait until some time after the payment was due, and then forcing her to persuade the department to replace it. The court found that the welfare department's delay in payment placed an unreasonable burden upon the woman. The court also took judicial notice that the welfare department's policy caused emotional and financial stresses detrimental to family life.

Two Maryland cases involve application of a welfare department policy under which mothers find they cannot obtain welfare aid for part of their family, since the State of Maryland requires that all or none of the family be on welfare. Both cases involve mothers who have children by successive husbands.

Dorsey[11] involves an applicant for welfare who resisted the welfare department's requirement that the one child who was being supported by its father at a level above the welfare standard be placed on welfare so that support payments made for her could be used for the entire family and, in effect, the welfare department would save money.

Johnson[12] concerns a Connecticut policy under which those children in a family who received Social Security benefits on their father's account were not allowed to keep the excess money over what would be a welfare standard for them. Rather, this excess was applied to reduce the payment made by the welfare department to their siblings. The court held that federal jurisdiction did exist.[13]

> Since welfare cases by their very nature involve people at a bare subsistence level, disputes over the correct amounts payable are treated not merely as involving property rights, but some sort of right to exist in society, a personal right.

The claim that an otherwise constitutional welfare regulation was administered unconstitutionally with denial of equal protection and taking of property without due process of law was ordered to be considered by a single-judge court.

In addition to welfare the federal government, through its laws, discriminates against women in matters concerning social insurance and taxes. For example, several categories of employment are excluded from unemployment compensation in most states. These include areas of employment where women are a substantial part of the labor force: employment by state and local governments, nonprofit organizations, and domestic work.

In addition, women are disqualified for benefits under unemployment compensation if they leave work due to pregnacy and maternity, or because of domestic or marital obligations. In seven states—Alaska, Arkansas, Idaho, Maine, Minnesota, Montana, and Utah—a man may leave his job because of domestic or marital obligations and still receive benefits.[14] In every state, and at the federal level, there is currently a drive to put maternity leave into the same category as absence for any other temporary disability.

Women are generally denied unemployment insurance if they must move to be with their husbands; yet a woman's refusal to follow her husband to a new residence is considered desertion and can be used as grounds for divorce.

An employer can discharge an employee for pregnancy any time he chooses, regardless of her state of health or willingness to work. In Wisconsin, for example, she cannot collect unemployment compensation under any circumstances for ten weeks before and four weeks after the birth of the child.[15] Although this type of law is being struck down in state after state, there are still states where an employer has no obligation to grant a woman employee a leave of absence for maternity, with or without loss of seniority upon her return. Ailing men and those in military service are frequently granted long leaves of absence with continuing benefits, sometimes over a period of years.

It is interesting to note that women workers are punished for becoming mothers. Actually, women workers are punished even before they become mothers, or even contemplate such. And many women workers are punished for *their capacity to become mothers* alone. I was once denied a job, writing a newsletter for a Chicago bank, because I was "engaged," and hence, according to the personnel manager, I would get married and have babies and quit the job. Law firms, interviewing women law graduates, have been known to ask them if they are "on the pill."

This becomes even more grossly unfair and irrational when one bears in mind that in our society women are trained to be mothers from the day they are given their first doll. Any woman who decides to eliminate child-raising from her life has a lot of explaining to do; any woman who includes child-raising in her life has lost a lot of wages and benefits.

Currently, before ratification of the ERA, an employer is within legal rights in insisting a woman employee retire at an earlier age than a man, and receive smaller benefits under a company-sponsored retirement plan.

Domestic workers in private homes, most of whom are women, are not protected under unemployment compensation and may miss out on Social Security benefits due to laxness on the part of their employers in failing to file appropriate forms and contributions for the employee's Social Security account.

The federal Social Security laws discriminate heavily against women. A woman who has been employed most of her life and has contributed regularly to her Social Security account may receive nothing from her account if she elects to receive benefits from her husband's account instead. Or she may receive lesser retirement benefits than the never-employed wife or widow of a man who happened to earn more as a worker than the employed woman.

A woman who has been married to an employed man

for any term less than twenty years, if divorced, is not eligible to receive any retirement benefits from his account in her old age. This, despite the fact that during the period she was married, her "job" was being his housekeeper.

Until the 92nd Congress (1971–72), women in their old age were not entitled to live as comfortably as men. A widow who became entitled to benefits at age sixty-two or after received only 82½ percent of the retirement benefit her husband would have received had he lived. The federal law, therefore, was saying to a woman that she should live on less money than a surviving widower or a retired single male.

One would think that a couple's retirement benefits should be greater if they were both employed outside the home and both contributed to the Social Security system. Not true! An aged couple may receive less in total monthly benefits if both husband and wife worked than a couple whose benefits are based on the same total earnings derived from the husband's employment alone.[16]

For example, if only the husband worked and had average earnings of $7,800 per year, benefits paid to the couple at age sixty-five would be $323 monthly, $218 to the husband and $105 to the wife. If both worked and had average earnings of $3,900 each per year—a combined yearly income of $7,800—their benefits would be $134.30 each, or a total of $268.60, $54 per month less than the one-earner family.

In effect, it is the contributions of employed wives which support the Social Security system, a system whose benefits accrue in large measure to noncontributing dependents.

In October 1972, for the first time, the Supreme Court ruled that discrimination on the basis of sex is "inherently suspect." They did so in the case of an Air Force lieutenant who was denied a dependency allowance for her husband. A male serviceman would automatically have been entitled to benefits for his wife. The decision means that in cases where individuals are treated differently because of their sex, the government bears the burden of justifying the distinction.

The Court accepted the argument that it is illegal to allow servicemen to draw housing and medical allowances for their wives, but require women in uniform to show that their husbands are dependent on them before they are eligible.

The Declaration of Independence states, "All men are created equal." This would be an accurate statement of our country's priorities—if it were amended to read "white men." Nowhere does this priority show itself more cogently than when women and minority men try to make changes in the current quota system in employment and in politics.

After enormous political, legal, and legislative struggles, the affirmative action plans were born. They are designed to eliminate the present results of past discrimination, by requiring employers to set up goals and timetables for the hiring and promotion of women and minority men.

In his 1972 Labor Day message, President Nixon told the white-run construction industry and others which have balked at hiring blacks and women—just what they wanted to hear. He said that so-called quotas (to redress discrimination) are un-American. What he chose to ignore is that we currently have a quota system operating—one that makes it possible for the positions at the top to be held primarily by white males. He took the guts from the "goals and timetables" provisions of Revised Order #4.

Revised Order #4 had been around only since April 1972, but during that time industry and universities had begun to quake in their boots. Specifically, many had hired consultants to help them plan for the inclusion of minorities and women in their previously "exclusive" white male clubs. A personal experience illustrates the impact of Nixon's Labor Day speech: I had been hired, on a one-day-a-month basis, by an international corporation, with headquarters in the East, to consult on affirmative action. We were doing consciousness-raising with the executives, looking at hiring and promotion procedures and the like. After Nixon's Labor Day speech, I was "fired." Or, rather, some verbiage was given on why my September visit was not possible. I spoke to the personnel manager on the phone: "I guess you heard Nixon's Labor Day speech." He laughed, and agreed that that was why my services were no longer required. Apparently the company was no longer frightened.

William H. Brown III, then chairman of the Equal Employment Opportunity Commission, a 1968 appointee of President Johnson, spoke out against the Labor Day speech. Nixon had said:[17]

> The quota hiring, which favors black employment, is a dangerous detour away from the traditional measure of a person on the basis of ability.
>
> . . . quotas are as artificial and unfair a yardstick as has ever been used to deny opportunity to anyone.

For more than a month after Nixon's speech, Brown was silent. On October 27, 1972, he sent the following memo to his staff:[18]

Recent newspaper accounts regarding statements by President Nixon on the issue of affirmative action and quotas have led some Commission employees to question whether there has been or will be any change in the Commission's policy of requiring certain types of remedies for discrimination in employment.

The purpose of this memorandum is to assure you that, regardless of what interpretations may have been placed on these news reports, there has been and there will be NO change in the policies of this Commission concerning appropriate remedies for the elimination of discrimination in employment.

. . . When discrimination is found to exist, it is the law itself which demands no less than full and appropriate relief . . . Remedies for discrimination may appear to some to be awkward, inconvenient, even burdensome perhaps. But if such is necessary to eliminate discrimination, Title VII demands no less.

Brown's term on the EEOC expired in 1973. Nixon of course could have removed him at any time as chairman, but kept him even though EEOC attacked (to some extent) his Republican friends such as American Telephone & Telegraph.[19] (As with all other presidential appointees, Nixon asked for Brown's stand-by resignation as chairman the day after the election.)

President Nixon did indeed ban minority employment hiring quotas from all agencies and departments of the federal government. He asked for a complete review by all agencies to ensure that no quota systems are in effect.[20] The Civil Service Commission has repeatedly asserted that there are no quotas for the hiring of minorities in the federal government.

In October 1972 the National Organization for Women charged a complete sellout of women and minorities by the Nixon administration. It condemned the systematic gutting (in September and October of 1972) of the affirmative action programs.

Wilma Scott Heide, national president of NOW, attacked President Nixon[21] for sabotaging the goals and timetables provisions of affirmative action:

> One of NOW's major accomplishments last year was our success in persuading the Department of Labor to issue Revised Order #4, which requires federal contractors to devise and implement affirmative hiring and promotion programs for women and minority men. The heart of these programs are the goals and timetables companies and educational institutions establish for themselves to overcome sexist and racist patterns of employment.

> The whole debate on "quotas"—the propaganda code word now being used to refer to hiring goals—is a smokescreen designed to maintain the status quo, which gives white males a monopoly on opportunity and upper level jobs and leaves women and minority men on the bottom or on the outside where they have always been.

Former Equal Employment Opportunity Commissioner Aileen Hernandez joined with Ms. Heide in the condemnation:

> President Nixon himself has said that the key element in a program to eliminate discrimination is "taking action to redress the effects of past discrimination." While he made this statement on June 11, 1972, in connection with minority housing problems, it's clear to us it should be extended to the crucial area of employment, without which one may have no house.

It is revealed, by this and other actions of the Nixon administration, that law and order is *not* a priority. The administration utilizes a selective law-enforcement policy, practically ignoring human rights laws and executive orders as they apply to women and minority men.

The essence of the new Nixon policy on hiring is a dependence upon "good faith" of the employer, which is, in the words of NOW and the NAACP, "utterly meaningless." For all practical purposes, the Nixon administration has scuttled the federal contract compliance program which dates back to 1941.

Further evidence of this administration's retreat on any progress which had been made to end sexism is the forced resignation[22] of Elizabeth Duncan Koontz, Director of the Women's Bureau of the U.S. Department of Labor. Ms. Koontz had been the only officially designated voice of working women in the administration.

Probably the federal government attitudes which affect laws on women most are those of the Justices of the U.S. Supreme Court. In September 1971, Ms. Nixon was reported to be "talking it up" with her husband about appointing a woman to the Supreme Court. The administration, however, could not find a woman who had the "desired constructionist philosophy and sufficiently distinguished legal background."

When Nixon first began seeking nominees for the Court, he said he was looking for the best man. After protests from the Women's Political Caucus, he amended his language; this did not change his choice. Rumor had it that Nixon could not find a woman good enough for the Court. Congresswoman Bella Abzug pointed out that the problem was that Nixon could not find a woman *bad* enough for the Court.

What kinds of attitudes do the men Nixon appointed have toward women?

A group of NOW members met Lewis Powell and asked him if he intended to look out for women's rights when he was on the bench.[23] He replied: "I always look after the ladies." He then talked about his youngest daughter, who is in law school. She would not get married, he said, until her fiancé promised her he would "*let* her finish law school." (One of the women, Alice Frandsen, suggested that she might *let* him finish too.)

William H. Rehnquist is either confused as to his views on women's equality, or else he chooses to speak on the subject in clouded terminology.[24] When he testified before the House Judiciary committee, in hearings on the Equal Rights Amendment, even the committee members were confused:

> *Mr. McClory.* Since the answer to the question with regard to whether or not women would be subject to the draft seems to be "yes," it would be helpful if the Attorney General would express some kind of positive opinion on what the impact of the equal rights amendment would be, because I can't interpret your answer to indicate one way or the other, and I would like to know. I think it is important to us to know what our highest legal authority feels.

> *Mr. Rehnquist.* I fully agree with you, sir. Unfortunately, the Attorney General works with the same language everybody else works with and the value of his opinion generally comes just like the value of any lawyer's opinion, from an examination of precedents and other similar cases and in this situation he is, unfortunately, writing on a clean slate. To simply take these words and say they do or do not apply to a particular situation, is not the sort of opinion that a lawyer ordinarily feels very comfortable giving.

During the same hearing,[25] Justice Rehnquist came out against the Equal Rights Amendment, although he was the administration's representative testifying "for it."

Mr. Wiggins. Let's directly confront the question. Do you feel the constitutional amendment is necessary to implement the federal policy you have enunciated, that is, no discrimination on the basis of sex?

Mr. Rehnquist. No, I don't. I think one could do it by statute.

Mr. Wiggins. Then, I think my observation is correct. Your answer indicates that the amendment is unnecessary and my query is why you are in support of an unnecessary amendment?

Mr. Rehnquist. Because the President has committed himself to it, and the importance of a general statement in the Constitution establishing the principles of equality of women outweighs the disadvantages that might flow from enactment of the amendment.

It is generally a toss-up as to whether women will fare better in male-dominated courtrooms, or in male-dominated legislatures. Almost a hundred bills were introduced into Congress in 1971–72 that would have benefited women—all of them except eight died with the 92nd Congress. Of the eight, Nixon vetoed the child-care bill—on the grounds that it would lead to "destruction of the American family."

One bill allows for deduction of household help and/or child care up to $400 per month, depending on the number of children and the income of the parent or parents combined. A second is the provision that increases the cash benefits for widows from 82.5 percent of their husband's payment to the full 100 percent.

Bella Abzug (D.-New York) introduced the following three bills into the House.

HR 15389: to prohibit discrimination by financial institutions or any other persons on the basis of sex or marital status, relating to federally financed mortgages;

HR 15391: to prohibit discrimination by any federally insured bank, savings and loan association, or credit union, against any individual on the basis of sex or marital status;

HR 15392: to amend the Truth in Lending Act to prohibit discrimination by creditors against individuals on the basis of sex or marital status.

The National Organization for Women has urged[26] the Bureau of the Budget to withhold any appropriations to the Department of Labor that would be expended on any funds which do the following:

(a) Enforce sec. 1910.141(f) of Subpart J of the Occupational Health and Safety Standards (36 CFR 10594) headed "retiring rooms for women" or any other standard applying only to women.

(b) Make any grant under the Occupational Health and Safety Act (29 USC 655) to any state that has safety laws, rules, or standards applicable only to women.

(c) Print or distribute copies of the publication "Teach Them to Lift" (Bulletin 100, or any other publication including implications that weight-lifting restrictions can or should be applied on the basis of sex).

(d) Fund any manpower training program, including any Job Corps Center, limited to one sex, or to fund any such program that does not affirmatively seek to enroll both sexes in training for jobs traditionally considered appropriate for one sex.

(e) Spend any funds for apprenticeship training, as long as the affirmative action program does not require efforts to eliminate sex discrimination.

(f) Fund any survey of, or related to, employment, unemployment, or under-utilization that does not include women, or publish any data from such a survey that does not include breakdown by sex.

That the U.S. Department of Labor has indeed been spending money on the above kinds of activities places its activities directly in opposition to the spirit and the letter of Title VII of the Civil Rights Act of 1964, executive orders, court decisions, and state fair employment laws.

The activities listed as (a) through (c) are to correct conditions and provisions that have already been found by the EEOC and the federal courts to violate Title VII.[27] Funds supporting the programs suggested by (d) and (e) violate Title VII, Revised Order #4, and the consent decree entered in *Thorn v. Richardson.*[28] In *Thorn* the government agreed that training programs which exclude women or prefer men are unconstitutional, and stipulated to a settlement, withdrawing its appeal to the Circuit Court.

The concept outlined in (f) is clearly necessary. Anyone who has reviewed Department of Labor statistics in search of data regarding employment, unemployment, or under-employment of women is impressed by their inadequacy. We will gladly stipulate—we who comb Department of Labor statistics for information on the status of women—that when the day comes that no one notices what sex you are when you apply for a job, separate statistics will not be needed. Today, that is hardly the case. In order to require compliance with the goals and timetables of Revised Order #4 (insofar as they still exist, following the President's Labor Day message), it is necessary to have far more statistics on women than the Department of Labor now publishes.

After a long fight for the right to buy a savings bond without declaring whether or not one has a husband, the Treasury Department announced that it will no longer require the titles of "Miss" or "Mrs." on savings bonds sold to women. However, the department still acknowledges[29] that while women buyers will be required to give their Social Security numbers, the same requirement will not be made of men. A reason was given: "With the enormous volume of bonds that have been issued, . . . identification problems are by no means uncommon." With men, evidently, the problem of identity is not too great.

Government benefits continue to be distributed unequally to men and women. The Supreme Court, using its version of the Equal Protection Clause, refused to review[30] a federal court case which had upheld a higher rate of benefits for women than for men under the Social Security laws, using traditional equal protection doctrine to state that only patently arbitrary classifications are barred by the Equal Protection Clause.

But, it is only when we look at the employment patterns of women in the United States that we can see how *federal policy*—deliberate and knowing—in all branches of government, including the judiciary—has denied women not only their dignity but their money.

Chapter Four
Money and Employment (1):
A Breach of the Duty
of Fair Representation

If it is a male from 20 to 60 years of age, the equivalent is 50 shekels of silver by the sanctuary weight; if it is a female, the equivalent is 30 shekels.

    The Lord, talking to Moses in Leviticus 27: and 4

Announcing a "grim picture" for women workers, Elizabeth Duncan Koontz, head of the Labor Department's Women's Bureau, reported Federal figures showing that a woman working full time in 1955 made, on the average, 64 percent of a man's income. The comparable figures for 1970 (the latest available) show that she is now making only 57 percent as much as a man.

    —*The New York Times,* DECEMBER 31, 1972

The man, more robust, is fitted for severe labour, and for field exercise; the woman, more delicate, is fitted for sedentary occupations, and particularly, for nursing children . . . Man's larger brain size, 3 pounds, 1.73 ounces, as opposed to the average female brain size of 2 pounds, 12.83 ounces gives him decided intellectual superiority.

    —1800–1810 *edition of the Encyclopaedia Britannica*

✖✖✖ Employers adhere so religiously to the Biblical injunction about paying women three-fifths of what men earn that we must assume they all read Leviticus before preparing the pay scales. What is a fairly well kept secret is that unequal pay is *illegal*.

Since the passage of the Equal Pay Act of 1963, it has been against federal law to pay women less than men. However, white men administer the Equal Pay Act, and white men are faring best with pay. Government reports show[1] that the median full-time earnings of white men is $7,396; of black men, $4,777; of white women, $4,279; and of black women, $3,194.

There are a lot of "old husbands" tales about the 31.5 million working women in the United States. These myths, combined with an apparent disrespect for law and order (when it comes to human rights law), aid employers in justifying not hiring women for high-paying jobs, not promoting them, and paying them unequal wages.

One myth is that women are always out sick and take much more sick leave than men. However, the truth is that the national average for sick leave for women is 5.9 days. For men it is 5.2[2] days. This slight discrepancy might well be accounted for by the fact that social mores dictate that it is the mother who stays home with a sick child.

In addition, men are absent more frequently for the shorter illnesses. The Labor Department interprets this to mean that women do not stay home from work for minor illnesses; that it is only major illnesses of greater length that cause them to be absent.

Other reports show that workers in boring jobs tend to have higher absentee rates than those workers who love their jobs.[3]

Another disability of women workers which helps to keep them from good jobs is the idea that women won't travel or move to a new geographic location. In the chapter on family law it will be shown that women who do not live in their husband's choice of domicile are guilty of desertion. This rather vicious circle has been used effectively to keep women from the executive suite.

Furthermore, men in certain kinds of employment do not move either. A study published in 1969[4] on the characteristics of federal executives—98 percent of whom were men—showed that more than half spent their entire government careers in a single agency.

Motherhood is used against women employees even more than marriage. Myth has it that women don't have the same commitment to a job as men, because women only plan to work until they get pregnant. This conjures up the image of the young wife working merely to purchase the new drapes or furnish the nursery.

Forty-two percent of all mothers in the United States work outside the home. Many are new mothers, and whether they return to work or not has a lot to do with their companies' maternity leave policies and ability to provide child care. The overwhelming number of mothers I have talked to who do not work say that they stay at home because they could not afford a private baby-sitter on the salary they would earn, and that child-care facilities are simply not available.

One out of every ten women heads a family. Eight percent of the women who work have husbands with incomes of less than $3,000 a year. Twenty-two percent have husbands with incomes of between $3,000 and $7,000 annually.[5]

The average number of years of employment for men is 43 years; for single women it is 45 years. For women with children it is 25 years.[6]

Women workers who are married and have children have *two* full-time jobs. Women in Russia, for example, who have achieved much greater job equality than women in the United States, still do not achieve, for the most part, the key or top jobs. Studies done to find out why revealed that whereas the Russian woman has the opportunity to advance on the job, promotions there, as elsewhere, involve overtime work. And the Russian woman simply cannot do much overtime work, since she is saddled with the entire burden of shopping (which takes a long time in the Soviet Union), cooking, doing the laundry, and cleaning. Her husband does not share in these tasks in post-Revolution Russia any more than he did in pre-Revolution Russia. He—like his American brothers—spends his "spare" time advancing on the job, or in leisure-time activities.

A study of time budgets in forty-four metropolitan areas of the United States found that the total time spent by married workers on paid work, commuting to work, housework, and family tasks averaged 65.5 hours a week for men and 72.4 hours for women.[7] Among working couples with children, fathers averaged 1.3 hours more free time each weekday, and 1.4 hours more on Sunday than mothers. Among married couples without children, both of whom were employed, husbands averaged .7 hours more free time a weekday and 1.1 hours more on Sunday than their wives.

Is the longevity of women affected when their career is employment rather than homemaking? It is well known that generally men in our society die younger than women. Since women and men in a working environment are under more similar stresses and strains, does the life span even itself out? Or, expressed differently, do men die younger in our competitive society because they are in the "rat race"? Apparently not.

A recent study[8] analyzed the 1965–70 mortality among all female TIAA (Teachers Insurance and Annuity Association) annuitants aged sixty-five and over. It compared the mortality of those who obtained their

TIAA annuities through employment with those who became annuitants as wives of participants. The mortality rates were virtually the same at all ages, regardless of whether the women had entered upon their annuities as retired staff members or as wives of retired staff members.

Before beginning an analysis of the laws which protect women workers, those which guarantee equal pay, and which, at least one hopes, can end sex discrimination in employment, we should pay brief attention to the major problem in our job market: unemployment. The problems which women face on their jobs are part of this larger problem, because, in the end, men workers are scared to death they will lose their jobs. And they are not paranoid; they do lose their jobs.

But even when there are jobs, the resistance to hiring women is tremendous. All discrimination laws must be looked at in the light of how, and by whom, they will be enforced. President Nixon appointed Peter J. Brennan as Secretary of Labor. He was president of the New York Building and Construction Trades Council, and has a nationwide reputation as a foe of affirmative action. This, needless to say, does not bode well for women workers.

Dorothy Haener, a leader both in the labor movement and in the women's movement, has been with the United Auto Workers since 1953. She makes some observations on sexism in employment:[9]

> There was a period in the Detroit area when we had employers going down to Appalachia to recruit workers for jobs that were within commuting distance of Detroit, and they were coming back with white males. When we raised strenuous objections, we got them to hire men from the inner city, but it still took a couple of years before this employer would start hiring women.

When you pay an assembler $4 or $5 an hour, they just feel it's a man's job. There was another case in Indiana. There had been layoffs in a plant, and women had the right to bump into janitors' jobs. The company said this was a man's job, since it required heavy lifting. While all this was being worked out, the company just arbitrarily farmed out the work to an outside contractor. This contractor brought in groups of *women* to do the work, and they were paid roughly half of what the male janitors in the union had been receiving. When the rate was less, women could do the work. After this there wasn't any more argument, but it points up how conditioned we are to accept the status quo.

Ms. Haener discusses the kinds of conflict which women workers face:[10]

The woman who is working faces two kinds of pressures from home. One is that she really has two jobs. Besides what she does at work, she still has the cooking and cleaning to do, and the family to take care of. The younger generation seems to be making some compromises in this direction, but in the older generations, the woman still carries the full load at home. Second, the woman's husband often feels guilty about the fact that his wife has to work. Although he accepts that necessity for financial reasons, he still feels that her place is in the home the rest of the time. Many women have a difficult time getting active in union affairs because their husbands object to their going to meetings of an organization which is predominantly male, or because their husbands want them to come home right after work.

While the union can be a powerful force against sex discrimination in hiring, wages, seniority, job classification, and upgrading, most unions do not do as good a job

as they could and should for women, because women
are not adequately represented in the executive and
policy-making bodies of the labor organizations.

As Letty Cottin Pogrebin points out:[11]

> If labor leaders weren't overwhelmingly male, unions
> might better represent women workers. Men do not
> easily support or strike in sympathy with women's is-
> sues such as child care centers or maternity benefits. If
> we are to win these important battles, more women must
> take an active role in union politics and stop electing
> men to do their bargaining for them. As matters stand,
> women's demands are the first things traded away at
> the bargaining table.

Today, there are three crucial issues which women
union members are pressing for within their organizations. First is child care. The union should be lobbying
for the bill which President Nixon vetoed. The union
should have its own facilities, or else negotiate with employers to provide them.

Second is maternity provisions. Many contracts do
not even include paid disability for delivery, or reinstatement to the same or similar work. Women must
insist on health insurance coverage for childbirth and
possible complications. Unions with large female membership, like the American Newspaper Guild, the American Federation of Teachers, the National Education
Association, and the International Ladies' Garment
Workers Union have taken the lead in these areas.

Third is the Equal Rights Amendment. The most
organized and vocal foe of this amendment has been
male organized labor, although many unions, including
the United Auto Workers, the American Federation of
State, County and Municipal Employees, the American

Federation of Teachers, and the National Education Association, are committed to its support.

The failure of most unions to support the ERA, and the almost routine bargaining away of women's rights at the collective bargaining table, raises serious questions of union violations of the duty of fair representation.

The doctrine of fair representation arose when the Supreme Court confronted the fact that whereas collective bargaining was a strong and powerful tool—the only tool workers could use against strong and powerful employers—it could indeed ignore the rights of the minority: black workers, women workers.

The right to collective bargaining was won through a hard and bloody struggle. It represents the recognition that one worker cannot confront one employer and obtain any kind of equity. Before collective bargaining was developed as a right, the courts had to more clearly define the right to contract of employer and employee.

The constitutional right of employers to conduct their affairs with their workers without government interference was established in 1905 in *Lochner v. New York*.[12] A New York statute had prohibited employment in a bakery for more than sixty hours in one week, or ten hours in one day. The conviction of Lochner for employing a baker for more than sixty hours in one week had been affirmed by the New York Court of Appeals. The Supreme Court reversed. It held that the statute necessarily interferes with the right of contract between employers and employees, concerning the number of hours in which the latter may work. The Court discussed the importance of determining which shall prevail— the right of the individual to labor for such time as he may choose, or the right of the state to prevent the individual from working, or from entering into any contract to work, beyond a certain time prescribed by the state. The Court, not particularly sensitive to the realities of life for the working class, seemed not to take into account that the baker probably could not get the job in the first place unless he agreed to work the number of hours specified by the employer.

The balancing of interests, as perceived in 1905, was the right to contract versus the right of the state to its police power. It took many years for the Court to recognize that the right to contract has no meaning unless the parties to the contract are in an *equal bargaining position*. Justice Harlan's dissent in *Lochner*[13] touched on what was to be stressed in later court decisions:

> . . . all things considered, more than ten hours steady work each day, from week to week, in a bakery or confectionery establishment, may endanger the health and shorten the lives of workmen, thereby diminishing their physical and mental capacity to serve the state and to provide for those dependent upon them.

Harlan, however, also wrote the opinion in *Adair*,[14] which held that for Congress to forbid an interstate railroad to discharge an employee for union membership denied due process. Harlan wrote:

> . . . any legislation that disturbs that equality [the right to join a union] is an arbitrary interference with the liberty of contract which no government can legally justify in a free land.[15]

Employees were again left to their own devices by *Adkins*,[16] where the Court held 5 to 3 that any regulation of wages violated the Due Process Clause of the Constitution.

These decisions were overruled in *West Coast Hotel*,[17] where the Court expressly recognized the unequal bargaining position of workers. *West Coast Hotel*, in 1937, led to a whole series of court decisions and legislation which, on the one hand, tried to give workers the handicap they needed to bargain effectively and, on the other hand, recognized that contracts have no meaning between two parties when one is a captive to the agreement and the other has effective freedom.

The collective bargaining agreement is, therefore, what each worker owns. A key provision of each collective bargaining agreement is the seniority provision; this provision gives the worker his or her rights to the job and to promotion.

Title VII of the 1964 Civil Rights Act[18] prohibits discrimination in employment on the basis of race, color, religion, sex, or national origin. Early in the interpretation of Title VII, courts were confronted with the problem of how to handle the present results of past discrimination. Or, how to grant equal employment opportunity to persons who would have much better jobs today had they not been kept from proceeding up the ladder of job opportunity yesterday.

This attempt to be fair to women and minority groups comes into instant conflict with the whole system of seniority. While seniority has never been considered a permanent vested right, it is a bargainable right. Those who have bargained for it, and have it incorporated into their collective bargaining agreements, will not react lightly to having their rights to seniority disturbed in an attempt to achieve justice for women and minority men.

In my view, the real villain is not the white, probably ethnic, worker, who is holding on to his job for dear life. Although he will not stand by while minority men (he has been suspicious of them all his life) and women (he thinks their place is in the home) try to work their way into his union and then into his job, this man is as much a victim of an unworkable system as is his (economically poorer) minority or female counterpart.

The real villain is the economic system which does not guarantee full employment. The seniority problem is exceptionally severe now because the white male worker knows that many of his friends are losing their jobs. In spite of the fact that there is a need for much work to be done in this country, there are not enough jobs.

The white male worker is not equipped—educationally or politically—to see that all workers are potentially in the same position: dependent for their bread on an economy they cannot control or affect.

President Nixon's order to reduce the federal payroll is stifling equal employment in the public sector. According to the Civil Rights Commission:[19]

> Any forced reductions in employment levels through job terminations are likely to affect most significantly those employees with least seniority, a disproportionate number of whom are minority-group citizens.

Of course it will affect women also.

The key tool for women's lawyers, in fighting seniority systems, is a section of Title VII which mandates that any seniority system must be bona fide.[20]

> (h) Notwithstanding any other provision of this title, it shall not be an unlawful employment practice for an employer to apply different standards of compensation, or different terms, conditions, or privileges of employment pursuant to a bona fide seniority or merit system, or a system which measures earnings by quantity or quality of production or to employees who work in different locations, provided that such differences are not the result of an intention to discriminate because of

race, color, religion, sex, or national origin. Nor shall
it be an unlawful employment practice for an employer to give and to act upon the results of any professional developed ability test provided that such test,
its administration or action upon the results is not designed, intended or used to discriminate because of race,
color, religion, sex or national origin. It shall not be an
unlawful employment practice for any employer to
differentiate upon the basis of sex in determining the
amount of the wages or compensation paid or to be
paid to employees of such employer if such differentiation is authorized by the provisions of section 6(d) of
the Fair Labor Standards Act of 1938, as amended by
29 U.S.C.A. 206 (d).

What this section means is that (1) the only seniority
system which can be upheld is a bona fide seniority system—and any seniority system which is based on discrimination is not bona fide; and (2) the employer may
differentiate on the basis of sex, if sex is a bona fide
occupational qualification for a job. There have been a
million words written on what is a bona fide sexual occupational qualification. Probably there are only three:
sperm donor, wet nurse, and human incubator.

Seniority provisions appear in 90 percent of union
contracts.[21] Seniority governs promotion, layoffs, shift
preference, transfer, overtime, vacations, parking spaces,
pensions, holidays, and sick leave. Probably the area
which concerns most workers in connection with seniority is whether or not they keep their jobs. Skilled
workers have always had ways to restrict their market;
it is the unskilled and the semi-skilled workers who must
rely on seniority rights.

Seniority is the sole consideration in 25 percent of
employment contracts with respect to layoffs; it is the
determining factor in an additional 41 percent.[22]

More than any other provision of the collective agreement, including union security provisions under existing law, seniority affects the economic security of the individual employee covered by its terms.[23]

This economic security is primarily assured by the elimination of arbitrariness. One cannot be fired because one is a union organizer, or because one does not curry favor with the boss, or because the employer doesn't like working with women or minority men.

A landmark pre-Title VII case, *Steele v. Louisville & Nashville Railroad*,[24] held that a union which excluded blacks from membership without notice to them, and amended the collective agreement so as to restrict and exclude black workers from railroad employment, violated its duty of fair representation under the Railway Labor Act.

The question in *Steele* was whether the Railway Labor Act imposes on a labor organization, acting by authority of the statute as the exclusive bargaining representative of a craft or class of railway employees, the duty to represent all the employees in the craft without discrimination because of their race and, if so, whether the courts have jurisdiction to protect the minority of the craft or class from the violation of such obligation.

Mr. Steele, a locomotive fireman working for the railroad, was excluded from membership in the Brotherhood (union) because he was black and persons of his race were excluded in the union's constitution and its practice. The Court, while holding for Mr. Steele, did see that a union cannot possibly represent to the fullest the needs of each individual member in the union.

This does not mean that the statutory representative of a craft is barred from making contracts which may have unfavorable effects on some of the members of the craft represented. Variations in the terms of the contract based on differences relevant to the authorized purposes of the contract in conditions to which they are to be applied, such as differences in seniority, the type of work performed, the competence and skill with which it is performed, are within the scope of the bargaining representation of a craft, all of whose members are not identical in their interest or merit.[25]

The Court, in 1944, was still holding that persons could be refused membership in the union (presumably because they were female or black), but that the union had to *nonetheless* represent them in negotiations with the company.

While the statute does not deny to such a bargaining labor organization the right to determine eligibility to its membership, it does require the union, in collective bargaining and in making contracts with the carrier, to represent nonunion or minority union members of the craft without hostile discrimination, fairly, impartially, and in good faith. Wherever necessary to that end the union is required to consider requests of nonunion members of the craft and expressions of their views with respect to collective bargaining with the employer and to give them notice of and opportunity for hearing upon its proposed action . . .

We conclude that the duty which the statute imposes on a union representative of a craft to represent the interests of all its members stands on no different footing and that the statute contemplates resort to the usual judicial remedies of injunction and award of damages when appropriate for breach of that duty.

Section 7 of the National Labor Relations Act gives employees "the right to be free from unfair or irrelevant or invidious treatment by their exclusive bargaining agent in matters affecting their employment." Section 8(b) (1) (A) of the same Act "prohibits labor organizations, when acting in a statutory representative capacity, from taking action against any employee upon considerations or classifications which are irrelevant, invidious, or unfair."[26]

A relevant case for attorneys of women employees to use is *Miranda Fuel*.[27] This was the first case where the National Labor Relations Board held that breach of the duty of fair representation is indeed an unfair labor practice of a union and, if acquiesced to by the employer, is also an unfair labor practice by the employer.

There is no clear statement in the legislative history of Title VII, but the whole tenor of the debate indicates that whites will not be bumped to make room for black employees, and men will not be bumped to make room for women employees. One exception occurred in *Kaiser Aluminum*,[28] where whites were bumped, but only in retaliation for the blacks being bumped by a prearranged deal between the union and management.

Title VII is still far from being inclusive. However, since the passage of the Equal Employment Opportunities Enforcement Act of 1972, Title VII has become a much more effective tool in ending discrimination. The Act now covers private concerns that employ fifteen or more people, state and municipal governments and agencies, educational institutions (public and private), labor organizations, and employment agencies. The fact that it covers labor organizations, combined with the federal mandate to the unions on the duty of fair representation, is effective ammunition for women workers who wish to go after their unions for discrimination.*

* The Act still exempts religious institutions with respect to religious discrimination.

Prior to March 1972, the EEOC had no enforcement powers. It could not file lawsuits on behalf of persons bringing charges; a charge could be filed only by a person aggrieved. Now an individual or organization may file on behalf of a person aggrieved. Such a charge need not show the name of the person aggrieved, but must be accompanied by an affidavit, which the Commission must keep confidential, setting forth enough detail and/ or examples of discrimination so as to avoid charges based on hearsay.

Keeping complaints confidential is a key, perhaps *the* key, to using the laws on sex discrimination in employment. The Department of Labor has a fine record in this regard. Under the Equal Pay Act of 1963[29] it keeps the name of a person making a complaint a secret. Retaliatory firing or harassment on the job are so well known that any woman who really needs her job probably will be afraid to file charges against her employer.

Prior to March 1972, charges had to be filed within 90 days of the discriminatory act, and lawsuits had to be filed within 30 days of receipt of notice from EEOC that conciliation had failed. Now, charges must be filed within 180 days of the act of discrimination and suits within 90 days of receipt of notice that conciliation has failed. Most discrimination, however, is a continuing act; charges against the employer can be brought at any time, as long as the complaint states that it was in fact going on within the 180-day period.

A tremendous weapon was given women as of March 1972: federal employees are now covered by Title VII. If a woman files a charge of discrimination and is not satisfied with the decision of the agency making the finding, or if after 180 days no action has been taken, she may file suit against the government in the Federal District Court.

Title VII prohibits the establishment or maintenance of seniority lists or lines of progression based on sex or race. The placement of jobs in a line of progression may constitute sex or race discrimination where such placement has a disproportionate impact on women or minority men, and is not warranted by business necessity.

In *Bowe v. Colgate-Palmolive Co.*,[30] back pay was awarded and a preliminary injunction issued on remand, in connection with a seniority system based on sex. *Bowe* attacked not only the seniority system, but arbitrary job assignments in the plant. A group of women employees complained of layoffs that resulted when Colgate refused to permit them to exercise their seniority to claim jobs involving the lifting of weight beyond a stated maximum. The court found sex discrimination in violation of Title VII and ordered the lower court to award compensatory relief to all the victims of the discrimination. Though the court said it would have to determine for each victim individually what job level she would have attained had she been permitted to exercise her seniority, the Court of Appeals expressly mandated such relief for every victim whether or not she filed charges with the EEOC and whether or not she joined in the suit.

The Court of Appeals ruled, in addition, that employers may not exclude women from jobs requiring the lifting of thirty-five pounds or more. In reversing a decision of the Federal District Court for the Southern District of Indiana (the Colgate plant is at Jeffersonville, Indiana), which had approved Colgate-Palmolive Company's practice of allowing only men to work on such jobs, the Court of Appeals stated that the lower court's decision was "based on a misconception of the requirements of Title VII's anti-discrimination provisions."

The court further declared that Colgate:[31]

must notify all of its workers that each of them who desires to do so will be afforded a reasonable opportunity to demonstrate his or her ability to perform more strenuous jobs on a regular basis. Each employee who is able to so demonstrate must be permitted to bid on and fill any position to which his or her seniority may entitle him or her.

Prior to this decision, jobs reserved for men at the Colgate Jeffersonville plant were paid at wage rates which *began* at the *highest* rate payable for jobs open to women. The effect of the court's ruling is to give women equal opportunity to bid for the better-paying jobs on the basis of their individual capabilities and to prohibit their exclusion from these jobs because of sex.

It is unclear to what extent matters political influence matters judicial. The excellent 1969 Colgate decision followed two years of picketing, demonstrating, and a consumer boycott, initiated by the National Organization for Women. Cavalcades of cars, in cities throughout the country, went from supermarket to supermarket, leafleting the shoppers (mostly women) and urging them not to buy Colgate products until Colgate stopped discriminating against its women workers. The actual extent of the boycott was never measured; we do know that Colgate was humiliated by the press coverage, and that the judges who decided the case must have been aware of the considerable public sentiment about it.*

* In 1968, I went to Jeffersonville, Indiana, with 20 other national NOW board members from all over the country, to protest the harassment, firing, and other economic and social indignities which the company was inflicting on the women plantiffs in this case. We had reservations in the Holiday Inn in Louisville, Kentucky, right across the river from the plant. When we arrived we found that our reservations had been canceled. They were reinstated only after we assured Holiday Inn that we would take immediate and drastic action.

Where plant-wide seniority has been in effect, it may be possible to correct a segregated seniority system merely by integrating the system. However, where departmental or gang job seniority is a factor in determining transfers and promotions, additional adjustments in the system are necessary to eliminate the effects of past discrimination. Otherwise, women and minority men with long years of plant service will remain excluded from certain jobs, gangs, and departments.

The key case that applies the definition of training to the seniority problem is *Quarles v. Philip Morris*.[32] The plaintiffs, Douglas H. Quarles and Ephraim Briggs, alleged that Philip Morris, by its employment practices and collective bargaining agreement, refused to hire, promote to supervisory positions, pay, advance, and transfer black employees on the same basis as whites. The Court held that the company had not engaged in discriminatory hiring practices after January 1, 1966 (the effective date of the Civil Rights Act of 1964), but that the plaintiffs were discriminated against with respect to advancement, transfer, and seniority. (They had been hired prior to January 1, 1966.)

This case decided that present consequences of past discrimination are indeed covered by the Civil Rights Act. In the Philip Morris plant, most of the opportunities for advancement or for exercising other privileges depended on *departmental seniority*, rather than employment seniority. (Before January 1, 1966, the company had black departments and white departments, the black departments invariably being those with dirtier work and less pay.) Thus, after the departments were integrated, a black with ten years' employment seniority transferring under a note of intent from a black department to a white department (in order to earn more money), took an entry level position with departmental seniority lower than a white employee with years less employment seniority.

The legislative history of Title VII indicates that a discriminatory seniority system established before the Act cannot be held lawful under the Act. Only bona fide seniority systems are upheld.

The case that has possibly gone farthest in the direction of affirmative action to end the results of past discrimination is *Commission for Human Rights v. Farrell*.[33] Prior to *Farrell*, the Equal Employment Opportunities Commission had held that it would regard a union policy which discriminated in favor of family members (with no racial intent) as unlawful only "if it intended to or has the effect of perpetuating *prior* racial, religious, or ethnic discrimination deemed unlawful by the federal act."[34] The key phrase here is "has the effect," since many discriminatory activities can be shown to be performed without any so-called evil intent.

Farrell indicated that a union which had discriminated against blacks could not give preference to the relatives of its all-white members, because such a preference would perpetuate the prior unlawful discrimination and could too easily be used as a mark to cover discrimination on the prohibited grounds. It is probable that the judge in *Farrell* was influenced by a newly enacted New York statute that was to take effect within a week of the decision. The act specifically prohibits the selection of persons for apprenticeship programs on "any basis other than their qualifications as determined by objective criteria which permit review." As a result of *Farrell*, the nepotistically inclined sheet-metal workers in New York State were forced to include "outsiders" in their apprenticeship program.

In analyzing a given case of sex discrimination, and deciding which avenues to use in fighting it, distinction should be made between the requirements under the Executive Orders (11246, as amended by 11375; Order #4) in which affirmative action to end discrimination is mandated, and Title VII, in which it is not.

Title VII has explicit language denying any requirement of so-called preferential treatment:[35]

> Nothing contained in this title shall be interpreted to require that any employer, employment agency, labor organization, or joint labor-management committee subject to this title grant preferential treatment to any individual or to any group because of the race, color, religion, sex, or national origin of such individual or group on account of an imbalance which may exist with respect to the total number or percentage of persons of any race, color, religion, sex, or national origin employed by any employer, referred or classified for employment by any employment agency or labor organization, admitted to membership or classified by any labor organization, or admitted to, or employed in, any apprenticeship or other training program, in comparison with the total number or percentage of persons of such race, color, religion, sex, or national origin in any community, State, section, or other area, or in the available work force in any community, State, section, or other area.

The fact that the Philadelphia Plan was upheld[36] proves definitely that affirmative action programs are required by Executive Order 11246. On September 29, 1969, the Labor Department had put into effect the Phladelphia Plan, under which federal contractors in the Philadelphia area would have to make good faith efforts to meet specific percentage goals for minority group employment in six construction trades. The percentages ranged from 4 to 9 percent the first year, to 19 to 26 percent the fourth year. The plan was held to be neither unconstitutional nor violative of Title VII of the Civil Rights Act, but rather an appropriate requirement of affirmative action.

In a recent unprecedented decision,[37] a Court of Appeals held that unilateral racial discrimination on the part of the employer violates section 8(a)(1) of the National Labor Relations Act where it has the effect of "producing a docility in its victims which inhibits the exercise of (section 7) rights." Section 7 deals with the rights of employees; Section 8(a)(1) states that it "shall be an unfair labor practice for an employer to interfere with, restrain, or coerce employees in the exercise of the rights guaranteed in section 7."

Under a federal court order, the Lawyers Constitutional Defense Committee of the American Civil Liberties Union Foundation recovered costs for protracted litigation that had secured the desegregation of the labor force at the Crown-Zellerbach plant in Bogalusa, Louisiana. The costs were borne by the employer and the plant's union.[38] The case held[39] that Crown's job seniority system carried forward the discriminatory effects integral to the company's former employment practices; that the safe and efficient operation of the Bogalusa mill did not depend upon the maintenance of the job seniority system (a business justification can often take the burden off the employer); and that to the extent that Crown and the all-white union insisted upon carrying forward exclusion of a racially determined class, without business necessity, they committed, with the requisite intent, an unfair employment practice as defined by Title VII.

The remedy imposed by the Court of Appeals in the case will probably be the model of how to reconcile equal employment opportunity today with seniority expectations based on yesterday's built-in racial discrimination. The court ordered that when a black applicant has the same qualifications as a white applicant to handle a particular job, the Civil Rights Act requires that black seniority acquired in a black "job line" be equated with white seniority in the newly integrated job line.

The Court in *Local 189* (the Crown-Zellerbach case) goes even farther than did the Court in the Philip Morris case:[40]

> Several facts are evident from the legislative history. First, it contains no express statement about departmental seniority. Nearly all of the references are clearly to employment seniority. None of the excerpts upon which the company and the union rely suggests that as a result of past discrimination a Negro is to have employment opportunities inferior to those of a white person who has less employment seniority. Second, the legislative history indicates that a discriminatory seniority system established before the act cannot be held lawful under the act. The history leads the court to conclude that Congress did not intend to require "reverse discrimination"; that is, the act does not require that Negroes be preferred over white employees who possess employment seniority. It is also apparent that Congress did not intend to freeze an entire generation of Negro employees into discriminatory patterns that existed before the act.

Millions of women and minority men see Title VII as a good, but basically unused, weapon in the war against discrimination in employment. It is possible that the last sentence of the above quote cannot be reconciled with the rest of the paragraph. The only way to avoid freezing an "entire generation" of black and female employees into the discriminatory patterns of the past is simply to assert that all existing seniority systems are not bona fide. And this is probably the case. In this way we can have our legislative history, and "eat our cake too."

Local 189 advances three theories for deciding how far the employer must go to undo the effects of past discrimination.[41] "A complete purge of the 'but for' effects of previous bias would require that Negroes displace white incumbents who hold jobs that, but for discrimination, the Negroes' greater mill seniority would entitle them to hold. Under this (1) *freedom now* theory, allowing junior whites to continue in their jobs constitutes an act of discrimination." The "freedom now" theory involves so much bumping that it is doubtful that it could be used.

The company and the union in the case each advanced the (2) *status quo* theory: the employer may satisfy the requirements of the act merely by ending explicit racial discrimination. Whatever inequalities would still exist, due to past practice, would, in effect, be forgotten. The status quo theory goes against what the court mandated in the *Quarles* case, and clearly does not solve the problem, either legally or politically.

A compromise theory of (3) *rightful place* construes the act as prohibiting the future awarding of vacant jobs on the basis of a seniority system that "locks in" prior racial classification. White incumbent workers cannot be bumped out of their present position by blacks with greater plant seniority; plant seniority is asserted only with respect to new job openings.

The "rightful place" theory is currently being used by some universities. While they are not bumping their white male professors to make room for women and minority men, department chairmen are advised that any new appointments they make will be looked upon more favorably if the new teachers are females or minority males. When I, for example, asked a law school representative who was recruiting for teaching jobs why he was interviewing me (who had just graduated from law school), he replied that the only teachers they can hire are women.

In the first years following the passage of Title VII, the EEOC took the position that the merger of related lines and free transfer from formerly black to formerly white departments was required, but failed to question the legality of the continued application of job and departmental seniority rules, or the related progression and transfer that prevented black or women workers from ever reaching the level of their white male counterparts.[42] Thereafter the EEOC reversed its position and adopted the view that job or progression line seniority in formerly segregated plants is unlawful.[43]

In exploring the legal remedies for women suffering employment discrimination, we have not yet fully explored the advantages of challenging the discrimination as a violation of the National Labor Relations Act, rather than using Title VII or the Equal Pay Act. Probably it is most effective to use *every weapon* available, including the whole legislative arsenal, and definitely not ignoring political and social pressure.

In reading the next chapter, which explores some of the leading cases on employment discrimination, it may be useful to bear in mind the question of why the duty of fair representation has not been used with regard to the millions of women workers. Does the answer lie in a complex interpretation of federal labor legislation, or perhaps in a more simple interpretation: the sex of the union officials?

Chapter Five
Money and Employment (2):
Sex and the Job Market

Pan Am sought . . . to explain in psychological terms why . . . most airline passengers of both sexes prefer to be served by female stewardesses. [The] . . . environment, said Dr. Berne, creates three typical passenger emotional states with which the air carrier must deal; first and most important, a sense of apprehension; second, a sense of boredom; and third, a feeling of excitement. Dr. Berne expressed the opinion that female stewardesses, because of the nature of their psychological relationship as females to persons of both sexes, would be better able to deal with each of these psychological states.

. . . He explained that many male passengers would subconsciously resent a male flight attendant perceived as more masculine than they, but respond negatively to a male flight attendant perceived as less masculine, whereas male passengers would generally feel themselves more masculine and thus more at ease in the presence of a young female attendant. He further explained that female passengers might consider personal overtures by male attendants as intrusive and inappropriate, while at the same time welcoming the attentions and conversations of another woman. He concluded that there are sound psychological reasons for the general preference of airline passengers for female flight attendants.

—Diaz v. Pan American World Airlines, Inc.,
311 F. SUPP. 559 (S.D. FLA. 1970);
REVERSED, 442 F. 2D 385

✂✂✂ It has been jokingly said that the first uses of Title VII as a tool for ending sex discrimination will be in the two or three instances of employment discrimination against men. Were that true, it would be no joke. We do know that the downright *funniest* legislative history and case law has come to us with reference to the whole concept of bona fide occupational qualification.

To those of us who are trying to eliminate the whole concept of sex roles from our lives, the lawyers, judges, and expert witnesses (like Dr. Berne) are voices from another century. Unfortunately, they speak from the same century as do most of the employers in the country.

The *Diaz* case was reversed, and now men and women alike can get jobs as flight attendants. The reasoning in the lower court case, however, is important as we examine the rationale behind sex discrimination in employment. Where women are denied so-called men's jobs, we assume the major rationale is that men enjoy keeping control of the higher-paying, higher-prestige jobs. In addition, sex role stereotypes enter into the picture, with the never-ending specter of Russian women sweeping the streets of Moscow as what we don't want here in America.

One of the major networks recently did a feature on women in the Soviet Union. Women doctors (75 percent of the doctors are female) received a scant flash of the camera. The program dealt heavily with women digging ditches, working in mines—doing the kinds of work that no one really enjoys. It was as if a feature on men workers in the United States showed men cleaning up the parks, but omitted any mention of U.S. Senators and bankers. The obvious intent was to show how bad it is when women get job equality.

The whole subject of men and women doing work interchangeably—Diaz wants to be a flight attendant—brings up, in addition to economics, the issue of sex role stereotypes. Why is the idea of a male nurse funny? Why did one of my law professors tell me that a woman law professor is a contradiction in terms? Why did one of my friends howl in shock when I suggested he buy his four-year-old nephew a doll?

Both women and men have not only been instilled with rigid unworkable notions about what they themselves should be and do—they have been instilled with equally idiotic ideas about the opposite sex. Many men get extraordinarily nervous at the very idea of a woman executive or college professor. Many women actually scorn a man who doesn't exhibit the Tarzanlike qualities—physical or psychological—that we have been trained to think mean "manliness."

The implications of this for frustrated personal lives, unliberated sex lives, and generations of generally unhappy women and men are enormous. The courts cannot hope to cope with this insanity. But the legal and judicial process *can* cope with the economic insanity which ensues. And, the results of sex role stereotyping are indeed economic.

Women who finish college and attend graduate school are earning 65 percent of men's salaries.[1] ($9,581 versus $14,747).

When the pay received in the total work force is broken down by sex, 1.1 percent of women working received $15,000 or more, compared to 13.5 percent of men. Within the $15,000-or-more job category there were 5.05 million jobs. Of these, only 3 percent were held by women in 1970.[2]

As Patricia Carbine writes in *The New York Times*:

> The truth is that a white woman with a college degree makes less than a black man with a high school degree.
>
> As women have learned from the blacks and other minorities asking to be "let up" into the system—controlled, let's face it, by white males—nothing even begins to happen until there is both legislation and enforcement.
>
> . . . Most businessmen, confronted with women's new consciousness of their worth, now concede that it is reasonable—albeit revolutionary—that equal work merits equal pay. In practice, however, the law is flaunted and reason ignored. That's why women are being forced to turn to the courts and government agencies to press for their rights.[3]

The Labor Department alone has found more than $53 million to be due in back pay. It expects the caseload to increase now that the Equal Pay Act has been broadened to cover salaries of 15 million executive, administrative, and professional employees.

The *Diaz*[4] case was an individual and class action for an injunction and damages under Section 706(f) of Title VII of the Civil Rights Act of 1964,[5] and under Rule 23(b) of the Federal Rules of Civil Procedure. Title VII prohibits sex discrimination in employment; Rule 23(b) deals with the provisions for maintaining a class action. (It should be noted that according to William H. Brown III, the chairman of the EEOC, the agency set up to administer Title VII, there were 5,800 sex discrimination charges filed in 1971, and 10,400 filed in 1972.)[6]

The issue was whether an airline violates Title VII in following the policy of hiring only persons of the female sex as flight cabin attendants. The lower court found the airline could do so; the decision was reversed on appeal.

The case centered around the definition of bona fide occupational qualification. Pan Am argued that their decision was not based on stereotyped thinking, but rather on pragmatic judgments. They used expert witnesses, such as Dr. Berne, to illustrate their pragmatic judgment-making process.

Another expert witness, Dr. Raymond A. Katzell, is an industrial psychologist and chairman of the Department of Psychology of New York University. He is also coauthor of *Testing and Fair Employment* (sic), and a frequent consultant to government agencies and industrial institutions. Noting that the flight attendant's work involves not only a "mechanical" aspect but an "intangible" aspect concerned with those interpersonal activities which are designed to contribute to passenger comfort and a physical and psychological sense of well-being, Dr. Katzell concluded that women are better at being flight attendants than men.

His reasons are fascinating. He testified that whereas some men do possess benevolence, genuine interest in the comfort of others, and a lack of perceived aggressiveness—these qualities are found more often in women.

> . . . It would be quite infrequent to find a man possessing each of these traits to at least as high a degree as the average woman.[7]

Such a statement from an expert in human development gives us cause to wonder about how we are training our male children—to be lacking in benevolence and a genuine interest in the comfort of others, and without an absence of perceived aggressiveness? But in addition, it leads one to wonder why the majority of psychiatrists, who certainly must possess these human characteristics, are male, and why, in addition, the expert witnesses for Pan Am are male?

Diaz lost in the lower court because the court reasoned that the compassion of a female was the same kind of obvious bona fide occupational qualification as requiring a Jewish person for the job of rabbi.

> . . . since the Court, not the EEOC, has the final responsibility for making findings of fact and for interpreting the statute in this action under Section 706, which must be tried here *de novo*, the Court cannot in justice accept the EEOC's interpretation which it finds to be inconsistent with the statutory language and the legislative history. The Court believes that the "bona fide occupational qualification" exception made by Section 703 for religion, sex, or national origin (but not for race or color) was consciously and deliberately intended by Congress to permit employers to establish general job qualifications based on one or more of these factors—and not necessarily related to basic job skills —in the very limited circumstances defined by subparagraph (e) of that Section.[8]

The legislative history of the Civil Rights bill shows that many Senators did not think women and men are equally suited for jobs. Senators Clark and Case, the floor managers of the bill, submitted a memo to the Senate during the debate, which explained the exception:

> . . . First, it would not be an unlawful employment practice to hire or employ employees of a particular religion, sex, or national origin in those situations where

religion, sex, or national origin is a bona fide occupational qualification for the job.

. . . Examples of such legitimate discrimination would be the preference of a French restaurant for a French cook, the preference of a professional baseball team for male players, and the preference of a business which seeks the patronage of members of particular religious groups for a salesman of that religion.[9]

With a legislative history like this, we can only hope that in interpreting Title VII, the courts will not look too often to the legislative history.

The *Diaz* lower court did, however, look to the legislative history, stating that the clear import of it is that customer preference can provide a rationale for an employer's selecting employees on the basis of their sex where the preference is a legitimate one. Using this reasoning, law firms could refuse to hire women lawyers, since most of the clients of the law firm are male businessmen, who presumably would prefer a male attorney.

The Supreme Court let stand the Fifth U.S. Circuit Court of Appeals decision that Pan Am could not limit the job to women only. Chief U.S. District Judge Charles D. Fulton of Miami had ruled for Pan Am in 1970, but was overruled in April 1971 by the Circuit Court in New Orleans. The case was overruled on a rejection of customer preference as a basis for hiring.

We do not feel that the fact that Pan Am's passengers prefer female stewardesses should alter our judgment.[10]

The key case on bona fide occupational qualification is that of *Lorena Weeks v. Southern Bell Telephone & Telegraph Company.*[11] Ms. Weeks charged that the telephone company would not consider her for the job of switchman, purely on the basis of her sex. The court found that the company violated the Civil Rights Act when it refused to consider a female employee's application, since the employer had failed to meet the burden of proving that sex is a bona fide occupational qualification, and that females would be unable to be safe and efficient switchmen.

The lower court in the *Weeks*[12] case had found for the company, using in part the EEOC's own interpretation of Title VII's bona fide occupational qualification exception as applied to weight-lifting.

> Restrictions on lifting weights will . . . [be honored] except where the limit is set at an unreasonably low level which could not endanger women.[13]

The Court of Appeals found that females were not restricted by maximum weight-lifting under a new state law; that there was no evidence to support the employer's contention that the job would be too strenuous; and that an employer may not impose its own weight limit for female employees. In addition, the court found that Southern Bell's contention that emergency work could require Lorena Weeks to use heavy equipment or be subject to late-hour call-outs was a speculative smoke screen for discrimination.

There was no dispute in the case that Ms. Weeks was denied the switchman's job because she was a woman, not because she lacked any qualifications as an individual. The job was awarded to the only other bidder for the job, a man who had less seniority than she. Under the terms of the contract between her union and Southern Bell, the senior bidder was to be awarded the job if other qualifications were met.

The EEOC 1968 position on weight-lifting was reversed in 1969. The EEOC in 1969 held that

> state protective laws have ceased to be relevant to our technology or to the expanding role of the female in our economy. Because such laws tend to discriminate rather than protect, the Commission will not regard them as a defense to a Title VII charge.[14]

Once the issue of state protective legislation was removed from the case, the court was left with the question of whether Southern Bell, as a private employer, had satisfied its burden of proving that the particular requirements of the job of switchman justified excluding women from consideration. The court used the test first enunciated in the Colgate case.[15]

> We conclude that the principle of nondiscrimination requires that we hold that in order to rely on the bona fide occupational qualification exception an employer has the burden of proving that he had reasonable cause to believe, that is, a factual basis for believing, that all or substantially all women would be unable to perform safely and efficiently the duties of the job involved.

Southern Bell didn't meet the burden. The record revealed that night work—one of the reasons given for not allowing women to work as switchmen—was in fact required of other women employees. The court enunciated perhaps the most complete and eloquent statement ever made on the subject of self-determination for women workers:[16]

> . . . Title VII rejects just this type of romantic paternalism as unduly Victorian and instead vests individual women with the power to decide whether or not to take

on unromantic tasks. Men have always had the right to determine whether the incremental increase in remuneration for strenuous, dangerous, obnoxious, boring or unromantic tasks is worth the candle. The promise of Title VII is that women are now to be on equal footing.

So, Lorena Weeks was given the power to decide to be a switch(wo)man. And she is on the job today.

Often women and minority men fail to qualify for jobs because of unreasonable, unrelated educational and testing requirements. In *Griggs v. Duke Power Co.,*[17] a unanimous court barred an employer from establishing as a precondition for employment or advancement, any testing system or formal educational requirements which are not necessary for the job for which application is made. The holding was clear in that it was not intended to guarantee a job to every person regardless of qualification. It *was* intended to remove past barriers that have operated to favor white employees. This decision upheld the EEOC guidelines on job-related tests. Tests can be related neither to any arbitrary condition ("I like to have high school graduates working in my plant. They understand more"), nor to a future promotion ("We hire engineers for the assembly line because we staff our executive departments with persons who start on the assembly line, and one needs to be an engineer to be in the executive department").

Griggs is a meaningful holding in eliminating the "good intent" standard as a crutch for the discriminating employer. The absence of discriminatory intent ("We want high school graduates. Many blacks don't graduate from high school. Therefore, we hire mostly whites") does not redeem employment procedures that are unrelated to measuring job capacity.

The *Griggs*[18] holding is also very relevant for female employment patterns:

> Congress has not commanded that the less qualified be preferred over the better qualified simply because of minority origins. Far from disparaging job qualifications as such, Congress has made such qualifications the controlling factor, so that race, religion, nationality, and sex become irrelevant. What Congress has commanded is that any tests used must measure the person for the job and not the person in the abstract.

This applies to women in a number of ways. One of the problems for women in employment is not the lack of high school diplomas, a problem which has often plagued minority men. However, job qualifications are often set up so that women *cannot* meet them. To give one example, for executive positions community experience—such as leadership in the Rotary, Elks, etc.—is often looked upon with favor. We simply must use the *Griggs* rationale, and insist that work in the League of Women Voters is equally applicable. Another example is in the academe: deans and directors are chosen on the basis of educational and administrative experience that women are not *allowed* to get. You can be the president of the university if you have been a dean, but women are not chosen to be deans. It sounds like Alice in Wonderland but, again, using the *Griggs* test of *job relevance* alert lawyers for women who insist on these jobs may succeed.

The EEOC guidelines on the availability of jobs for both sexes are reasonably specific.[19]

As a general rule, all jobs must be open to both men and women. Jobs must be open to both sexes unless the employer can prove that sex "is a bona fide occupational qualification reasonably necessary to the normal operation of that particular business or enterprise." The term—bona fide occupational qualification or BFOQ—is being narrowly defined by the Commission and the courts, with the burden of proof that sex is a BFOQ for the job in question falling on the employer (or union or employment agency) involved. Following are some examples of preferences, limitations, specifications and restrictions that are legitimate under Title VII and those which are not.

Jobs may be restricted to members of one sex:

For reasons of authenticity (actress, actor, model).

Because of community standards of morality or propriety (restroom attendant, lingerie sales clerk).

In jobs in the entertainment industry for which sex appeal is an essential qualification.

Jobs may not be restricted to members of one sex for any of the following reasons:

Assumptions related to the applicant's sex; *e.g.*, some or most of the members of one sex are unable or unwilling to do the job.

Preferences of co-workers, employers, clients or customers.

The job was traditionally restricted to members of the opposite sex.

The job involves heavy physical labor, manual dexterity, late-night hours, overtime, work in isolated locations, or unpleasant surroundings.

The job involves travel, or travel with members of the opposite sex.

Physical facilities are not available for both sexes. Only in cases where the expense of providing additional facilities is prohibitive, can this be used as an excuse.

The job requires personal characteristics not exclusive to either sex such as tact, charm, or aggressiveness.

The responsibility for most jobs being made available to both sexes lies with both the employer and the employment agency—the employer with regard to hiring; the employment agency with regard to receiving, classifying or referring applications for employment.

According to the EEOC guidelines, all employees are entitled to equality in all conditions of employment, including: retirement, hire, layoff, discharge, recall, opportunities for promotion, participation in training programs, wages and salaries, sick leave time and pay, vacation time and pay, overtime work and pay, medical, hospital, life and accident insurance coverage, optional and compulsory retirement age privileges, and pension benefits.

The EEOC has stated that employers may be permitted to effect gradual adjustment of certain plans that provide for earlier optional retirement of women, since the immediate removal of the earlier retirement option would be unfair to women close to retirement.

With respect to maternity leave, EEOC has taken the position:

Section 1604.10   Employment Policies Relating to Pregnancy and Childbirth.

(a) A written or unwritten employment policy or practice which excludes from employment applicants or employees because of pregnancy is in *prima facie* violation of Title VII.

(b) Disabilities caused or contributed to by pregnancy, miscarriage, abortion, childbirth, and recovery therefrom are, for all job-related purposes, temporary disabilities and should be treated as such under any health or temporary disability insurance or sick leave plan available in connection with employment. Written and unwritten employment policies and practices involving matters such as the commencement and duration of leave, the availability of extensions, the accrual of seniority and other benefits and privileges, reinstatement, and payment under any health or temporary disability insurance or sick leave plan, formal or informal, shall be applied to disability due to pregnancy or childbirth on the same terms and conditions as they are applied to other temporary disabilities.

(c) Where the termination of an employee who is temporarily disabled is caused by an employment policy under which insufficient or no leave is available, such a termination violates the Act if it has a disparate impact on employees of one sex and is not justified by business necessity.

The Equal Pay Act of 1963[20] was enacted as an amendment to the Fair Labor Standards Act. The law provides that covered employers shall not discriminate "between employees on the basis of sex by paying wages to employees . . . at a rate less than the rate at which he [sic] pays wages to employees of the opposite sex . . . for equal work [requiring] equal skill, effort, and responsibility . . . except where such payment is made pursuant to (i) a seniority system; (ii) a merit system; (iii) a system which measures earnings by quantity or quality of production . . . provided, that an employer who is paying a wage rate differential in violation of this subsection shall not, in order to comply with the provision of this subsection, reduce the wage rate of any employee."

The *Wheaton Glass*[21] case, with its $900,000 payment to women glass workers, is a fine example that the Equal Pay Act works. The U.S. Court of Appeals in Philadelphia upheld, in 1971, the U.S Department of Labor's right to obtain more than $900,000 in back pay, including interest, for some 2,000 women employees of the Wheaton Glass Company of New Jersey.

The money represented underpayment of wages to the women in violation of the Equal Pay Act. In denying a second appeal from the company, the U.S. Third Circuit Court of Appeals affirmed the decision of the U.S. District Court of New Jersey, which had ordered:

(1) That the women selector-packers' wages be increased to equal the men's rate.

(2) Payment to the Secretary of Labor, for distribution to the women, of back wages dating from March 1, 1965, to the date their wage rates were equalized.

(3) Payment of interest at 6 percent on the back wages.

(4) That money due unlocated employees be paid to the district court clerk for deposit with the Treasurer of the United States.

A key and important issue in the case was that the women had been doing work that was comparable but not exactly the same. The court ruled that substantially the same work demands equal pay; and that a company cannot get around the Equal Pay Act by assigning slightly different tasks to women and to men workers.

The first equal pay decision involving a retail food

supermarket was also won in 1971. The U.S. District Court, Middle District of Pennsylvania, ruled that Food Fair Stores, Inc., must pay women and men cashiers the same rate under the federal Equal Pay Act.[22]

Food Fair operates several hundred establishments in several states, including the stores in Scranton and West Hazelton, Pennsylvania, which were involved in the court case. The case centered around *job titles*. It held that "a rose by any other name smells as sweet," or, rather, that whatever the employer chooses to call the job—if men and women are doing the same work, they must be paid the same amount of money.

The court held that although male cashiers were designated as *clerk-checkers* at the stores, and women cashiers as *checkers*, their duties were substantially equal. Food Fair attempted to justify the higher pay for men cashiers on the basis of their performing miscellaneous tasks in addition to cashiering. The court found that the women also performed additional duties.

> Considering all the subsidiary activities actually performed on occasion by front-end clerk-checkers, neither the time expended for performance, nor the nature of the additional tasks actually performed, introduce any substantially greater skill, effort, or responsibility into the front-end clerk-checkers jobs than to the checkers jobs.

Different pay scales had been established for male and female clerks under a 1963–65 Food Fair collective bargaining agreement. The agreement set higher wage rates for the male clerks, and the higher rates continued under subsequent agreements. It should be noted that 1963 was prior to the passage of the Civil Rights Act, but well after the duty of fair representation of unions had been established.

The Corning Glass Works was ordered, in 1971, to pay 946 men and women workers $536,581 in back wages on grounds that they were discriminated against in their pay on the basis of sex.[23] The ruling, handed down by Judge John T. Curtin of the U.S. District Court, applied to all Corning plants. The firm has three plants in Corning, New York, and two dozen others elsewhere in the country.

The Court found that 677 women employees were underpaid $526,825 and 269 men workers were underpaid $9,756 between November 1, 1964, and June 27, 1971. The men were daytime inspectors who received less pay than some women inspectors working at night.

Corning had to pay 6 percent interest, plus giving pay raises to those workers still working on the jobs involved in the litigation. In 1967, the U.S. Department of Labor filed suit, charging the Corning Glass Works with violating Equal Pay provisions by paying women inspectors on day and afternoon shifts 18¢ an hour less than men inspectors on the night shift. (Prior to 1966, women employees were not allowed to work on the night shift.)

The court held that a 1969 collective bargaining agreement signed with the American Flint Glass Workers Union continued prior sex-based, illegal wage practices. It ordered that all inspectors involved in the litigation be paid the higher rates in order to comply with the act.

The court noted that the collective bargaining agreement then in effect expired in 1972 and that "whatever new agreement is entered into, it is important that the negotiations be carried out with the understanding that future violatons of the Act may be the subject of contempt proceedings."

An extremely important work concept—that of *ef-*

fort, in relation to equal pay—was defined in the *Daisy Manufacturing*[24] case. It was the first decision under the Equal Pay Act where a court ruled that in measuring effort for purposes of the act both mental and physical demands must be taken into consideration.

In *Daisy*, the U.S. Court of Appeals, 8th Circuit, in St. Louis, Missouri, upheld a lower court ruling under the Equal Pay Act that the Daisy Manufacturing Company, of Rogers, Arkansas, must pay ninety women employees the same rate as it pays men. The decision resulted in the women's getting back pay, plus interest, retroactive to June 11, 1964. The court also ruled that the women's wage rates must be raised to the same level as the men's.

In the original suit, the U.S. Department of Labor charged that Daisy was paying some of its women employees less than men employees for substantially equal work. Daisy claimed it was paying the men more because their jobs required greater physical effort and responsibility.

While the district court agreed that this might be so about some of the male employees, it found that some of the women's jobs required greater mental effort in the form of stress caused by fear of injury while operating high-speed machines, and that this offset the greater physical effort exerted by the men. Daisy manufactures air rifles, noise guns, and related products.

The appeals court based its decision on its earlier ruling in *Hodgson v. American Can Company-Dixie Products Division*.[25] This 1971 decision had upheld all the district court's rulings, except its denial of prejudgment interest on the back pay. The case was remanded to the district court for computing the prejudgment interest from the time back pay was "wrongfully" withheld.

According to the court in *Daisy*, the payment of interest issue was resolved in *American Can*, where it was held:

> From the inception of the discrimination, American Can was unjustly enriched, and the female employees damaged. During the entire period, American Can had the use of the money, and therefore equity and justice require payment of interest for its use. The interest should be allowed from the dates of the underpayment.

The *American Can* decision not only gives guidelines for the law on payment of interest, but it suggests the use of a common law tool for lawyers arguing sex discrimination cases. The time-honored contracts concept of *unjust enrichment* can and should be used against employers who make profits at the expense of their female workers.

One of the commonest forms of discrimination to women employees has recently been struck down by the Equal Pay Act. Women in sales are notoriously underpaid, usually receiving about half of what men in sales earn. This is accomplished by job-sorting. For instance, in a department store women are often assigned to sales jobs for which there is no commission supplement (they sell greeting cards), while men are given the sales jobs which include commission supplements (they sell refrigerators).

In a precedent-setting decision that has broad implications for the retail industry, one of Alabama's largest department stores was ordered, in 1971, to pay women workers the same as men. The ruling came in a federal court case initiated by the U.S. Labor Department under the Equal Pay Act.

Finding that the jobs of salespersons in the men's, women's, and children's clothing departments are "substantially equal" at Loveman's Department Store[26] the court concluded that the store "has engaged in a continuing routine practice of hiring its saleswomen at a lower wage, while at the same time denying them an opportunity to perform on a commission basis.".

This is one of the first court decisions in the area of sex discrimination between male and female salesclerks. The order, signed by U.S. District Judge Frank M. Johnson, provided for women's salaries in thirty-one departments at the store to be raised on parity with men.

Restitution pay was ordered for saleswomen for as far back as October 2, 1967, with the amount and rate depending on the company's male pay policy. Citing the store's pattern of wages, the court ordered that saleswomen with at least eight years of retail sales experience who sell women's and children's clothes and related items be raised by $.57 an hour and that they be paid a 2 percent commission on net sales.

Women with less than eight years' experience were increased by $.15 an hour, with restitution back to April 1, 1968. The pay of women and men doing alterations was also equalized.

The judge ordered the Secretary of Labor to provide a restitution of pay and for 6 percent interest to each affected employee or former employee.

Another recent large settlement was received by the women employees and former employees of the Square D Company in Lexington, Kentucky.[27] More than $748,000 in wages and interest was awarded to 1,600 women, in a case brought under the Equal Pay Act by the Labor Department.

The company was found in violation, having withheld equal wages from the women between May 3, 1965, and October 23, 1972. Judge MacSwinford of

the United States District Court for the Eastern District
of Kentucky ordered the payment after the Supreme
Court denied Square D's petition to review the case.

In June 1972, the Higher Education Law extended
the Equal Pay Act protection to 15 million executive,
administrative, and professional employees, and outside
salespersons. Section 906 (b) (1)[28] of the new law
extends benefits of the Equal Pay Act, which previously
had exempted such groups from its protection.

According to Assistant Secretary of Labor Richard
J. Grunewald, who directs the Employment Standards
Administration (ESA) which administers the Equal
Pay Act:[29]

> Women will benefit more than men in the newly cov-
> ered occupations because, where sex discrimination is
> found, it is nearly always women who are discriminated
> against.

The Equal Pay Act has been enormously effective in
helping women get back pay and equal pay for their
current jobs. However, our greatest legislative victory
was Title VII of the Civil Rights Act of 1964, which
became effective on July 2, 1965. Relief under Title VII
can be obtained both from the Equal Employment
Opportunities Commission (EEOC) and the Department of Justice. Whereas the commission processes
charges through conciliation, the Attorney General is
authorized to institute a lawsuit whenever he has "reasonable cause to believe that any person or group of
persons is engaged in a pattern or practice of resistance
to the full enjoyment of any of the rights secured by
Title VII."[30] The Attorney General may institute a suit
whether or not a charge has previously been filed with
the EEOC. Pursuant to section 706(e) of the act,[31] the

Attorney General may also, in the discretion of the court, intervene in civil actions brought by charging parties if he certifies that the case is of general public importance. This all sounds more effective than it has been, since the priority of the Attorneys General in the years since 1964 has clearly not been injustice to women.

The Southern gentlemen who were attempting to defeat the entire Civil Rights Act by inserting the "sex amendment" were relying on the assumption that both below and above the Mason-Dixon line, men shared similar views on women, even if their Northern colleagues seemed determined to pass the title on race. But the joke was on them. The bill passed, and they then had to confront dual abominations: a federal law guaranteeing equal employment opportunity for women *and* minority men.

The amendment was introduced by Howard W. Smith, an eighty-one-year-old white male from Virginia, and Chairman of the Rules Committee of the U.S. House of Representatives.

He called it "my little amendment."

> This amendment is offered to prevent discrimination against another minority group, the women, but a very essential minority, in the absence of which the majority group would not be here today. Now, I am very serious about this amendment . . . I do not think it can do any harm to this legislation; maybe it can do some good. I think it will do some good for the minority sex. I think we all recognize and it is indisputable fact that all throughout industry women are discriminated against in that just generally speaking they do not get as high compensation for their work as do the majority sex.

Representative Smith was confused on his statistics: women are the majority sex (53 percent of the population).

Representative Smith had voted against bills guaranteeing equal pay for equal work regardless of sex.[32] During the debate in Congress over the "sex amendment," there was so much laughter (from all those grown-up men) that hardly any speaker could be heard. Emanuel Celler, former Congressman from Brooklyn, New York, who was finally defeated in November 1972 by Elizabeth Holtzman, a woman lawyer who won his seat, discussed his home life, on the floor of the House:[33]

> I can say as a result of forty-nine years of experience—and I celebrate my fiftieth wedding anniversary next year—that women, indeed, are not in the minority in my house.
>
> . . . I usually have the last two words, and those words are, "Yes, dear."
>
> . . . *Vive la différence.*

No doubt the few women who then sat in the House were radicalized by the debate.

Katharine St. George, former Congresswoman from New York, said that she, indeed, would be glad to abolish laws regulating working conditions and hours of employment for women:[34]

> Women are protected—they cannot run an elevator late at night and that is when the pay is higher.
>
> They cannot serve in restaurants and cabarets late at night—when the tips are higher—and the load, if you please, is lighter.

So it is not exactly helping them——oh, no, you have taken beautiful care of the women.

But what about the offices, gentlemen, that are cleaned every morning about 2 or 3 o'clock in the city of New York, and the offices that are cleaned quite early here in Washington, D.C.? Does anybody worry about those women? I have never heard about anybody worrying about the women who do that work.

The addition of that little, terrifying word "s-e-x" will not hurt this legislation in any way.

Late in the afternoon of February 8, the amendment was voted upon. When the tellers announced 168 for the amendment, 133 against it, a woman in the House gallery cried, "We made it! God Bless America!"

She was promptly removed by the guards.

The two most typical weapons used against women's equality are trying to make us look like fools or ignoring us. I have found in my women's movement experience that if a news item simply cannot be made to look fool-ish, the press will ignore it.

When Title VII, *including sex*, passed the House of Representatives, *The New York Times* (*the* record of world events, giving us all the news that's fit to print) had only this to say: "The civil rights forces had to accept some unexpected amendments."

On July 2, 1965, the Civil Rights Act of 1964 went into effect. The Equal Employment Opportunity Commission was set up to administer Title VII, under the direction of Franklin D. Roosevelt, Jr. It could hardly be said that the men at the EEOC were thrilled about the "sex" amendment. Women who work at the EEOC today report that among the men at the agency, sex discrimination is still not a priority, and it is often a joke.

Apparently consciousness-raising is still needed among those who enforce the discrimination laws.

The commission's first executive director, Herman Edelsberg, told reporters at his first press conference that he and other men at EEOC thought men were entitled to have female secretaries. Edelsberg publicly labeled the sex provision a "fluke . . . conceived out of wedlock."[35]

The New York Times ran an editorial bemoaning the end of the good-old-American-tradition of sexism.

> Better if Congress had just abolished sex itself. A maid can now be a man. Girl Friday is an intolerable offense. The classic beginning of many wondrous careers in the Horatio Alger fashion—Boy Wanted—has reached its last chapter.[36]

As we have seen, the Equal Pay Act creates the opportunity for women to collect back pay and equalize wages. But Title VII deals with *opportunity* for equal employment, and for that reason is potentially a much stronger tool for us to use. If American women were to collect reparations for the wages we never earned because we never got near to getting the job—the whole American economy would be overturned. Billions and billions of dollars would be involved. If we were to collect reparations not only for the money we never were allowed to even dream of earning, but also for the humiliation of being second-class citizens in the job market—the handmaidens of American business and government service—more billions and billions of dollars would be paid out.

The Equal Pay Act provides that unions shall not "cause or attempt to cause" an employer to commit a violation.[37] Numerous collective bargaining agreements contain provisions contravening the principle of equal pay for equal work. But, as Leo Kanowitz[38] points out, the phrase "cause or attempt to cause" (as any students of the law of torts would quickly recognize), is rife with interpretative problems.

The Department of Labor has issued an Interpretive Bulletin on the Equal Pay Act, stating that covered labor organizations and their agents

> must refrain from strike or picketing activities aimed at inducing an employer to institute or maintain a prohibited wage differential, and must not demand any terms or any interpretation of terms in a collective bargaining agreement with such an employer which would require the latter to discriminate in the payment of wages contrary to the provisions of section 6(d) (1). Section 6(d) (2), together with the special provision in section 4 or the Equal Pay Act of 1963 . . . are indicative of the legislative intent that in situations where wage rates are governed by collective bargaining agreements, unions representing the employees shall share with the employer the responsibility for ensuring that the wage rates required by such agreements will not cause the employer to make payments that are not in compliance with the equal pay provisions.[39]

A Wisconsin case illustrates the laxity of the standard that unions must meet, not to be in violation of the act. In a decision of the Wisconsin Industrial Commission,[40] applying its own state fair employment practices act,[41] which contains no "cause or attempt to cause" language, but which does prohibit labor organizations from discriminating on the basis of sex, the commission, though finding that a union discriminated against the female complainants by signing a contract that established different wage rates on account of sex, let the union off rather easily. It held that the union "need not be jointly liable for back pay because the record shows it made a valid attempt to eliminate the discriminatory practice of wage differentials."[42] The "valid attempt" apparently consisted of union proposals, during new contract negotiations, that the same rate be paid to both sexes engaged in similar work—a proposal that had been rejected by the employer.

With such rulings, it is possible that a company and a union can subtly collude for a long time—each agreeing to veto equalizing proposals submitted by the other —so that the status quo remains and neither the company nor the union is found in violation of fair employment practices acts.

In the Colgate case,[43] the Title VII charge was filed against the employer and the union. The court found that even if a technical basis existed for imposing liability on the union, it "has been most assiduous in seeking to protect the rights of the [plaintiff women employees] and to secure relief for them. Although named as a defendant by the plaintiffs, it has been aligned with them and against the defendant Colgate. Under these circumstances, a judgment requiring the Union to recompense the plaintiffs, or to indemnify Colgate for the very actions which the Union has protested [maintenance of separate male and female seniority lists to which the union had *originally agreed in a contract*] would not be warranted." (emphasis mine)

Good faith is not enough, and there is much evidence that even good faith is lacking. A woman in Portland, Oregon, writes me[44] about her recent experiences with the Public Dock Commission. She worked up through the ranks to just below the position of traffic manager, but was not allowed to take that position, even though there was no one with her experience (male or female) to take it. It was given to an inexperienced young man because, as the commissioner put it, "The work involved meeting the captains of ships and it would not look good for a woman to go to the dock to meet a captain."

Chapter Six
Money and Employment (3): Credit

Whether or not a widow or divorcee has worked in the past, she has difficulty getting credit unless she has established her own credit record—a feat that is almost impossible, since a married woman can seldom obtain credit in her own name.

—CONGRESSWOMAN MARTHA W. GRIFFITHS (D.—Michigan)

They told me I can't get a loan on a house because my wife's salary doesn't count. My wife does not count as a human being. When I heard that, I went wild.

. . . Let's face it, I was no believer in Women's Lib and all that about the bras. Like most guys, I couldn't care less.

. . . Now I know what these women are fighting for.

—RICHARD CARROLL

❦❦❦❦ Richard Carroll, thirty-three, is a Con Edison senior coordinator. His wife, Christine, thirty-one, has worked as a bookkeeper for ten years. Their combined income is $16,500, more than enough to get the maximum mortgage they would need in order to buy the $30,000 Long Island house they selected.

Carroll approached two local institutions for a mortgage based on the two incomes and, as had happened during three years of trying previously, he was turned down. He also went to the New York Civil Liberties Union, where lawyer Eve Cary took the case to the State Division of Human Rights.

New York State law prohibits financial institutions from discriminating against an applicant for credit because of race, creed, color, national origin, or sex. In New York State and elsewhere, however, lending institutions flatly refuse to count a woman's salary if she is of childbearing age, as a matter of "general policy." Another in the line of existential traps for women: penalize them if they don't bear children, penalize them if they do, and penalize them if they *can*.

There is no doubt that after obtaining a mortgage, some women may become pregnant or may stop work. But after obtaining a mortgage a man may quit his job, or get laid off, or get fired, or get sick. To flatly refuse to consider the salary of all women of childbearing age, instead of considering applicants on a case-by-case basis is a classic example of discrimination.

The Carroll family has one child, age ten. Ms. Carroll does not plan to stop working.[1] Carroll said most of the institutions to which he applied over the three-year period turned them down without even questioning their plans for the future.

He did tell one loan officer, "We're married eleven years now. That's long enough to know what we're doing. We have *one* kid, see? My wife is a person. She doesn't drop a litter every year."[2]

The bank said the only way they would count Ms. Carroll's salary is if she were over thirty-eight or if an affidavit were produced proving she had had a hysterectomy. Mr. Carroll apparently doesn't like discussing matters gynecological in front of strangers.[3]

. . . And he's saying all this about my wife in front of
three witnesses. He didn't even try to camouflage it . . .
I really wanted to give it to the guy right there. I'm a
very violent man.

Instead of demolishing the particular loan officer, Carroll took the advice of Carole DeSaram, of the NOW
Employment Committee, and Eve Cary, and filed a
lengthy and detailed complaint with the New York State
Division of Human Rights. His is one of more than a
hundred similar complaints which the National Organization for Women has been gathering to fight sex discrimination in lending and credit. DeSaram says she
feels Mr. Carroll's case has singular clout because "he is
Mr. America."

The cases gathered by NOW include complaints
against both private lending institutions and the Federal
Housing Administration; from married, divorced, and
single women who have had trouble getting mortgages.
The cases keep coming in, despite two recent changes by
the FHA, which guarantees home loans, and the Federal
National Mortgage Association, which buys conventional mortgages from banks and lending institutions.

In 1965, the FHA revised its guidelines, advising that
it would consider 100 percent of the wife's salary in insuring loans. Prior to 1965, the guidelines suggested not
counting a woman's salary if she was of childbearing
age.

In February 1972, "Fannie Mae" (the Federal National Mortgage Association) issued new guidelines for
conventional mortgages. The new policy calls for adding
the couple's earnings to arrive at "total effective income." This means that lending institutions could count
both salaries, knowing that they had met the Fannie

Mae guidelines, and therefore could sell the mortgages to Fannie Mae.

Harry Pearson, who represents the U. S. Savings and Loan League, a trade association, said it appeared from studies that most institutions are considering all of a woman's income, but since there is no federal law banning sex discrimination in lending, "We can't tell the associations what to do."[4] He said he expected more sex discrimination state laws to come out of committee.

But according to the complaints, most lending institutions have not changed their standards. Some refuse to count any of a woman's salary; others count only a portion.

John V. Piro, a Brooklyn real estate dealer, told *Newsday*[5] that the FHA, contrary to its written policy, does not count a woman's (entire) income:

> I deal with the FHA all the time. In reality they don't give it [a loan based on two full salaries] to you.

He cited one recent case of a couple who were refused an FHA insured loan. They had two children, cared for by the wife's mother, who lived with the family. After the birth of the second child, the wife returned to her job, which she had held for eight years, after a few weeks' maternity leave. Each spouse made about $9,000 a year; they wanted a $27,000 mortgage with $5,000 down. Piro said:[6]

> Any man with that total income would pass right through if he were sole provider. After they requested a personal interview with the FHA and had a rehearing, the agency said they would credit her for only half her income. By this time the contract period was over and the couple lost the house.

Divorced and widowed women are up against an even bleaker situation. Banks ask them to get co-signers. As long as he is male and over twenty-one, the co-signer is approved.

Piro's partner, Evelyn Polisar, is divorced and earns $45,000 a year. She was turned down by four lending institutions when she went for a $40,000 mortgage on a $65,000 house. One bank told her to "let her boyfriend sign."

A Delaware woman was first denied a low-income mortgage on a federal program because the combined income of her earnings and her husband's was too high. She was then denied an FHA loan because they refused to count her income and said her husband's income alone was too low.

She told the National Organization for Women:

> Further discussions revealed that they would not be able to count the woman's income under this program (FHA and the Veterans Administration housing) unless I would consent to sterilization. They suggested that I have my tubes cut. In that event they would credit half of my income. They also informed me that it would not be enough if my husband were to agree to a vasectomy (which is less costly and less difficult than tying tubes), because "you can still get pregnant."

Another case deals with a divorced woman with a high salary who was turned down by several New Jersey lending institutions. They said it was because the house was unsound. She whipped out an engineer's report attesting that the house was in perfect condition. Next they complained that the neighborhood was "bad." The neighborhood in no way could be considered risky.

Barbara Shack of the American Civil Liberties Union reports on a case of a single woman, living with her parents and applying for a mortgage based on her own and her father's income. The woman said she did not intend to marry or to leave the home. The bank told her they could not consider her income because she was of marriageable age.

Shack concludes:

> Credit is an American way of life. Society functions on credit and women have been systematically denied it. The time has long passed when women are to be systematically viewed as baby machines and all the assumptions that flow from the stereotype. The classification has interfered with their access to fundamental rights and privileges.

> What seems to be happening now is that the banks seem to be becoming more sensitive to criticism. If a fuss is made, they may capitulate.

After the Carrolls had filed their complaint,[7] one of the institutions named in it agreed to pass on their mortgage. They also received an unsolicited letter from the Chase Manhattan Bank inviting them to apply. Ironically, in their three-year search for a mortgage, Chase was one of the banks that had summarily turned them down.

Obviously, a blanket refusal to consider the full income of women does not make *economic sense*. Putting aside considerations of equality, even if the parties did default on their mortgage, the lending institution would lose nothing. Since most persons put at least 20 percent down on a home, if the lending institution had to foreclose and auction the house, it would lose no money. If the house depreciated, the down payment would more than make up the difference. For example, if a woman puts $10,000 down on a $40,000 house, the bank is owed only $30,000. Even in a declining market, the bank could easily get $30,000 at auction.

The current real estate market happens to be such that the house would most likely have appreciated. The bank would then get what it is owed, plus legal fees, and the defaulter would get the overage.

Two incomes are also a safeguard in times of high unemployment. If only one person in the family has a job, and loses it, the family's entire income is cut off.

A Florida study[8] shows how the potential for motherhood is used against us, time and time again. A mortgage company vice-president says:

> We look at the woman's life from an overall point of view. If she is a professional type person and she and her husband have not had any children nor do they expect to have children, then their combined income can be considered when they apply for a home loan.

> It would help a woman's case if she is of the child bearing age to have a doctor's statement that she cannot have children.

> . . . You can't expect that she will not become a mother.

It is not just mothers and potential mothers who are discriminated against in obtaining credit. It is all women. According to Congresswoman Griffiths:

> Banks, savings-and-loan associations, credit-card companies, retail companies, retail stores, and even the Federal government discriminate against women in extending credit. And, they discriminate against women in all stages of life—whether single, married, divorced or widowed; with or without children; rich or poor; young or old.

Women have found that companies that extended them credit in their own name before they married refuse to do so after they marry. An NBC newscaster in Chicago had charge accounts at most of the major stores there. After she was married, she requested that her accounts be changed to her new name and address. One store immediately closed her account; the others sent her application blanks to open new accounts—in her husband's name, based on his credit rating.

As Lynne Litwiller, former national task-force coordinator on taxes and credit for NOW says:[9]

> Married women become financial "nonpersons"—"children" who have no identity of their own.

Even for a married woman who doesn't object to having retail and credit card accounts in her husband's name, the system can cause problems if her husband dies, or if they separate or get divorced. An Illinois woman in her forties, the head of her family, wanted to buy a home for herself and her children. She was told that to get a mortgage she would have to ask her seventy-year-old father, who was living on a pension, to co-sign it.

Legislation would obviously be the most effective weapon, but if past experience is any guide, progress on this front may be slow. Only a handful of cities, such as Minneapolis and St. Paul, have laws prohibiting discrimination against women in credit. New York is one of the few states which has laws banning discrimination against women in credit. They were passed late in the 1973 session.

Hearings held by the National Commission on Consumer Finance in 1972 documented the massive problems women face in applying for credit. Three bills introduced by Representative Bella Abzug during the

92nd Congress would outlaw discrimination against women in financial and credit transactions by:

1) prohibiting discrimination by financial institutions or any other persons on the basis of sex or marital status in connection with federally related mortgage transactions;

2) amending the Truth-in-Lending Act to prohibit discrimination on the basis of sex or marital status in the extension of credit;

3) prohibiting discrimination by any federally insured bank, savings and loan association, or credit union against an individual on the basis of sex or marital status in credit transactions and other activities.

Since women are the shoppers for the family, the reasoning behind denying us credit cannot be explained. Moreover, the failure of lenders to regard women as credit-worthy in their own right means that married women who subsequently become divorced, separated, or widowed have no prior record of credit transactions —thus providing the rationale for a refusal to lend to them at all!

The main reason that many lawsuits have not been brought directly challenging discrimination against women in granting credit is that, until the *Reed*[10] decision, women had not been held to be persons, entitled to equal protection under the Fourteenth Amendment. With the *Reed* opinion, and with the Equal Rights Amendment (soon, we hope, to be ratified by the thirty-eight states necessary to amend the Constitution), the situation will be different.

Currently, many women find that after they are separated or divorced their credit has been *automatically* canceled. Widows find that it is easier to open charge accounts in their dead husbands' names than in their own. (This gives rise to the conclusion that a dead man is considered a better credit risk than a live woman.)

Colorado state law gives married women credit for being persons in their own right—and gives them credit. One statute states:[11] "The expenses of the family and the education of the children are chargeable upon the property of both husband and wife or either of them and in relation thereto they may be sued jointly or separately."

The U.S. Report for Colorado on the Legal Status of Women in the United States states:[12] "A wife may contract debts in her own name and upon her own credit . . . as if unmarried."

The Colorado statute states:[13]

Any woman while married may contract debts in her own name and upon her own credit and may execute promissory notes, bonds, bills of exchange and other instruments in writing, and may enter into any contract the same as if she were sole;

and in all cases where any suit or other legal proceedings shall be instituted against her, in any judgment, decree, or order therein shall be rendered or pronounced against her, the same may be enforced by execution of other process against her the same as if she were sole.

With such good laws on the books, one wonders how it is with women and credit in Colorado. Not so good.

One woman, president of a public relations firm, and recently divorced, reported that when the joint accounts were ended, she could not get credit in her own name.[14]

Another woman, who is a realtor married to an attorney, applied for credit in her own name at Penney's. After three weeks of not hearing from them, she called.

The credit manager asked her if she was having marital difficulties; then asked who was the breadwinner of the family.

When the whole issue of credit arose in the women's movement, many women, including myself, thought it was a superficial one. For years, I have thought that one of the saddest symbols of the brainwash of women is that we have all been convinced that we must be heavy consumers. Thus, when the credit discrimination topic came up, while I recognized it was indeed discrimination, I could not get too excited about it. I had hoped that, with the revolution, we women would simply stop buying all that junk—in anybody's name or with anyone's credit card, even our own—whatever the ramifications would be for the American economy.

However, I have seen the error of my ways. Being able to buy a house, or a car, or a dress, or get a bank loan to go to school or on a trip is indeed part of actively participating in life. And it certainly can be said that credit is the American way of life. Whereas we are hoping to change the American way of life, we want to be able to enter it (or reject it) at times of our own choosing.

A good example of the childlike status given to women is the defense of "excusable ignorance" that we can use as an answer to actions in commercial law. In the Uniform Commercial Code, the codification of commercial law that has been adopted by forty-eight states, an important section deals with the rights of a holder in due course.[15]

A holder in due course is a person who takes a commercial instrument for value, in good faith, and without notice that it is overdue or has been dishonored, or of any defense against or claim to it on the part of any person.[16] In other words, one is responsible for one's participation in a commercial transaction unless one has a defense, such as being an infant or being insane.

Paragraph 2(c) is of special interest. It discusses as a defense that the person did not have reasonable opportunity to gain knowledge of what she/he was doing.

Rights of a Holder in Due Course. To the extent that a holder is a holder in due course he takes the instrument free from

(1) all claims to it on the part of any person; and

(2) all defenses of any party to the instrument with whom the holder has not dealt except

 (a) infancy, to the extent that it is a defense to a simple contract; and

 (b) such other incapacity, or duress, or illegality of the transaction, as renders the obligation of the party a nullity; and

 (c) such misrepresentation as has induced the party to sign the instrument with neither knowledge nor reasonable opportunity to obtain knowledge of its character or its essential terms; and

 (d) discharge in solvency proceedings; and

 (e) any other discharge of which the holder has notice when he takes the instrument.

It follows the great majority of the decisions under the original Uniform Negotiable Instruments Law in recognizing the defense of "real" or "essential" fraud, sometimes called fraud in the essence of fraud in the factum, as effective against a holder in due course.[17] The common illustration is that of the maker who is tricked into signing a note in the belief that it is merely a receipt or some other document. The theory of the defense is that his signature on the instrument is ineffective because he did not intend to sign such an instrument at all. Under the provision stated above, the defense extends to an instrument signed with knowledge that it is a negotiable instrument, but without knowledge of its essential terms.

What categories of persons are deemed to be likely not to understand the essential terms of a commercial document? The code continues:

> The test of the defense is that of excusable ignorance of the contents of the writing signed. The party must not only have been in ignorance, but must also have had no reasonable opportunity to obtain such knowledge. In determining what is a reasonable opportunity, all relevant factors are to be taken into account, including the age and *sex* [emphasis mine] of the party, his intelligence, education and business experience; his ability to read or to understand English; the representations made to him and his reason to rely on them or to have confidence in the person making them; the presence or absence of any third person who might read or explain the instrument to him, or any other possibility of obtaining independent information; and the apparent necessity, or lack of it, for acting without delay.

> Unless the misrepresentation meets this test, the defense is cut off by a holder in due course.

So, according to commercial law, women may be placed in somewhat the same category as the foreign born, when it comes to understanding the English words in a document they are signing.

The Internal Revenue Code is based on the premise that most women are married and do not work, or if they do, earn much less money than their husbands. As more and more women work, and as they increasingly earn more money, the code will have to be revised—to make it equitable. Now, a substantial new deduction for child care is allowed under the provisions in the tax bill that became effective January 1, 1972. In other words, permissible deductions could be claimed in the 1972 income tax returns, due April 1973.

The new provision enabled working mothers to deduct up to $4,800 a year for hiring baby-sitters, cleaning help, and full-time maids. Deduction was allowed for the cost of child-care center tuition. The provision allows working parents to deduct up to $400 a month for hiring household help to care for children under fifteen, or for a disabled family member. Up to $200 a month can be deducted for out-of-home care for one child, $300 for two, and $400 for three or more. The deduction is available to families in which both parents are working, if they file a joint tax return, and to working single-parent taxpayers. To claim the full deduction, total family income must be $18,000 or less; lesser deductions may be claimed by families with incomes up to $27,600, under a formula that reduces the permissible deduction $.50 for every dollar of income above $18,000.

The relevant provision in the Internal Revenue Code, section 214, was originally enacted in 1956, and permitted the deduction of certain dependent care expenses incurred by a "woman or a widower."[18] This was subsequently changed to include husbands whose wives were incapacitated or institutionalized, but it was not until January 1, 1972,[19] that the section applied to all similarly situated taxpayers regardless of sex. In addition, a 10th Circuit case, *Moritz v. Commissioner*,[20] dealt with the pre-1972 law, and held that the former section 214 was unconstitutional, and that a single male who hired help to care for his invalid mother was entitled to the benefits of the section.

If a taxpayer has a child under fifteen (or other qualifying dependent, such as an invalid spouse) in her/his household, deductions can be made up to $400 per month for household and dependent care services rendered in the taxpayer's household, if they enable her/him to be gainfully employed. If the services are rendered outside the taxpayer's house (e.g., child-care center), the maximum deduction is $200 per month if taxpayer has one qualifying dependent, $300 for two, and $400 for three or more. Each dollar of the taxpayer's adjusted gross income over $1,500 per month reduces the maximum deduction for that month by $.50. Thus, if taxpayer adjusted gross income is $2,300 or more in a month, there can be no section 214 deduction for that month. Finally, the person being employed to furnish the household or dependent care services cannot be a relative of the taxpayer. Relatives are defined by the Code:[21] all of the obvious ones (up to, but not including, aunts, uncles, nephews, and nieces) and close in-laws and step relatives, as well as any dependent who lives in taxpayer's house, are included.

Under existing rate schedules, a husband and wife earning similar incomes will pay a higher tax than if they were unmarried. For example, if husband and wife have equal gross incomes and total taxable income (gross income minus business expenses and the like, minus personal exemptions, minus either itemized personal deductions or standard deductions) of $32,000, they will pay $8,060. If each were single and had $16,000 of taxable income, each would pay $3,830. The real disparity is even worse, however, because if single, each could take a full standard deduction, while a married couple gets only one between them (each gets a half if they choose to file separately).

This, however, does not mean the rate schedule discriminates against persons who get married. If the incomes of the husband and the wife are widely disparate (as is clearly the case with most men and women), the couple is better off married—at least for tax purposes. Thus, if the wife's taxable income is $32,000 and husband's is nothing (or vice versa), the couple will pay $8,660. If both were single, the woman would pay $10,290. The pre-1971 rate schedule was purely "pro-marriage." If incomes were equal, being married neither saved nor cost taxes; if incomes were disparate, marriage saved even more money than under the present rates.

Why not simply make everyone file individual returns? Tax specialist Richard Abt suggests the following considerations:

Because of progressive rates, it is obviously desirable to shift income to persons with lower incomes. All sorts of schemes were developed to accomplish this, with "husband and wife schemes" particularly easy to pull off, since the donor had little risk of not having use of the money if needed. Then several states enacted community property laws. This had the effect of dividing incomes evenly between husband and wife for, among other things, federal income tax purposes. Married residents of such states were at a distinct advantage over residents of other states—they had perfect income splitting, by virtue of state law, with no need for artificial schemes. While similar legislation was being introduced throughout the country, Congress decided to do something about it. It then changed the income tax laws to permit joint returns, with tax being equal to twice that which an individual earning half that amount would have to pay—i.e., complete income splitting.

This of course greatly discriminated against single persons who could not split their incomes with anyone. The current schedule makes some modification—lowering the rate single taxpayers have to pay, thus decreasing the advantages enjoyed by married couples with disparate incomes, but creating a disadvantage for married couples with equal income. In other words, the code regulations currently in use give a greater advantage to a couple where the partners earn disproportionate amounts, than where they earn similar sums.

The "fair" answer is not clear. Perhaps married persons should be allowed to pick either set of schedules. However, this would bring us to where we were before —discrimination in favor of married persons—only at lower rates. Perhaps we could allow any two persons to file joint returns. But this would mean a rush on unemployed students as tax partners for Rockefellers.

Most of the sex discrimination that exists in the federal income tax code is the result of state property law. For example, if someone puts assets (e.g., stock) in trust for beneficiaries for ten years or longer, the income from the assets is taxed to the beneficiaries rather than to the donor. Wealthy persons often set these up for their children. The purpose is income splitting, the root of the joint return problem. The children are of course in lower tax brackets, and there are often several children. However, if the money is actually used for the donor's benefit, the entire income of the trust will be taxable to the donor.

If the money is used to pay for the education of the children, or their food and clothing, the entire income of the trust will be taxed to the father. Under most states' laws, the father (increasingly the laws are obligating both parents for support of children) is obligated to pay for such items for the children. The trust, therefore, would have discharged the *father's* obligation, and therefore the income from it will be taxed to him. If, on the other hand, the mother is the donor of the trust, the income can be used for the education, etc., of the child, without any fear of its being taxable to her. This is true whether or not the father is around; therefore it presents a case of discrimination against men.

As women continue to work, and begin to earn sums of money equal to what men earn—and also perhaps as fewer of them marry—the Internal Revenue Code will no doubt be changed to reflect that change in social organization.

As of 1967, thirty-five states had comprehensive laws prohibiting employment discrimination on the basis of race, religion, or national origin. Thirty of these states provide for administrative enforcement; the remainder provide criminal penalties. Eleven states and the District of Columbia forbid discrimination on the basis of sex.[22]

Attorneys for women are making progress (and law) by filing with state fair employment practices commissions. One example is the case of Alice Waterman, who wanted to be a dogcatcher.[23] Ms. Waterman charged that she was discriminated against on the basis of sex when she was not hired for the job of animal control warden for the Village of Northbrook, Illinois. After she applied for the job, a man the same age as she (twenty), but without any experience with animals, was hired. Her experience with animals included working as a stable hand, working for a veterinarian, and personally owning dogs and horses.

On May 1, 1972, a public hearing was held and Ms. Waterman was found to have been discriminated against. This was the first public hearing held on sex discrimination under the new Illinois law, which had added "sex" as a covered category.

The Village of Northbrook appealed the ruling of the hearing officer, but in the meantime they hired her for the job; she began work on July 15, 1972. On appeal, the Fair Employment Practices Commission affirmed the hearing officer's finding in favor of Alice Waterman.[24]

Another Illinois job discrimination case is that of Virginia Wisdom.[25] She charged that the Rush Presbyterian St. Luke's Medical Center discriminated against her by sex when, on November 30, 1971, she asked to apply for a position as security guard, and was refused an application.

The hospital made a motion for judgment on the pleadings against her, saying they were exempt from the law, which provides:[26]

> . . . the term "employer" does not include any not for profit corporation or association organized for fraternal or religious purposes, nor any school, educational or charitable institution owned and conducted by or affiliated with a church or religious institution.

The hospital asserted it was not an employer within the meaning of the statute because it was a "school, educational or charitable institution," affiliated with the Presbyterian Church.

The hearing examiner ruled[27] that it was not "affiliated" within the meaning of the statute, and hence was not covered. The reasoning of the examiner if used as a precedent could indeed change the status of most private hospitals in this country: since the hospital has doctors, staff, etc., and handles patients of all religions, it is not "affiliated" with the Presbyterian Church.

The Chicago want-ads case, although lost in the

courts, turned out to be a victory for the women's movement. For years, the women of NOW have been picketing, demonstrating, negotiating, and otherwise trying to get the newspapers to integrate their help wanted columns.

Originally, the EEOC had ruled that the newspapers could designate the help wanted columns as "male" and "female." They finally reversed their position on the grounds that women simply do not look for employment in "Help-Wanted—Male" columns. In addition, it has been shown conclusively in many cities that the jobs listed for men are at considerably higher salaries than those listed for women, thus perpetuating sex discrimination in employment at the first juncture of the employment situation.

To demonstrate this point, members of New York NOW visited the offices of the then head of the New York City Human Rights Commission, Simeon Golar. We brought thousands of newspapers to his office, with the segregated want ads underlined in red, showing the pay differentials, and left them in the middle of the floor.

The Illinois case was brought against the five Chicago daily newspapers.[28] Filed under Title VII of the Civil Rights Act, it charged that when the newspapers print help wanted ads, they act as employment agencies within the meaning of the statute. Therefore, for them to segregate the columns violates the law.

The U.S. District Court ruled in favor of the newspapers,[29] saying that they were not employment agencies within the meaning of the statute. However, Judge McGarr did say that he thought plaintiff's request was one "whose time has come."

Apparently it had come, because one month later, after the notice of appeal was filed by attorney Charlotte Adelman on behalf of NOW and the ACLU, the five

Chicago papers—*Daily News, Sun Times, Defender, Tribune,* and *Today*—integrated their want-ad columns. They called it a "voluntary action."

In summer 1973, the Supreme Court ruled, in a case brought against the Pittsburgh press, that ordinances prohibiting sex-segregated want ads are *not* a violation of the First Amendment rights of newspapers. The Pittsburgh Human Rights Commission had ruled earlier, and had been supported by the state courts, that in running these segregated ads, the newspaper aided and abetted sex discrimination.

Following the Supreme Court decision, many newspapers throughout the country integrated their want ads, most without so much as an editorial explaining the change. This, of course, was a tremendous victory for the women's movement—NOW had been actively protesting segregated want ads since 1967.

In a Washington, D.C., case the ACLU secured a federal court decision awarding more than $30,000 in damages to fourteen victims of racial discrimination in job promotion in the D.C. Department of Licenses and Inspections.[30]

The New York Civil Liberties Union recently won a decision from the New York City Human Rights Commission, which held that the New York Philharmonic had engaged in discriminatory hiring. Changes in the hiring procedures were ordered.

The Washington, D.C., Civil Liberties Union is challenging discriminatory hiring practices by the District Police Department. The New Jersey Civil Liberties Union brought a series of actions to halt construction of a medical school and a U.S. post office because of discrimination against black employees by contractors and craft unions. In another New Jersey case, the contractors are appealing a lower court decision upholding an integration plan.

The New York Civil Liberties Union, in 1972, challenged several employment practices, charging sex discrimination.[31] In *Chamberlain v. Indian Valley Realty Corp.*, NYCLU unsuccessfully challenged the Holiday Inn's power to fire Mary Chamberlain, who was working as a Little Fox (similar to a Bunny), because she was allegedly too flat-chested. In *Matter of Sullivan and Smolens*, the New York law that had excluded girls from being newspaper carriers was attacked. The New York State legislature passed a law later to allow children of both sexes to carry papers.

In *Brennan v. Nassau County Civil Service*, NYCLU challenged the civil service requirement of two years of college for female police trainees, while male trainees were required to have only high school diplomas. In *Doyle v. Sidewalk Cafe* and in *Griffin v. Parker*, policies were challenged that, on grounds of differential sex roles unrelated to job performance, required short hair on men while permitting long hair on women.

The Appellate Division upheld a New York State Supreme Court ruling that two women working as audiovisual technicians at Hunter College must each be able to lift a 25-pound barbell above her head with one hand.[32]

Marilyn Sontag and Sophie Stepinoff contended in a court suit that the Civil Service weight-lifting requirement discriminated against women. The judge ruled that the test was a fair one, because the women had to lift twenty-five-pound projectors. Both women had been employed for over a year, and had performed their jobs in a satisfactory manner. Both were required to take the Civil Service examination, and both passed the written examination.

In order to pass the physical examination each woman had to run an obstacle course in twenty seconds, lift a twenty-pound weight overhead with the left hand, and a twenty-five-pound weight with the right hand. Each failed to lift the twenty-five-pound weight satisfactorily, and therefore failed the test. They had never in the course of their work been unable to perform the physical duties required, or been called upon to lift heavy weights above their heads. Both have been replaced by other employees.

This is a clear-cut case of a test (in this instance, lifting twenty-five pounds over one's head) that is unrelated to the job. The sole effect of that particular test was to bar women from employment in a job in which they had already proven their abilities through actual performance.

Since private pressure to win sex discrimination cases requires organization, money, and knowledge, various legal problems must be resolved before total enforcement of Title VII can begin to take effect.

In *Lea v. Cone Mills*,[33] litigants who were successful in obtaining an injunction under the Civil Rights Act, barring an employer from refusing to hire a black woman, were entitled to recover counsel fees, even though they were not seeking employment for themselves. In this case, a civil rights organization went to every employer in town, filing complaints. The court held that such behavior constituted an acceptable cause of action.

In *Piggie Park*,[34] the court held that "when a plaintiff obtains an injunction, he does so not for himself alone, but also as a 'private attorney general,' vindicating a policy that Congress considered of the highest priority. If successful plaintiffs were routinely forced to bear their own attorney's fees, few aggrieved parties would be in a position to advance the public interest in invoking the injunctive powers of the federal courts." *Piggie Park* also involved mass complaints, which had been typed on the same typewriter, using the same words.

Is the duty of fair representation being breached by most unions and most employers? I think so.

In *United Rubber*,[35] the union had refused to process grievances of eight black employees in its bargaining unit at the Goodyear Tire & Rubber Company of East Gadsden, Alabama. Local 12 had been the exclusive collective bargaining representative of the employees; until March 1962, three separate seniority lists—white male, black male, and female—were maintained, although the separate listings were not mentioned in the contract. The union committee concluded, therefore, that no contract violation existed, and that the union had no grounds for complaint against the company.

Unfair labor practices were filed against the union. The court concluded that where the record demonstrates that a grievance would have been processed to arbitration but for arbitrary and discriminatory reasons, the refusal to so process it constitutes a violation of the union's duty to represent its members "without hostile discrimination, fairly, impartially, and in good faith."[36]

In New York State, for example, the union has complete control, and one must first bring an action against the union for breach of the duty of fair representation. Under federal law,[37] since *Vaca v. Sipes* in 1967, the employee can sue the employer after he has shown that the union has breached the duty of fair representation. In the *Crown Zellerbach*[38] case, review by the U.S. Supreme Court was denied (even though there was a split of opinion between the 5th and 2nd circuits), to determine whether or not a breach of the duty of fair repre-

sentation is an unfair labor practice, under the National
Labor Relations Act.

Griggs[39] has clearly spoken about the validity and uses
of testing and formal requirements (a high school di-
ploma, for example). It is interesting to note that the
EEOC guidelines[40] are less stringent than are the court's
guidelines in *Griggs*.

EEOC Employee Selection Guidelines

The use of any test which adversely affects hiring, promotion, transfer or any other employment or membership opportunity of classes (race, sex, etc.) protected by
Title VII constitutes discrimination, unless:

(a) the test is validated and evidences a high degree
of utility,

(b) the person giving the particular test can demonstrate that alternative, suitable, hiring, transfer, or promotion procedures are unavailable for his use. Where
technically feasible, a test should be validated for
each minority group for which it is used. Under no
circumstances will the general reputation of a test, its
author or its publisher . . . be accepted in lieu of evidence of its validity.

Under the EEOC guidelines, if no other means of
selecting employees is available, the employer can use a
(perhaps inadequate) test. In the case of the two women
who had been performing their jobs successfully for
a year, the test of being able to lift twenty-five pounds
over their heads was obviously an invalid one.

Since judging the future ability of workers is at best an
art, this guideline gives an available "out" for potential
discriminators. One other section[41] of the EEOC guidelines, however, is effective ammunition against an employer trying to avoid hiring or promoting minority men

or women. This will be effective as a guideline in cases where the qualifications were once simple (or vague), and have become more complex.

> No new test or other employee selection standard can be imposed on a class of individuals protected by Title VII who but for prior discrimination, would have been granted the opportunity to qualify under less stringent selection standards previously in force.

Anyone working actively to get jobs for women and minority men in areas where they have never worked before will be confronted with the accusation that the standards are "being lowered" by federal law. It is my view that such imputations are sexist and racist. Nonetheless, the weighing of seniority versus ability is a significant problem.

The court has spoken on the subject in several cases. In any discussion of seniority, particularly seniority made complicated by the requirement of incorporating Title VII mandates, the phantom always appears of unqualified workers rising to the top, while excellence goes unrewarded. An umpire's decision in *General Motors*,[42] for example, outlines one possible procedure:

> (a) An outstanding employee, "head and shoulders" above others in ability, merit and capacity, is entitled to promotion irrespective of seniority consideration. If necessary, management should have no difficulty in pointing out the factors that account for his superior qualification.

> (b) When such an outstanding employee is not available, management may select several employees whose "ability, merit, and capacity" are adjudged by management to be approximately equal. The individual in the

group with greatest seniority may then be selected for the promotion.

The "head and shoulders" provision is, at best, vague. If a proper method is for management to take a group of employees who are approximately equal in ability, merit, and capacity, and select from them those with the longest seniority for the purposes of promotion, the method of selection is considered proper. If, however, a single employee is promoted out of line seniority, management must show that this employee is not merely slightly better qualified than longer seniority employees, but that she or he is "head and shoulders" above.

"No seniority clause will ever be written that will be completely self-executing,"[43] wrote an arbitration scholar. Needless to say, the entrance of Title VII into the problem will not make resolution any easier.

No discussion of employment and pressing sex discrimination complaints is honest if it does not confront the issue of retaliatory firing. A rather sobering decision in early 1971 brings into focus a very real problem which a woman or minority male worker may face when asserting federal rights: *she or he may get fired.*

In *EEOC v. Woolco*,[44] the court held that neither the Civil Rights Act, the commerce clause of the U.S. Constitution,[45] nor the All-Writs Act empowers the EEOC to obtain an injunction against an employer requiring him to cease discrimination and reinstate a discharged employee who has been fired in retaliation for filing an EEOC complaint.

Federal courts have held, however, that employees cannot be fired for violating a rule that requires racial discrimination. In *Smith*,[46] hospital employees were fired when they refused to abide by a policy which allocated black jobs and white jobs. They were ordered reinstated; they had broken only an illegal rule.

However, in a recent Supreme Court decision,[47] Maryland's common law ban on strikes by public employees was upheld, even though the public employees were striking to protest their employer's racial discrimination. They were fired for failing to return to work. The Court held that they must find other means, *even if they are slower means* (emphasis mine), of enforcing their rights. The Court said it was for the legislature, not for them, to find an exception to the no-strike provision. Given the racial composition of Maryland's state legislature, it seems unlikely it will make such an exception.

In this country, making provisions for persons who have been "handicapped" is not unique. The blind, for example, are afforded all kinds of economic and social privileges, in recognition of the hardship of their lives. Under the provisions of the Universal Military Training and Service Act,[48] returning veterans are entitled to reclaim their civilian positions without loss of seniority. This can, and often does, mean the displacement of newly hired workers. After World War II, returning (male) veterans displaced tens of thousands of women who had worked in private and public employment while they were overseas. Since exclusion from the military has been considered a "privilege" for women, the issue of veterans' preference (particularly in a time of underemployment) has always struck me as ironic.

A recent case, which will probably be a model for sex discrimination suits in the future, is that against AT&T. James Baldwin warned, in 1962, "A bill is coming in, that I fear America is not prepared to pay."

A bill did come in, for *four billion dollars*, monies that AT&T owed its female employees for discrimination during the last eight years (computed from the time the

Civil Rights Act went into law). AT&T was prepared to pay only $38 million of the bill. Whereas that is a fraction of the money owed, it still represents the largest sex discrimination settlement in the history of the world. So it is a victory.

According to the Equal Employment Opportunities Commission, which filed the suit against American Telephone and Telegraph, women employees in the Bell System with the same age, education, and experience as males are paid $500 million per year less than the men.[49]

AT&T has so far to go that when several of us from NOW were negotiating the back-pay issue, they told us they had an "emotional hang-up" on the whole subject of back pay. (We told them that, being women, we of course understood emotional hang-ups, and that we had one on the back-pay issue also.) In the company's press release, designed to show how progressive they are on opportunity for equal advancement and equal pay, they (inadvertently) included sexist remarks about how women are more comfortable in nonexecutive positions.

The $38-million agreement provided for increased pay and advancement opportunities for women and minority men. The pact with the Department of Labor and the EEOC provides that AT&T and its twenty-four operating companies make one-time lump sum payments totaling $15 million to 15,000 workers who the EEOC claimed were victims of "pervasive and systematic discrimination."

Another $23 million per year will go into wage adjustments, aimed at elevating women and minority men to equal standing with white men in similar jobs. In addition, the agreement called for new hiring practices aimed at getting more men as operators and clerks and more women into outside craft jobs. It also provides for a broadening of management opportunities.

Richard F. Schubert, solicitor of labor, termed the settlement "dramatic and historic," and one which "will probably constitute a model for civil rights agreements for many years to come."[50]

Bell, the largest private employer in the United States, has 780,000 employees. The agreement, which was entered as a consent order in the U.S. District Court in Philadelphia, does not affect two of its divisions, Bell Laboratories or Western Electric.

This landmark case shows that it is indeed possible at least to attempt to redress the injury done to persons who fail to apply for jobs that pay well because the company's policy of not hiring persons of their class is well known. It serves as a warning to other companies which systematically discriminate that they too will be open to liability.*

The most dramatic effect of the AT&T case was the financial restitution to women who work as telephone operators and clerks, and who—but for discrimination —might have applied long ago for the much better-paying jobs installing, maintaining, and repairing telephone equipment, indoors and out.

It is impossible to tell exactly which women would have applied for these jobs if they had been open to women in the past. The company and the government, therefore, agreed to operate on the assumption that the

* The same week as the AT&T decision, the government ordered Bethlehem Steel to make fundamental changes in the seniority system in effect at its plant near Baltimore, in order to offset the effects of years of discrimination against blacks. This is also a landmark case, because it imposed the views of an outside party (the government) on what the company's seniority rules should be—a matter that has long been regarded as one of the most important of all the issues that should be determined solely by collective bargaining between management and the union, here the United Steel Workers.

first 10,000 women who successfully applied for such
jobs now would be (for the purpose of settlement) the
women who would have sought them earlier if there had
been any point in it. These 10,000 women will receive
lump-sum restitution payments of up to $400 each, in
addition to the higher pay they will start earning as soon
as they are established in craft jobs. (Pleasant though it
is to receive $400 in the mail, no one would argue that it
can compensate a person for decades of underemployment.)

For many of 3,000 women whom the company has
hired for craft jobs since two years ago (when government actions against AT&T began), there will be back-
pay settlements totaling $7.5 million.

In addition, raises totaling $23 million in the first
year will be paid to 36,000 women and minority men
who had been moved into better-paying jobs without
having their seniority from their old jobs counted.

The company also committed itself to hiring certain
minimum percentages of women and minority men for
jobs in the immediate future. The agreement also required that at least 10 percent of those hired as telephone operators, and at least 25 percent of those hired
as clerks, be men. According to *The New York Times*,[51]
"the idea is to erase the stigma that these are 'women's
jobs.' " We have some educating to do if such reasoning
is included in a *pro-woman* decision.

Since the telephone company made *$2.5 billion in
profits* in 1972, the settlement will hardly break them. It
will, however, give hope to many millions of underpaid
and underemployed women workers in this country.

The AT&T case brings clearly into focus the issue of
the duty of fair representation. The Communication
Workers of America, which represents most telephone
workers, has fought the EEOC case since the start; it

has also failed miserably in achieving contracts which even approach fairness for its female and minority men workers. Joseph A. Beirne, president of the union, contacted President Nixon,[52] telling him that the agreement "ignores and disrupts" the union's contract relationship with the company. He asked Nixon to block the case. Obviously, Beirne has not been negotiating fair contracts. I believe this kind of sellout of women employees will be tested in the courts in the years to come.

Despite decisions like AT&T, all is not bright for the woman worker. She is hired by men, fired by men; her rights in the union contract are negotiated by men. It is a male-run federal agency which decides if her employer and her union have treated her unfairly; it is a male judge who decides whether the government agency is correct.

To be able to properly handle women's cases in court —whether they be cases of sex discrimination in employment or cases involving subtler forms of sexism—one must understand one fact of female existence: all women are poor.

All women are poor. Even "rich" women have gotten their money from men—husbands, lovers, fathers. And when these ornately attired women cease to please (even the male banker who is administering the trust), they find they aren't rich any more.

In the last few chapters we have seen how a woman trying to earn money of her own is at the mercy of the prejudice of male employers, male union leaders, male administrative agency heads. In the next chapter we will see how personal wealth is also out of the province of women. We are given control over enough money to buy a car, but not a Senate seat.

And, until we sit in the seats of power and control, all women, even those who live in big houses, will be poor.

Chapter Seven
Estate Law:
The Power of Sex
After Death

It must be remembered that the point of honour which decrees that a man must not under any circumstances accept money from a woman with whom he is on certain terms, is of very modern growth, and is still tempered by the proviso that he may take as much as he likes or can get from his wife.

—PREFACE TO HENRY FIELDING'S *Tom Jones*

❧❧❧ Louisa Strittmater died on December 6, 1944. Her will, dated October 31, 1944, disposed of her entire estate to the National Women's Party. She had been a member of the New Jersey branch of the National Women's Party since 1925, and had worked as a volunteer in its New York office from 1939 to 1941.

Ms. Strittmater considered herself to be a militant feminist. She was born in 1896, and lived "an apparently normal life"[1] with her parents until their deaths about 1928. She never married.

Her heirs contested the will on the ground that the gift to the National Women's Party was the consequence of an "insane delusion." The usual standards for testamentary capacity are not particularly strict. As the cases outline, the person writing the will must know the natural objects of her/his bounty, know the property held, and know to whom it is being given.

> Mental weakness is not inconsistent with testamentary capacity. A less degree of mental capacity is requisite for the execution of a will than for the execution of contracts and the transaction of ordinary business. One may be capable of making a will yet incapable of disposing of his property by contract or of managing his estate.[2]

> The condition of being unable, by reason of weakness of mind, to manage and care for an estate, is not inconsistent with capacity to make a will.[3]

Evidence that the testator was eccentric, old, ill, weak, deaf, dumb or blind, or that the provisions of the will are unnatural, is admissible on the issue of testamentary capacity, but such evidence will not necessarily invalidate the will.

Under the Uniform Probate Code[4] "Contestants of a will have the burden of establishing lack of testamentary intent or capacity, undue influence, fraud, duress, mistake, or revocation."

Apparently, then, the testator can be in pretty bad shape, and still have the will stand up in court. Not in such poor shape, however, as to leave one's money to the National Women's Party.

The evidence offered in the case was as follows. Ms. Strittmater's doctor, a general practitioner, testified that she suffered from paranoia, the "Bleuler type of split personality." Allowed into evidence were journals which Ms. Strittmater had kept since 1935. Also allowed into evidence were notations she had made in the margins of her personal books. According to the court, these indicated that she looked forward to the day when women would bear children without the aid of men and all males would be put to death at birth.

In August 1936, for example, she wrote:[5] "It remains for feminist organizations like the National Women's Party to make exposure of woman's 'protectors' and 'lovers' for what their vicious and contemptible selves are."

On the other hand, her relationships with her lawyer and bankers, all males, had apparently been "normal." Evidence was introduced that she had a poor relationship with her father. This was taken seriously by the judge, who was no doubt a father himself.*

The court found that the evidence sustained the finding that a militant feminist who regarded men as a class with an insane hatred, and who looked forward to the day when women would bear children without the aid of men, and when all men would be put to death at birth, lacked testamentary capacity, requiring the setting aside of probate of her will.

The court also took note of the fact that she used vile language and exhibited "feminism to a neurotic extreme." As far as the record shows, her views of men were derived *exclusively* from her private writings, and had in no way been broadcasted to the public.

The treatment of the Strittmater will can be evaluated only in relation to what is considered testamen-

* A recent example of the importance placed on the father-daughter relationship in determining the "mental health" of the woman, is *The Female Orgasm: Psychology, Physiology, Fantasy*, by Seymour Fisher. (New York: Basic Books, Inc.) Dr. Fisher found that the most significant variable in determining whether or not a woman would be sexually responsive was whether she had had an involved relationship with her father. Or, expressed in another way, if you don't get on well with your father, you won't learn how to get on well with other men, later in your life.

tary capacity in other kinds of wills—which didn't leave the entire estate to the National Women's Party. In a New Jersey case,[6] a husband totally disinherited his wife. Throughout his life, he had had violent outbursts about her allegedly carrying on with another man. These suspicions were found to be completely untrue. And yet the court found testamentary capacity. The will was admitted to probate.

In another case, the testator claimed to talk continually with the dead.[7] The court found testamentary capacity. The will was admitted to probate.

One Mr. O'Neil totally disinherited his daughters, his only heirs, and left all his money for the use of "worthy boys" on a nearby college campus. He had had delusions, proved unfounded and false, that one of his daughters was a prostitute, and that the other was poisoning him. The court found testamentary capacity.[8] The will was admitted to probate.

Louisa Strittmater's inability to determine the fate of her money is not atypical. The laws on estates, when examined, defeat one of the most prevalent myths surrounding women in America: that we control all the wealth.

Whereas the facts about job discrimination are at least vaguely known by the public, the popular wisdom has it that the money is in the hands of women, if not while husbands are alive, at least when they die.

In reality, money is sometimes in the names of women, but rarely in the control of women. The average husband makes sure that his son, banker, accountant, stockbroker, brother (all males) stands between his wife and her disposition of the family wealth.

The number of shares of stock owned individually by women stockholders equals only about 18 percent of the total, compared with 24 percent owned individually by men.[9] The remaining 58 percent is held by institutions, whose boards of directors are mostly or entirely male, or by brokers, who are almost exclusively male. According to *The New York Times,* February 4, 1973, 150 of the 5,000 registered representatives of Merrill Lynch, Pierce, Fenner & Smith, Inc., are women. There are 5,241 women brokers out of a total of 52,466 working for New York Stock Exchange member firms.

Women own less than 39 percent of all real estate privately held, in spite of the fact that they outlive men. Bank accounts, as well as stocks and other assets, are often placed in the names of wives, mothers, and other women, but only for tax purposes, and with no power attached.

If "the rich" are defined as persons with assets over $60,000, $2½ million of these fortunes are held by men, compared to $1½ million in the hands of women. Less than 3 percent of women with income from any source earn over $10,000 per year, as compared to 24 percent of men.[10]

More important is the fact that women are conspicuously absent from the ranks of stockbrokers, financiers, corporation and bank presidents, directors of major corporations, high government officials, and other elements of control over the wealth of our country.

A further disability of women is that while we often are responsible on paper for various financial transactions, we rarely can direct them. For example, wives traditionally sign joint tax returns with their husbands. A wife who has no income of her own, and who is financially dependent upon her husband will probably sign many papers, without questioning them. To say that she should not have signed papers she didn't comprehend is not enough; to say that women should understand their own finances would require a total revision of our work structure, our social mores, and the whole basis of the marriage relationship.

Our tradition has it that men control the finances; that women "do not understand these matters." An incident in the film *Diary of a Mad Housewife* illustrates this point: Jonathan Balser, the husband, takes all their joint assets and puts them into a vineyard in France. When Tina, the mad housewife, asks him about whether it is a good investment, he tells her that *he* handles the finances of the family. The vineyard fails; they lose all their money. Tina suggests they "cut down" on expenses, as her contribution to the solution of how to rectify their economic tragedy. She has gone from being rich to being poor—but she had no control over either condition.

A recent New York case deals with a woman whose husband was in a business which was found to be greatly in debt to the Internal Revenue Service. She had signed business documents and tax returns for years, but never understood what she was signing, or the nature of the financial dishonesty that was going on.

At any rate, the husband died in the midst of paying off his back taxes, but before the debt was fully paid. The IRS is now going after her funds, threatening to throw her out of her apartment, and so forth. She is in her seventies and has never worked. She is, naturally, panicked.

Another New York State woman married a man who had a preexisting debt of $1,500 to the IRS. While married, they held a home in joint tenancy. They divorced, she got the house, and now the IRS is threatening to take it, as payment on her ex-husband's debt. She is on welfare, and lives in the home with her five children. She too, naturally, is panicked.

It is not just unsophisticated women who have such

troubles. When Doris Day's husband died suddenly, five years ago, she could find neither his will nor any financial records. He had been her manager for years, and needless to say, she had quite a fortune to manage. She soon learned not only that all the records of her commercial life were nowhere to be found among his effects, but that *she owed* the Internal Revenue Service $450,000!

> Contracts, investments, wills, deeds, money, lawyers—motion-picture and TV star Doris Day never concerned herself with such bothersome business details. Her husband of 17 years, Martin Melcher, took care of them. Besides, thought Doris, all those financial and legal goings on were for men only. It wasn't a woman's place to butt in, to ask questions, to make a nuisance of herself. So even when she did have a question or suggestion, she kept quiet about it.[11]

Because of her bad experience, Ms. Day drew up a check list for wives. If a woman who makes as much money as she does could have been so ignorant of her own finances, she assumed less affluent women would be in similar trouble.[12]

1. Know that your husband has an up-to-date will, and know where it is. Sit in on the planning of the will.

2. Know what—and where—your husband's assets are. This includes a safe deposit box, brokerage accounts, life insurance and pensions.

3. Know what your husband's major financial liabilities are—including taxes.

4. Don't be naïve about financial matters. Look at income tax returns when you sign them. Read all contracts and papers before you sign them—even if your husband says "It's all routine, you don't have to read it."

5. Remember that your husband's financial affairs are really the whole family's affairs. Take an interest in your husband's business. Ask questions about things you don't understand.

Doris Day's suggestions, which appeared in the *Ladies' Home Journal*, are potentially of great value to women. If a wife is totally unfamiliar with the family finances because she does not see herself as one who understands money, these suggestions will be of help. But if the husband wants to have total control of the money in the household, a check list for wives will not help. Many, many women (I was one of them) know, for example, that their husbands spend much of the family income on stocks, but have no idea which stocks or how many. Other women, who are joint owners of stock, have to get the records of what is owned by subpoena, since neither their husbands nor the stockbroker will tell them what *they* own.

When I was studying estate law in law school, we were taught the management benefits of setting up a revocable trust. The primary strength, along with the fact that it saves probate expense, is that it can be used as a way to keep the money from the wife. The major thrust of the course seemed to be to teach the class (of a hundred males and a couple of females) how to keep money out of the hands of women, primarily wives. (The professor always thought it very funny when we studied a case which left money "to the girl friend.") The theory seemed to be—as stated by the male experts on estates, and carefully written down in notebooks by the male future experts on estates—to leave the wife enough money so that she can live nicely. After all, if after the husband's death, the widow has to buy her clothing at a second-hand store, it is assumed that he was not the big success he was thought to be. This means enough money for consumption goods is desirable. However, the cardinal rule is not to leave her with enough money for power. This is accomplished in a variety of ways. The most common is to simply leave the bulk of the fortune in the control of a banker, male relative, or stockbroker. The wife then has to get permission to get more than her monthly allotment. She can use what she gets for travel, country clubs, clothes. But if she wants to go back to school, she must go to the banker and ask for enough money for tuition. We have all heard of dozens of cases where the money was denied. If she wants to go into politics, and must go into the capital, she has to get permission. Often, the permission must be gotten from her own son—surely a humiliating event for a mother. Often, where there are sons and daughters, of similar age and intelligence, the sons control the money, and the daughters must ask their brothers for it.

Obviously, this whole discussion does not apply to most women, who live in families where there is no fortune, for females or for males. But in those families where there is a lot of money, it is clear that the women do not have equal, or sometimes any, access to it.

Estate law is the codification, the enshrinement, of paternalism as a way of life. In Roman law, *paterfamilias* was the head or master of the family. This word is sometimes employed, in a wide sense, as equivalent to *sui juris*, which means possessing full social and civil rights, and not being under any legal disability or the power of another.[13]

A person *sui juris* is called *paterfamilias* even when under the age of puberty. Just as we saw in the section on getting credit that a dead man was considered a better credit risk than a live and working woman, a boy under the age of puberty had more legal rights under Roman law than a grown woman.

In the narrower and more common use, a *paterfamilias* is any one invested with *potestas* (a Latin term meaning the power of the father over his children, the authority of masters over their slaves) over any person. It is thus as applicable to a grandfather as to a father.[14]

Another Latin concept, which originates in the French law, is that of *paterna paternis*, which means paternal estates to paternal heirs. This is a rule which signifies that such portion of a decedent's estate as came to him from his father must descend to his heirs on the father's side.

"Paternal power" is defined in *Black's Law Dictionary*[15] as the "authority lawfully exercised by parents over their children." "Paternity," of course, refers only to the state or condition of a *father*, having no connection to the mother.

Patria potestas, from Roman law, means paternal authority or power. This term denotes the aggregate of those peculiar powers and rights which, by the civil law of Rome, belonged to the head of a family in respect to his wife, children (natural or adopted), and any more remote descendants who sprang from him through males only. Anciently, it was of very extensive reach, embracing even the power of life and death, but gradually was curtailed, until finally it amounted to little more than a right in the *paterfamilias* to hold as his own any property or acquisitions of one under his power.[16]

Patrimony is defined as any kind of property: Such estate as has descended in the same family, and estates which have descended or been devised in a direct line from the father, *and*, *by extension* (emphasis mine) from the mother or other ancestor.[17]

All this should in no way imply that husbands and fathers are not often *generous* with their money, before and after their deaths. But it is an entirely different matter to have money because someone has decided to give it to you, than to have money because you are capable of getting it on your own.

Early deeds recognized the power of husbands over their wives. One, for example, from the town of Salina, New York,[18] in 1836, stipulates: ". . . the said Eliza on a private examination by me apart from her said husband acknowledged that she executed the same freely without any fear or compulsion of her said husband."

One hundred thirty-five years later, the same kind of problem exists, and a group called the "Women's Equalization Committee" in California was trying to rectify it.[19] The group was offering husbands a chance to give their wives legal equality in handling the family finances. For one dollar they supplied the legal forms for giving the wives a 50 percent share in control of the community property.

Under California law, although husband and wife share ownership of joint property, except real estate, the husband has the legal right to sell it without his wife's knowledge or consent. The law also gives the husband the exclusive power to choose where the family will live, and the wife must agree, or she will be guilty of desertion.

Where did these legal disabilities begin? In great measure, with the English common law. Under the common law of descent, devise, and the early formation of the trust, women were non-persons. Sir William Blackstone, an eighteenth-century English jurist, condensed the common law of descent into canons, which included:[20]

I. . . . Inheritances shall lineally descend to the issue of the person who last died actually seised, *in infinitum*; but shall never lineally ascend.

II. . . . The Male issue shall be admitted before the female. . . . But our law does not extend to a total exclusion of females . . . for, though daughters are excluded by sons, yet they succeed before any collateral relations.

III. . . . Where there are two or more males in equal degree, the eldest only shall inherit; but the females altogether.

VII. . . . In collateral inheritances the male stocks shall be preferred to the female; (that is, kindred derived from the blood of the male ancestors, however remote, shall be admitted before those from the blood of the female, however near,)—unless where the lands have, in fact, descended from a female.

These rules were apparently to insure that *one male* in the family (the eldest son) had control of the land. When the land went to the daughters, in the absence of sons, it was divided equally, since there was no attempt to create a dynasty, including lands, following the blood lines of a daughter.

Rules preferring the male stock, including the rule of primogeniture, were first applied to military tenures. (The rule of primogeniture states the superior or exclusive right possessed by the eldest son, and particularly, his right to succeed to the estate of his ancestor, in right of his seniority by birth, to the exclusion of younger sons and all daughters.)

Preference for the male stock made it likely that a person who held a military tenure would be fit for military service, an early instance of how being kept out of the army was no favor to women.

Preference for the eldest male made a single individual responsible to the overlord, prevented frequent partition of land, and provided a family leader with the economic power to hold the family together. The feudal system was based upon concepts of interpersonal loyalty (between lord and man) that weakened but did not replace the bonds of tribal and family affection that had been the strength of the English community before the Norman Conquest. The medieval Englishman had "confused" identifications and loyalties, and it was essential for a stable social *and economic* structure that the influence of the central government be thrown behind family and local police organizations.

If the eldest male child died without issue, the land passed to the male child next in age. If all male children of the intestate died without issue, female children inherited in equal shares. It was then *the husband* of the eldest female child who gave homage to the overlord.

In 1540, the English Parliament enacted the Statute of Wills.[21] That period, under the reign of Henry VIII, will be recalled as one in which the status of women was not high. The Statute of Wills provided, among many other things, that the will had to be in writing; a supplementary statute withdrew power to make wills of land from all married women, infants, and mental incompetents.[22]

No person lacked testamentary capacity (the ability to make a will) unless disabled by some special rule of law, by mental incompetence, or by infancy. A male could make an effective testament when fourteen; a female could make an effective testament when twelve. A married woman, however, could not make an effective testament because her husband acquired ownership of her chattels. A serf could not make an effective testament because the lord of his manor could seize his chattels.

Progress in modernizing the law of intestate succession was very slow. In 1925, the Administration of Estates Act,[23] which consolidated a number of earlier English statutory provisions affecting the administration of decedents' estates, also introduced a uniform table of descent and distribution.[24] The common law rules of primogeniture and preference for the male stock, and the common law marital estates of curtesy ("the life tenure formerly enjoyed by a husband in his wife's land inheritance after her death, provided they had issue to inherit," as defined by *The Random House Dictionary of the English Language*) and dower, were abolished. As amended by the Intestates' Estates Act, in 1952,[25] and the Family Provision Act, in 1966,[26] the Administration of Estates Act favors the surviving spouse. The surviving spouse takes all of the "personal" chattels of the intestate, which include furniture, household effects, and vehicles, but exclude money, securities, and business chattels.

Although English law was based on concepts and practices unsuited to American conditions, state legislatures adopted the substance of English statutes, and courts deferred to English precedent in construing the statutes so produced. Primogeniture, for example, gained a foothold in New York and several of the Southern colonies, but was abolished soon after the American Revolution. The ancestral property doctrine and the rules preferring male stock to female shared a similar fate in many states.

One interesting English doctrine—that of shifting estates—does not appear to be recognized in the United States, but it illustrates (along with a dead husband's being a better credit risk than a living wife) that sometimes an unborn brother takes land in preference to living sisters. A majority of U.S. jurisdictions currently permit children of posthumous fathers and children among collaterals (relatives that are not lineal—such as cousins) to inherit real or personal property, although such children must have been in embryo at the time of the death of the intestate.[27] In England, there was no requirement that the posthumous child in collateral relationship be in embryo at the intestate's death. This gave rise to the doctrine of "shifting estates." If, for example, the intestate died survived by sisters and parents, the parents could not take, and the land descended to the sisters in equal shares. If, however, a male child was born to the parents, although conceived after the death of the intestate, the land passed to the male child by the rule of primogeniture, the interests of the sisters being divested.

"Misconduct" on the part of the wife is often grounds for disqualification in taking (inheriting) under a will, or taking intestate. The English Statute of Westminster II[28] barred the dower of a wife who deserted her husband and committed adultery. Dower was not barred, however, if her husband "permitted her to return to his house" after she had committed adultery. This statute is part of the common law of several of the states, and has been the pattern for statutes in others.

The marital misconduct provision in the Statute of Westminster II does not bar a distributive share in personal property[29] or a share as heir in land,[30] although statutes in some states bar such claims when the spouse deserts.[31]

Nine states (Arizona, California, Hawaii, Idaho, Louisiana, Nevada, New Mexico, Texas, and Washington) have community property laws. The system proceeds on the assumption that property acquired during marriage (other than by gift or inheritance) is the product of joint efforts of the husband and wife, and each therefore has a half share. Property acquired before marriage or by gift or inheritance is classified as the separate property of the respective spouse. But *the husband is normally the manager of the community property and may transfer it during his lifetime.*

Each spouse has a power of testamentary disposition over his/her half interest in the community, except in New Mexico, where the wife has no such power.

If, for example, the husband earns money in a common law state, retires, and the couple moves to a community property state (this happens frequently, since California and Arizona are common retirement states), the wealth invested in the husband's name would be characterized as "separate" because at the time and place it was acquired (in the common law state), the wife had no community property right. When the husband dies, now domiciled in the community property state, the wife may end up with nothing. She has no community property interest because the property was acquired under a common law system, and she has lost the common law protection because the property is now governed by a community property law. This result can be avoided only by a statutory provision classifying such property as "quasi-community" (the California approach), i.e., treating it as though it were community property with one half passing to the surviving spouse on the death of the spouse who is the owner, or by enacting legislation affording some kind of forced share in separate property.

Most trusts are set up today to "protect women from themselves." And even if the husband has confidence in his wife to spend carefully after his death, there is always the fear of her remarriage to a spendthrift. As a Kentucky case expressed it:[32]

> . . . the petitioners were then married to men of idle and wasteful habits, and it was feared that the estate, which was the sole property of Mrs. Underhill, might be dissipated, and that its only purpose was to protect herself and her daughter from the habits and conduct of their respective husbands.

The most complete explanation of the role of women in sharing the wealth of the family can be gleaned from a textbook on trusts[33] that tells law students how to set up estates.

> For some understanding of why trusts are created, let us consider a typical trust limitation: settlor by his will leaves certain specified property to a named trustee in trust to pay the income to the settlor's wife for her life, and directs that at her death the trust terminate and the property be transferred to his descendants then living. Why should he utilize the trust rather than make a gift outright to his wife in fee or a gift to her of a legal remainder in the descendants? One obvious reason is that by carefully selecting the trustee the settlor can provide expert management of the property, *relieving the wife as beneficiary from the duties and responsibilities of management, and at the same time assuring that the property will not be dissipated with little or no inheritance left for the children.* [emphasis mine]

> Secondly, if you will recall the cumbersome nature of the legal life estate, and the difficulties which arise if a sale of the property becomes necessary, you can appreciate the advantage of having legal title in one person

who can, if the settlor so desires, be empowered to sell, with the proceeds being reinvested in other property.

. . . Had the property been given to the wife outright, there is the danger that *the wife may dissipate the capital fund either through unwise investment or through improvident expenditure.* [emphasis mine] In addition there is the possibility of remarriage, with a second husband not only helping her to spend the funds but also exerting influence (not undue!) to have the wife transfer the wealth to him either during lifetime or at death. The trust therefore serves to "conserve" wealth for the ultimate takers. Moreover, if the owner had chosen to give his property to his wife outright, although it would in normal succession pass to the children, there would be the cost and delay involved in the probate and administration of her estate.

. . . But we should note here that we can confer on the trustee power to make decisions "in his discretion" which the original owner would make if he were still alive. Thus, the settlor may feel that the probable income will exceed the needs of the wife; he can empower the trustee to determine the amount needed by her and distribute the excess income to the children.

A future lawyer has to be carefully taught: Don't leave trust powers in the hands of the wife of your future client (the settlor is always signified by "he") because (1) the estate may be too hard and complicated for her to handle; (2) she may squander the money (you know how women are with money); (3) she will probably acquire another husband soon, and he will help her spend your money unwisely; (4) since you want to leave it to your children anyway, why go through the administration costs and annoyances of having it pass through her estate first.

Thus we see the real position of women in estate law. And, ironically, it is supposed to be in the areas of wills and trusts that we women "really collect."

Another area of the law where we women are supposed to be collecting fortunes is family law. In the next chapter we will see the source, the nature, and the extent of such "fortunes."

Chapter Eight
Family Law:
The Man and the
Woman Are One

*By their mutual matrimonial consent and contract the
wife hath given up herself in this kind unto her husband, which she cannot retract.*
　　　　　　　—I HALE, *Pleas of the Crown* 628 (1800)

An unmarried man is glamorous. His mother
and aunts may provide him with an unwanted and un-
ending supply of telephone numbers, but nonetheless,
the world looks upon him with pleasure. Although he
probably lives in a pile of laundry and newspapers and
eats TV dinners, we all imagine him on an endless
stream of gourmet restaurant meals, accompanied by
an endless stream of affectionate starlets.

An unmarried woman is a failure. The women's liberation movement has partially succeeded in planting
the idea of options in the heads of women and men.
Nevertheless, if you are female and not married, it is
still assumed by the public (and by a surprisingly large
number of "liberated" people) that no male wants to
marry you. The question "So, what's new?", meaning
"Do you have any hot prospects for marriage?" is asked
of single women, widows, and women with brand-new
divorce decrees. Because of this social imperative to be
married, it is perhaps the marriage and divorce laws

which illustrate most accurately the actual status of
women in America.

Although every girl, from age sixteen on, is trained
in the School for Wives, such training is no indication
that she knows the legal implications of marriage. Before one can get a driver's license one must score 90
percent of the Rules of the Road. To get a marriage
license, one must have a blood test and pay a couple of
dollars. The National Organization for Women has suggested repeatedly that the marriage laws be supplied at
the Marriage License Bureau by each state, but so far
young lovers have been kept blissfully ignorant about
the legal relationship they are entering into. And, it is
young Mary Smith who becomes Mrs. John Doe; not
John Doe who becomes Mr. Mary Smith. The fascinating laws on names are explored in another chapter, but
while we are thinking about marriage, give some attention to the reaction you would get if you asked a man,
"And what was your name before you got married?"

For centuries, under common law, the husband and
wife were one. The couple became "two," according to
the Supreme Court, in 1960.[1] The *Dege* case marks the
change of mind of Justice Frankfurter, who held that a
wife could indeed be tried for criminal conspiracy with
her husband. Prior to that time, wives could not be so
tried, since they were assumed to be one with the husband, and therefore, could not conspire "with themselves." The case held that a husband and wife are not
legally incapable of violating 18 U.S.C. 371 (the criminal conspiracy statute), by conspiring with each other
to commit an offense against the United States.

Frankfurter wrote:

> None of the considerations of policy touching the law's
> encouragement or discouragement of domestic felicities

on the basis of which this Court determined appropriate rules for testimonial compulsion as between spouses . . . are relevant to yielding to the claim that an unqualified interdiction by Congress against a conspiracy between two persons precludes a husband and wife from being two persons. Such an immunity to husband and wife as a pair of conspirators would have to attribute to Congress one of two assumptions: either that responsibility of husband and wife for joint participation in a criminal enterprise would make for marital disharmony, or that a wife must be presumed to act under the coercive influence of her husband and, therefore, cannot be a willing participant.

Although one's first reaction might be that any decision which calls a husband and wife "two" rather than "one," must be based on sound, just thinking, we would do well to think about the meaning of "coercive influence." It is well understood in Labor law, for example, how much influence is wielded by employers who control the *source of income* of their employees. Decisions under the National Labor Relations Act are replete with language which shows the understanding that economic power over another's life is the ultimate coercive influence.

It is not necessary, for proof of a violation, to show by direct evidence that any particular persons were in fact successfully restrained or coerced; it is enough if it is shown that the employer's conduct has a natural tendency to do so.[2]

These cases generally hold that, in a broad sense, any expression of anti-union opinion by an employer has a tendency to interfere with, restrain, or coerce employees in the exercise of their rights of self-organization. The attitude of the National Labor Relations Board in the early days of the Wagner Act was that the employer should remain neutral so that the employees could exercise a free choice as to whether or not to unionize.

A good case can be made that just as the employee is dependent upon his employer for source of income—and hence is very unlikely to "cross" that source—wives are dependent upon their husbands for *source of income*—and are also very unlikely to cross that source. The implications for a wife in a criminal conspiracy case are enormous.

Charlotte Perkins Gilman said: "Women are in slavery because of economic dependence."[3] This slavery extends beyond household chores—to the psychological prison of being unable to have separate opinions about political issues, or to implications in criminal behavior.

> An employer's "opinion" about unionism expressed to his employees is not the same as his opinion on what doctor to use or about the international situation . . . When an employer addresses his antagonism toward unionism, however devoid his words may be of direct threats, there is always implicit the threat of economic compulsion if his wishes are not heeded . . . *Freedom of speech is possible only among those who approximate each other in equality of position.* (emphasis mine)[4]

As Judge Learned Hand put it:[5]

> What to an outsider will be no more than the vigorous presentation of a conviction, to an employee may be the manifestation of a determination which it is not safe to thwart.

The Supreme Court said, in a machinist's case:[6]

Slight suggestions as to the employer's choice between unions may have telling effect among men who know the consequences of incurring that employer's strong displeasure.

There is great doubt that the judges who wrote these opinions understood that the connection between worker and boss was similar to the relationship between wife and husband. But they did understand the significance of power.

Frankfurter, in the *Dege* criminal conspiracy case, states that the assumption that the wife is presumed to act under the coercive influence of her husband "implies a view of American womanhood offensive to the ethos of our society."[7] Justice Frankfurter had apparently not counseled many women. It is the observation of lawyers in divorce practice, for example, that even on the eve of the termination of the marriage, the wife simply does not want to offend her husband. In her desire not to make him angry, she often suffers economic disadvantage, but that does not outweigh the psychological conditioning which she has had—to please the man.

The case concludes:[8]

. . . Suffice it to say that we cannot infuse into the conspiracy statute a fictitious attribution to Congress of regard for the medieval notion of woman's submissiveness to the benevolent coercive powers of a husband in order to relieve her of her obligation of obedience to an unqualifiedly expressed Act of Congress by regarding her as a person whose legal personality is merged in that of her husband making the two one.

The dissent, which perhaps represents nonprogressive thinking for 1960, would not hold the wife responsible for criminal conspiracy. Justice Warren, writing for himself, Black, and Whittaker:[9]

> . . . A wife, simply by virtue of the intimate life she shares with her husband, might easily perform acts that would technically be sufficient to involve her in a criminal conspiracy with him, but which might be far removed from the arm's-length agreement typical of that crime.

The dissent then deals with Hawkins' medieval statement about will, which concludes:[10] ". . . because they are esteemed as one Person in Law, and are presumed to have but one Will."

Warren writes a feminist dissent, probably not because he understands the power of husbands, but on the basis of his view of the sanctity and privacy of the marriage relationship.

> . . . While it is easy enough to ridicule Hawkins' pronouncement in the Pleas of the Crown from a metaphysical point of view, the concept of the "oneness" of a married couple may reflect an abiding belief that the communion between husband and wife is such that their actions are not always to be regarded by the criminal law as if there was no marriage . . .

> I am not so easily persuaded that a rule accepted by so many people for so many centuries can be so lightly dismissed.[11]

The courts appear to recognize that while a wife cannot effectively cross her husband, a husband is not under the same pressure to concur with his wife. In a Pennsylvania case,[12] a wife was convicted of drunken driving, despite her reliance upon the presumption of compulsion resulting from her husband's presence in the car. Presumption of compulsion is a doctrine in the law which makes the assumption that when a husband and a wife are in a car driving together, she is doing his bidding, whether or not he has expressed any instructions.

In becoming Mrs. John Doe, Mary Smith gives up a wide variety of rights and freedoms, receiving in return "love," "companionship," social acceptance—and the right to be supported. On virtually every talk show about women's rights someone (usually the moderator, who claims to be paying alimony to several ex-wives all of whom refuse to remarry) glares knowingly and says "Alimony. Ahha—who says women don't have liberation and equal rights in this society? Look at alimony."

Let's look at alimony. Putting aside for the moment the important facts that most women who get divorced don't get alimony, that the payments awarded are usually too small for anyone to live on decently, and that many men effectively evade paying at all (despite the Uniform Reciprocal Support Act), it should be made clear exactly what alimony is. Alimony is the recognition by the legal system that most women *can't earn a living*.

Since one in three marriages ends in divorce (one in two in California), the state welfare systems cannot possibly be burdened by all the divorced women, most of whom have dependent children.

In a society where women are carefully taught from birth that they will be supported, are punished for aspiring to high-paying jobs, and in fact are making about half of what men make in any kind of job—alimony is not only desirable, it is necessary.

The myth that alimony is in some way unfair to men should be corrected immediately. The economics of female life, and the statistics on women's salaries, make alimony the only way to make sure they don't starve to death.

Ironically, since the passage of the Equal Pay Act (1963) and the Civil Rights Act of 1964 (Title VII), the difference between men's and women's salaries has widened. In 1955 the average female employee earned 64 percent of the wages paid to similarly employed men; in 1970 she took home only 59 percent as much.

The gap is even greater within certain broad occupational groupings. Women in sales work, for example, in 1970 averaged only $4,188 versus $9,790 for the typical salesman.

The median income of full-time employees in 1971[13] was $5,323 (women) and $8,966 (men).

Yet the actual salaries of, say, women lawyers as compared to men lawyers is a small part of the picture, and not the crucial reason why, until the sex role revolution is successful, women will have to be supported by men. The major factor is level of aspiration.

In any social class we care to examine, a young woman prepares for a job (if indeed she is preparing for a job at all) which pays a fraction of what the job her brother studies for pays. In middle-class families, while the sons go to law or medical school, the daughters study to be teachers or social workers. This means that as adults the men will be earning six to ten times as much as the women. While upper-class young men go into the family business at astronomical salaries, or work for others in "the group," their sisters work as bank tellers, or go to Katharine Gibbs to learn to be secretaries. While working-class young men are sent to training programs which will enable them to work at well-paying factory or construction employment, their sisters are often cleaning houses or waiting on tables.

Alimony comes from the Latin word "alimonia," meaning sustenance. Perhaps the proper way to look at alimony is not only as a way of sustaining the wife who is unable to support herself, but rather as *back pay*.

Based on the usual wage rates of housekeepers, cooks, dieticians, practical nurses, and chauffeurs, economists at the Chase Manhattan Bank estimate that the U.S. housewife holds the equivalent of a 99.6-hour-a-week job paying $13,391.56 a year. There are 28.3 million American women classified as "married, not in the labor force." They have no set hours, and no specified schedule for rest. They have no paid vacations guaranteed—and anyone watching the typical mother on a "vacation" trip will say they have no vacations at all. It has become increasingly prevalent for women to sign themselves into rest homes for a few weeks of recovery from "nervous exhaustion"—just to have a vacation.

While a woman is married, her husband has to support her, but the court is unwilling to determine the level of support at which she should be maintained. The political status of one who is dependent upon the charitable feelings of another for food and clothing is low indeed. A 1953 Nebraska case[14] is illustrative of the reluctance of the court to "pierce the domestic veil."

In this case, the wife, Mrs. McGuire, worked in the fields, did outside chores, cooked, cleaned the house, and did the washing. For a number of years she raised chickens, and sold poultry and eggs for money to buy clothing and the family groceries. Her husband was boss of the house and his word was law; he did not allow charge acounts and did not inform her of his finances or businesses. (He owned 398 acres of land, worth $83,960; he had $12,786 in the bank; and he had government bonds worth $104,500.)

When Mrs. McGuire asked her husband for money, he gave her small amounts; in the four years preceding her action for support he had not given her any money nor provided her with clothing. He had not, for four years, given her money to purchase furniture or household necessities. Their home (in 1953) had no bathroom, inside toilet, or kitchen sink.

> There is a pipeless furnace which she testified had not been in good working order for 5 or 6 years, and she testified she was tired of scooping coal and ashes. She had requested a new furnace but the defendant [Mr. McGuire] believed the one they had to be satisfactory . . . Use of the telephone was restricted, indicating that defendant did not desire that she make long distance calls.

The court held that while a wife lives with her husband, he can, in effect, determine the level of support he will give her. This, incidentally, bears no relationship to the level at which he chooses to support himself. His standard of living, in other words, can be much higher than hers.

> With reference to the proposition that the parties are living under the same roof, [the cases have held] that a wife had no right to the interference of the court for her maintenance until her abandonment or separation . . .

> In the instant case the marital relation has continued for more than 33 years, and the wife has been supported in the same manner during this time without complaint on her part. The parties have not been separated or living apart from each other at any time. In the light of the cited cases it is clear, . . . that to main-

tain an action such as the one at bar, the parties must be separated or living apart from each other.

The living standards of a family are a matter of concern to the household, and not for the courts to determine, even though the husband's attitude toward his wife, according to his wealth and circumstances, leaves little to be said on his behalf. As long as the home is maintained and the parties are living as husband and wife it may be said that the husband is legally supporting his wife and the purpose of the marriage relation is being carried out.

Dissenting Justice Yeager asked whether "there is any less reason for extending the right to a wife who is denied the right to maintenance in a home occupied with her husband than to one who has chosen to occupy a separate abode."

The answer to his question apparently is "yes." The Bible refers often to the unity of flesh of husband and wife. This doctrine was formalized for secular life by Blackstone, who expressed the feudal doctrine of coverture.[15]

By marriage, the husband and wife are one person in law; that is, the very being or legal existence of the woman is suspended during the marriage, or at least is incorporated and consolidated.

This state of legal disability was redressed to some extent by the Married Women's Property Acts, which first were enacted in Mississippi in 1839[16] and were later adopted by all American jurisdictions. By 1882 they had also become the law in England.

Leo Kanowitz, in his book *Women and the Law*, summarizes the effects of the legislation.[17]

Though the precise wording and scope of these statutes varied from state to state, they were all products of conscious and deliberate legislative efforts to redress property and contract relations between wives and husbands and to remove previous procedural disabilities of married women. Responding in great part to the rising tide of individual and organizational protest against the married woman's status of legal subjugation to her husband, these laws generally granted married women the right to contract, to sue and be sued without joining their husbands, to manage and control the property they brought with them to marriage, to engage in lawful employment without their husbands' permission, and to retain the earnings derived from the employment.

However, then as now, the rights of women were interpreted in the courts by men, and usually by men who had been raised in the male supremacist tradition.

A 1925 article in the *Harvard Law Review*[18] described the situation, which still prevails.

The interpretation of Married Women's Acts frequently fell into the hands of judges who as young lawyers had been educated in the legal supremacy of the husband.

It can be seen, therefore, that the dissenting judge in the *McGuire* case asks a rhetorical question. The difference in socio-political status between a married woman who lives with her husband and a woman who lives separately (and might create a financial burden on the state if she has no money) is enormous. That the court will not enter into the marital abode to set rules is more than a respect for the privacy of citizens. It is also a tacit acknowledgment among male judges, male legislators, and male attorneys (most of whom are husbands) that a husband should not be told how to treat his wife.

An interesting contrast to standard court procedure is the operation of the Jewish Conciliation Board of America, a private body set up for the purpose of resolving family disputes according to Jewish law and custom. The matters dealt with by the Board pertain to such as demands for increased support, interfering in-laws, and child-parent controversies. The parties are required in advance of the hearing to sign an arbitration agreement which stipulates the judicial enforceability of the award.[19]

Some states have made the wife secondarily liable for the family's support where she has sufficient means and the husband does not.[20] And, some of the statutes dealing with the responsibility for family expenses have gone so far as to make the property of both husband and wife jointly or severally liable for the "reasonable and necessary expenses of the family and the education of the children," without any right of indemnification by the wife against the husband.[21]

The Married Women's Acts did indeed improve women's rights to contract and to property in some instances, but the laws today are still examples of the denial of equal protection, both as it applies to basic civil and political rights, and in matters of family law and policy.[22]

Men and women do not have the same rights as to legal residence. The domicile of a married woman automatically follows that of her husband. If he has moved to a separate domicile, or deserted her, this can seriously affect her rights to vote, to run for public office, to serve on juries, or to have her estate properly administered.

The psychological and sociological implications of a woman's automatically being expected to follow her man are very far-reaching. A working woman is often reflexively excluded from a promotion because the employer thinks she will follow her husband if he moves. The aspiration level of women preparing for careers is severely handicapped, because in our mobile society the average wife can expect to be uprooted several times in her life at least, but in accord with her husband's, not her own, career advancement.

An aspect of the domicile question not often considered is the impact on the nonworking wife. Robert Seidenberg[23] has written a powerful analysis of the problems of uprooting that affect 40 million Americans each year. He suggests that although American corporate men indeed suffer the consequences of competetiveness and alienation in their lives, the greatest victims of deracination are their wives and children, who follow them around the country in the numerous moves imposed on families by the American corporate structure. A wife who is head of the Junior League or the League of Women Voters in her home community may find, when she follows her husband to a new city, that she can locate the same organization, but that she has lost her leadership. She will now be given the lowest, most menial job in the organization. Many women who move many times, finally just give up, and upon coming to a new community, simply cop-out and retreat to their homes.

In five states (Alaska, Arkansas, Delaware, Hawaii, and Wisconsin) a wife may take legal steps to establish separate domicile for any purpose. In thirteen additional states (California, Connecticut, Florida, Illinois, Indiana, Iowa, Maine, Massachusetts, Michigan, New Jersey, New York, North Dakota, and Wyoming), she may do so for voting purposes. In three of these (Maine, New York, and New Jersey) she may do so to hold public office.

The effects of the ratification of the Equal Rights Amendment on all of these laws, of course, will be dramatic. That they still exist does prove, however, that the Equal Protection Clause of the Fourteenth Amendment has not done its work for women.

In nine states, a wife can retain her original domicile for paying taxes (Alaska, Arkansas, Delaware, Florida, Hawaii, New Jersey, New York, West Virginia, and Wisconsin).

The total common-law legal disability, in which the husband was the complete symbol and representative for both persons, was improved by the Married Women's Property Acts. Today, however, laws in ten states still restrict a married woman's contractual rights (Alabama, Arizona, California, Florida, Georgia, Idaho, Indiana, Kentucky, Nevada, and North Carolina). In four states (California, Florida, Nevada, and Pennsylvania), a wife must get court approval before she can engage in an independent business. The Florida law requires her to file a petition stating her character, habits, education, mental capacities, and the reasons why the judge should grant her request. In New York, a woman who wishes to get a license from the Alcohol Beverage Control Board, to run a restaurant or bar, must have a male co-signer for the license. (A man applying for the same license does not need the co-signature of a woman.)

In Kentucky, a woman is generally barred from co-signing a loan without her husband. In Georgia, she cannot use her property as collateral for a loan. In Alabama, Florida, Indiana, North Carolina, and Texas, she cannot dispose of her property without her husband's consent.

In spite of the cultural pressures on a young woman to marry, single women are generally in better legal shape than their married sisters. A 1944 Florida Supreme Court decision summarized the peculiarity of a married woman's situation under the law:[24]

> A woman's responsibilities and faculties remain intact from age of maturity until she finds her mate; whereupon incompetency seizes her and she needs protection in an extreme degree. Upon the advent of widowhood she is reinvested with all her capabilities which had been dormant during marriage, only to lose them again upon remarriage. Intermittently, she is protected and benefited accordingly as she is married or single.

The laws governing marriage itself are not the same for males and females. Marriageable age, or age of consent, is earlier for girls than for boys in thirty-nine states, the most frequent minimums being eighteen for girls, twenty-one for boys.

As Kanowitz[25] points out:

> The establishment of a uniform minimum marriageable age for both sexes in all 50 states would assist tremendously in ameliorating male-female relationships by reducing the likelihood of earlier discontinuation of education for women and placing more equal emphasis on their responsibilities for participating in meaningful productive enterprise.

Except in the nine community property states (Arizona, California, Hawaii, Idaho, Louisiana, Nevada, New Mexico, Texas, and Washington), the wife is financially at the husband's mercy and at the discretion of the court upon divorce. In the forty-one common law states, all monies earned by a husband during marriage belong exclusively to him. No monetary value is attached to the wife's domestic services in helping to produce the family income or acquire property.

The $13,391 which full-time housewives should earn each year is not taken into account during the making of the separation agreement, or during the divorce award proceedings. Since women have no *legal right* to the family property, the aspect of the husband's "mercy" comes into play in the following manner: One or both parties want a divorce. The husband does not want to part with more of "their property" than he has to. If husband and wife can draw up a separation agreement prior to the trial of the divorce action, it can be merged into the divorce decree. If they cannot agree to terms of a separation agreement, each element (support, custody, distribution of property, etc.) must be hammered out in open court. The woman in such a case is not only subjected to a particular judge on a particular day (What was his morning coffee like? Does he "approve" of divorce? What are his views on women?), they are both subjected to the humiliating experience of relating their most intimate problems in open court. For this reason, most persons prefer to have the agreement drawn up beforehand and in private. Because the woman has high motivation to reach "agreement" on the separation agreement, and because in the forty-one common law states she has no *right* to any of the property of the marriage, she all too often is deprived of what *is hers*. While the marriage was in effect, she had no right to money for household services; upon divorce she has no right to collect back pay.

Contrary to popular belief, created by an occasional male movie star who is ordered to pay his ex-wife an astronomical sum in alimony, divorce laws do not favor women in the awarding of alimony and the custody of children.

More than one-third of the states permit alimony to be awarded to either spouse at the discretion of the court. (Alaska, California, Colorado, Hawaii, Illinois, Iowa, Kansas, Massachusetts, Minnesota, New Hampshire, North Carolina, North Dakota, Ohio, Oklahoma, Oregon, Texas, and Utah.)

Often child-support payments are camouflaged as alimony because taxes on alimony payments to an ex-wife are payable by her, not the ex-husband, while the total amount of alimony is subtracted from the ex-husband's income. Child support, on the other hand, is deductible only up to the $600 exemption allowed. By disguising child support as alimony, the husband enjoys a tax advantage.

In only a few states is the mother given automatic preference in custody of children, and then only if they are very young. There seems to be a preconceived notion that women are better with young children, and that men should have a controlling interest in the lives of older children. The general rule with regard to children in court proceedings is (appropriately) that custody, like other matters affecting children, should be awarded in accordance with the child's best interest.

There are, however, some extremely sexist ideas connected with the court view of what constitutes the child's best interest, and what constitutes a "fit" mother. Although it is assumed that fathers who are separated from their wives will engage in sexual activity with women, mothers who are separated from their husbands are not similarly assumed to have sexual desires. More specifically, if a woman goes to bed with anyone, she runs the risk of losing her children.

> Where the mother has been guilty of adultery, she was denied custody of her child and such denial would be effective until such time as she could convince the court

that she was free from all traits and tendencies that might adversely affect the child's welfare.[26]

The double standard goes far beyond rules of behavior which dictate that men *should* have intercourse before marriage, but that women should not. (This aspect of the double standard is perhaps disappearing, particularly among university-educated persons.)

That women define their own sexuality in terms of men is of course the prime example of the double standard. A man defines his manhood, even if he enjoys the sexual attentions of women, by what other men think of him. Women, on the other hand, define their "femininity" purely in terms of male approval. If men don't think you are sexy, you are not feminine, by definition.

(Even the sexual activity of a man and a woman is invariably defined in male terms. A purely sexual example of the double standard at work is that when a woman says, "We did it three times," she means that the male had three orgasms. She may have had sixty—or none.)

Chastity is a concept that has nothing to do with men. If you say a man is unchaste, no one knows what you are talking about. *Black's Law Dictionary* says, about "chaste": "Never voluntarily having had unlawful sexual intercourse; an unmarried woman who has had no carnal knowledge of men."[27]

One who falls from virtue and afterwards reforms is chaste within the meaning of the seduction statutes.[28]

An early New York case draws a distinction between wives and "mistresses" that is still very relevant in the law.[29]

Where prior chastity is not a necessary qualification for marriage, it may by insistence be made such, so that a marriage will be annulled for fraud where it appears that the defendant told the plaintiff before marriage that she had been the wife of a man then deceased, and that he was the father of her child, when in truth she had been his mistress and the child was a bastard. "Such a misrepresentation," said the court, "can afford ground for the annulment of a marriage for fraud because, as a matter of law it can be material upon the question of consent, which is essential to the contract of marriage." To reach any other conclusion is to say in effect that the fact that the woman, otherwise *acceptable* [emphasis mine], is unchaste cannot be sufficient motive for a man of average intelligence and prudence to refuse to consent to marriage. This doctrine would put a *Cyprian* [emphasis mine—means prostitute] on the marriage plane of a virgin, and make no distinction in respect to virtue as between a woman who had been a mistress and one who had been a wife.

Dr. Trude Weiss-Rosmarin, editor of the *Jewish Spectator*, recently charged that Mosaic laws on adultery and divorce (the common law is based on the Judaic-Christian tradition) have the *Playboy* philosophy toward married men and sexual promiscuity.[30] Women are treated as the property of men and not as persons with equal rights.

Technically, a Jewish husband is free to have sexual relations with women other than his wife so long as the other women are not married. (Until an eleventh-century decision of a rabbinic court, polygamy was acceptable under Jewish law.) But a married woman who has sexual relations with any man other than her husband is guilty of adultery and must be divorced by her husband even if he is willing to forgive her. On the other hand, a male who has sexual relations with a married woman is permitted to return to his wife, and she cannot sue him for divorce on that ground.

The typical Western attitude toward adultery—viewing any sexual relationship outside of marriage by either the man or the woman as infidelity—is the common view of most modern Jewish persons, but nonetheless, the earlier law cannot help but shape, consciously or unconsciously, all of our attitudes toward women and sex outside of marriage.

In addition, Judaism vests the authority of issuing a divorce in the husband, not in the rabbinic court. If he refuses to give his estranged wife a divorce, if he deserts her and cannot be located, if he disappears and there is no proof of his death, or if he becomes insane and thus is incapable of executing a legal document, such as a bill of divorcement, the woman remains an "Agunah"—a woman bound forever to her husband, from whom she cannot be divorced because Jewish law still adheres to the Biblical provision "He shall write for her a bill of divorcement."

In considering custody, the sexual behavior of the mother is thought to be relevant by the court, regardless of whether it actually influences the children or not. At this point, a fair comparison cannot be made between judges' views on the sexual behavior of mothers and fathers. This is because sex role stereotyping has convinced both men and women that child-raising is the mother's job. Therefore, there simply aren't that many cases where the father is fighting for custody.

The custody of a child should not be granted a mother who is morally unfit or degenerate.[31]

When on habeas corpus to determine the custody of children pending an action for divorce, it is shown that the children are boys not of such tender years that the mother is essential to their daily living; that the mother is indiscreet, intemperate of speech and infirm of temper, and associates with men whose influence is bad; but that the father offers to such children a home in refined surroundings, their custody should be awarded to the father.[32]

In the case that follows, the sexist language of the judge is as important in analyzing considerations relevant to the custody award, as is the unfortunate decision.[33]

On the trial of this divorce suit, Mrs. Bunim "admitted numerous deliberate adulteries . . . attempted to rationalize and justify those adulteries, denied any repentance therefor, and . . . testified to a deliberately false story as to consent by plaintiff (a reputable and successful physician) to the adulteries."

Despite the above facts, the lower court had awarded the two children of the marriage, daughters aged eleven and thirteen, to the mother.

There is an affirmed finding below that the husband is a fit and proper person to have such custody, and no such finding as to the wife, but a finding that "the interests and welfare of the children, the issue of said marriage, will be best served by awarding the custody to the defendant." We see in this record no conceivable basis for that latter finding, unless it be the testimony of the two daughters that, though they love their father, *they prefer to live with their mother.* [emphasis mine] Unless that attitude of these adolescent girls be controlling as against every other fact and consideration, this judgment insofar as it deals with custody, is unsupported and unsupportable.

. . . No decision by any court can restore this broken home or give these children what they need and have a right to—the care and protection of two dutiful parents. No court welcomes such problems, or feels at ease in deciding them. But a decision there must be, and it cannot be one repugnant to all *normal concepts of sex, family, and marriage.* [emphasis mine] The State of New York has old, strong policies on those subjects . . . Our whole society is based on the absolutely fundamental proposition that: "Marriage, as creating the most important relation in life," has "more to do with the morals and civilization of a people than any other institution" (*Maynard v. Hill*, 125 U.S. 190, 205). Defendant here, in open court, has stated her considered belief in the propriety of indulgence, by a dissatisfied wife such as herself, in extramarital sex experimentation. It cannot be that "the best interests and welfare" of these impressionable teen-age girls will be "best served" by awarding their custody to one who proclaims, and lives by, such extraordinary ideas of right conduct.

The states do have old and strong policies which reinforce the idea that a married woman is the physical property of her husband, right along with his automobile and power mower. Given the sociopolitical views of the judges, and of course their *sex* and marital status, it is no surprise that the girls were taken away from their mother and given to their "reputable and successful" father, the doctor.

The dissenting judge in *Bunim* points out that though the father was a successful doctor, he was "inordinately preoccupied with his professional duties; that, as a result, he gave little of his time or of himself to the children; and that not infrequently he treated them brusquely, impatiently and even intemperately. Likewise pertinent was proof that the wife was ever a good and devoted mother; that her *indiscretions* [emphasis mine] were unknown to the children; that she was deeply devoted to the children and truly concerned with their welfare; and that, for their part, the children returned her affection with an attachment that was, in the language of the trial court, 'almost Biblical' in its intensity."

"It is not logical to assume that a woman can be a good mother and an adultress at the same time," pronounces a case note in the *Notre Dame Law Review*.[34] The cases, as would be expected, do fall on the both sides. In *Hild*,[35] there was a presumption against awarding custody to a mother who had had relations with a man other than her husband. In *Grimditch*,[36] custody was awarded to the mother because her children were unaware that she had relations with men other than her husband. In *Shrout*,[37] the "mother's misconduct simply one of factors to be considered along with others relevant to determining what is best for child; woman who had children bring beer to her while she was in bedroom with paramour held unfit."

Besides fitness, the relative financial standing of the contestants is often looked to by the court in determining "the best interests of the child." Given the relative financial standing of men and women in our society, particularly if the women are mothers of young children, one can see that even in the area of custody, often thought of as one which discriminates in favor of women, men are at an advantage.

All other things being the same and the welfare of the child being certain of equal promotion with either parent, it seems that the father, as the *head of the family* [emphasis mine], may be viewed with presumptive favor.[38]

The courts will not hesitate to award the care and custody of very young children to the wife, as against the right of the husband, where the wife has shown herself to be a *proper person* [emphasis mine] and is able to discharge her duty toward the child.[39]

A child of the tender age of six is entitled to have such care, love, and discipline as only a good and devoted mother can usually give and the custody should so remain until the child has passed the infantile stage.[40]

The "mental health" of the mother is of course considered. It is interesting to note what sometimes constitutes mental illness. A Michigan mother[41] was deprived of the custody of her three daughters, aged fifteen, ten, and nine, on the basis of conflicting medical evidence concerning her mental illness. One of the "signs" of her mental illness was that she had refused her husband visitation rights.

The grounds for divorce, for the most part, are the same for men and women. Where they are different, however, they favor the man. The only grounds for divorce common to all fifty states and the District of Columbia is adultery. Cruelty is recognized as grounds in forty-five states, but the definitions of cruelty differ widely. Incompatibility is recognized as a ground in only four states.

In Kentucky, a man can divorce his wife upon proof of one act of adultery, but the woman does not have the same right. Also in Kentucky, a wife may get a divorce from an alcoholic husband only if he has been wasting his money and not providing for the family; a husband can get a divorce from his wife on a charge of drunkenness alone.

A Nebraska divorce law deprives women who commit adultery of everything but their personal property. Men are not similarly penalized.

The National Organization for Women Equal Rights

Divorce Reform Bill[42] reflects a suggestion of marriage as an equal economic partnership, and gives the wife the right to equal division of property at divorce. It contains other provisions designed to give much-needed economic protection to wives and dependent children at various stages of matrimonial actions.

The purpose and intention of the bill is to recognize the financial, physical, and mental contributions of women to their marriages and to their husbands' achievements, business and professional success, and resulting income assets. This bill, in some form or other, will be presented to all state legislatures by NOW chapters.

It should be relevant, also, that in determining the position of the wife at divorce, it is not only her particular contributions to the marriage that should be taken into account. The legislatures and courts must begin to realize that each woman who gets divorced has been carefully trained from early childhood to consider marriage her career. She has been carefully trained not to aspire to well-paying professions; when she does in fact enter the work force she is not paid equally.

The answer to any man who suggests that alimony and support are unfair is that they are necessary adjuncts to a sexist society. When women are equal, we will not have to be supported. Until then, we will. There is a rising trend among chauvinist men who have learned the liberation rhetoric to demand, for example, that their wives supply half the household expense money. He earns $45,000, she earns $8,000—yet he still submits this ridiculous proposal in the name of equality.

NOW's Divorce Reform Bill is basically concerned with:

1. Equal division of marital property (community property).

2. Management and control of own share of community property in marriage.

3. Legal recognition of marriage as an equal partnership. (There are many who consider this to be impossible, given the status of men and women in the society; each comes to the marriage with certain political, social, and economic baggage, and combining unequals will rarely produce an equal partnership.)

4. Equitable alimony and child support, with cost-of-living increases.

5. Legal fees awarded to the wife before trial so that she can retain an attorney equal in ability to the attorney employed by the husband.

6. Security bond equal to one year's projected support payments.

7. Compulsory payroll deductions.

8. Compulsory financial disclosure.

9. A financial investigation and enforcement bureau, with authority to conduct pretrial investigations, subpoena records of income and assets, and enforce support orders.

10. A training and vocational guidance bureau for separated and divorced persons.

NOW has also encouraged insurance companies to consider writing family-marriage insurance. Resolutions to study this will be introduced into the New York State legislature by State Senator Donald Halperin and Assemblyman Richard N. Gottfried. It is suggested that such a policy be converted into retirement income if the couple stays married.

Probably the best solution for women who are getting divorced would be for each woman to decide whether she can be made autonomous and independent. This would involve a careful evaluation of her age, her education, the opportunities open to her, the job market, and (not least) her psychological state. If she felt that "rehabilitation" was truly possible, her ex-husband should be made responsible not for alimony, but for providing her with money so that she could prepare to lead her own economic life. I look forward to the day when the judge awards the wife money to live on until she completes law school, or until she finishes college and gets a well-paying job. Unfortunately, today the climate in family court is such that women fare much better appearing as helpless as possible.

This rehabilitation suggestion, of course, should in no way conflict with *back pay*, which wives should be entitled to at divorce, as a matter of justice.

The property of a married woman, since the Married Women's Acts, is hers.

> Property, real or personal, now owned by a married woman, shall continue to be her sole and separate property as if she were unmarried, and shall not be subject to her husband's control or disposal, nor liable for his debts.[43]

If she is a housewife with no private source of earnings, however, she has no power over money, and no way of accumulating equity, except through the whim of her husband. Household allowances, traditionally the money given by the husband to the wife to run their home, belong to the husband. The wife is merely his agent, and cannot, by saving or economizing, make any of the money truly her own.

> Where the husband, without making a gift, made a weekly allowance to his wife for the household, and she deposited it in a bank balance left after paying necessary

expenses, it would be proper in husband's action after legal separation to impress a trust on the fund in his favor.[44]

Many women of my generation rejected our mothers' suggestions that we "put away" money of our own, either from our earnings or from the household money. We felt that they (our mothers) had not had the benefit of the "true, communicating, I-Thou" relationships that we had. They had been raised on neither Martin Buber nor the "togetherness" ideals of *McCall's* magazine. So the women of my generation, upon divorce, found themselves penniless. The moral of this story is certainly not that women should be party to relationships that involve deceit—but rather that we should not be involved in relationships which place us in a psychological and economic position of dependency and helplessness.

In the management of a household, the wife is the agent for her husband, and any surplus arising out of the economy of the wife in the conduct and management of such household remains and is the property of the husband, unless *bestowed as a gift* [emphasis mine] upon the wife, and therefore where a wife saves without the knowledge of her husband a part of the household allowance furnished her by her husband, and invests it in property, the property is to be considered that of her husband and may be subjected to his creditors to the payment of their claims.[45]

If the woman who has separate earnings is in a better financial position than the housewife, she still is not equal to her husband. Earnings are part of the common holdings in the community property states.

In four of the community property states (Arizona, Louisiana, Nevada, and New Mexico) the community property is managed and controlled *solely* by the husband, and this includes all of the woman's earnings, which belong to the common fund. In California, Idaho, Texas, and Washington the wife may control her earnings.

A man need not pay wages to his wife who works in his business. This exemption, which is permitted in most states, does not apply to a husband employed by his wife, or to children who are employed by their parents. In no state does the law give the woman the right to tell her husband how to spend his earnings, or to claim his labors without recompense.

Married men and women do not have equal rights to property purchased by them with their individual earnings. Unless there is a title or a record establishing otherwise, property purchased by the wife—such as a car or television set—is generally considered to be the property of the husband, even if the purchase is made from her individual earnings.

A wife owns none of the property accumulated during marriage in her husband's name in the common law states. In some states, she has a "dower right" to one-third of his estate (one-half if there are no children) when he dies. In some states he has a comparable "curtesy right."

Alabama and Florida, while not giving a husband a statutory interest in the wife's property, specifically require him to join in the conveyance of her separately owned real property.

In the community property states where the husband has sole control and management of the property, he can legally dissipate the estate without the wife's consent or *knowledge*. Only Texas has eliminated this inequity by amending its community property laws to provide that "each spouse shall have sole management, control, and disposition of that community property which he or she would have owned if a single person."[46]

No chapter on marriage and divorce would be complete without a recording of a particular phenomenon which so many women experience: when she goes to divorce court she is a nervous wreck. She is losing her social status. She is almost invariably getting poorer. She is often losing her self-confidence ("Why couldn't I make this marriage work?"). Her advocates through this whole trauma are invariably male. She has probably consulted a male psychiatrist. She may have had counseling from a clergyman. Her divorce lawyer is probably male.

The social grouping in the hallways of family court is usually one cluster of three well-dressed, confidently chatting men: her lawyer, his lawyer, and her husband. Standing a few feet away, unfamiliar with the "business-like" talk of the others, is the wife. I am not here alleging that the three are in collusion, although this may happen on occasion. I am suggesting that the "male club" atmosphere which pervades family court is not a paranoid delusion. These men, who are all out in the world and used to the discussion of money and contracts and property rights, do have something in common, and the woman who perceives this is simply perceiving reality.

If American women are treated unfairly in the family courts of America, our courts are paradise compared to what American (and Sicilian) women encounter in the courts of Sicily.[47]

ROME—A young American mother, seeking to regain her 18-month-old daughter, is learning what it means to run up against Italian justice, Sicilian-style.

Her experience serves as a warning, U.S. officials say, to the problems American women can face when they marry foreign nationals and become subject to the laws of the husbands' countries.

The mother is an attractive, dark-haired Chicagoan, Judith Munat Ardizzone, 31, whose estranged husband, Dr. Giuseppe Ardizzone, 38, snatched their daughter Daniela, from the mother's home in Florence and took her to his family's home in Messina.

In Messina, the old Sicilian family of Ardizzone packs plenty of political punch.

Thus, though the wheels of justice grind exceedingly slowly in Italy, Dr. Ardizzone managed a series of lightning legal moves to gain custody of the infant.

Though never daring to charge that his wife was an unfit mother, since she had an unblemished reputation in Florence, he nevertheless claimed that she was "a feminist," and, according to Mrs. Ardizzone, cited among her flaws the fact that she read Germaine Greer's "The Female Eunuch."

So, despite the fact that the mother is almost invariably given custody of young children in Italian separation cases, a judge in Messina, Sicily, denied Mrs. Ardizzone temporary custody of her daughter in order to give the girl "an education in accordance with ours."

. . . She met her husband when he was a medical student at the University of Florence, and her salary helped finance his studies.

. . . "I tried to keep the marriage going, but it became impossible" [she said].

. . . The U.S. Embassy has monitored the case, but it is limited to making sure that an American woman gets the same treatment that an Italian national would before the court of law.

Chapter Nine
Criminal Law:
Free Our Sisters,
Free Ourselves

That is what is so bizarre about the American legal system. Where else in the world would stealing from a phone booth be considered more serious than polluting the earth?

—LAURA NADER, *July 16, 1972*

We demand that the rape of our women be taken as seriously as the rape of our land.

—WILMA SCOTT HEIDE, *February 20, 1973*

❧❧❧ Ten women on welfare were arrested on charges of petit larceny and possession of stolen goods in November 1970, after participating in what they termed a "shop-in" at Macy's department store in New York City.

They said they were among at least forty mothers who took children's clothing from the store without paying because, according to the women, their children did not have clothes for school.[1] All were members of the City-wide Coordinating Committee of Welfare Groups.

"We weren't hiding those clothes at all," said Ms. Jeanette Washington, a leader of the demonstration. She said the women rode down the escalators with the merchandise over their arms because they wanted to publicize the fact that they had no money to buy the clothes.

In a statement,[2] the Citywide Coordinating Committee said it had been trying without avail to get a clothing allowance of a hundred dollars for each child in school from the Board of Education's federal funds for the poor. It added that allowances were urgently needed because the Department of Social Services had eliminated a special grants program, which formerly provided money, as well as other services.

Following the incident, a Macy's spokesman said the store "cannot, under any circumstances, allow people to remove merchandise from its stores without paying for it." He added, "This is an illegal act."[3]

In night court the women pleaded guilty to reduced charges of criminal trespass and were paroled by the judge, who said that their action was "political." The district attorney and the arresting officer were angry that the women were getting away too easily. They singled out Jeanette Washington, a leader in the Welfare Rights Organization, and charged her with noncooperation with a police officer because she refused to have her picture taken when she was booked. These charges were thrown out.

President Nixon decided, in 1972, to permit prostitutes on service bases in Vietnam, to boost the morale of demoralized servicemen.[4] He did not, however, permit abortions in Service hospitals, so these women were on their own if they became pregnant.

California Assemblywoman March K. Fong was sitting at her desk in the assembly chamber, reviewing legislation which would appear on the day's agenda. It is common practice for members to consult each other about the many bills on which they must vote, and a male colleague turned to her and asked, "March, what should I do about this prostitution bill?"

She replied, "By all means, pay it."[5]

The laws and the taboos surrounding prostitution are not only antiwoman, they are hypocritical. The proof of this hypocrisy is that when one takes a careful look at the role of the nonprostitute women in the society—the secretary, the nurse, but especially *the wife*—one sees that the politics of her economic life are the same. Laws which govern wives and prostitutes are the legislative and judicial enforcement of patriarchy.

Whereas women are encouraged by the society to be wives, they are later punished legally and socially for becoming wives. Whereas women are often forced by the society to become prostitutes, they are later punished legally and socially for doing so.

The laws on female prostitution, like so many of the laws which govern human relationships, are designed to keep the family together—nuclear, patriarchal, and monogamous. Sexual relations outside of marriage are usually punished. Homosexual relations are usually illegal, even between consenting adults. The medieval contraception laws, and the abortion laws before the recent Supreme Court decision, have as one underlying assumption that sex for purposes other than procreation is not permissible. Needless to say, since women are the sex partners who get pregnant, these laws are not only puritan, but misogynic.

In family law, there is a clear trend that women are punished for having sex outside of marriage. This is not really puritanical America speaking, since men who have sex lives outside of marriage are considered normal, and often are admired. No one ever suggests that the unwed father needs psychiatric counseling.

In dealing with juveniles, the family court looks not only to the offense, but also to the life of the child as a whole. A determination is then made whether the court system should step in to "help the child," rather than to punish the crime. In evaluating whether a child is a juvenile delinquent, a PINS (person in need of supervision) case, or a wayward minor, sexual behavior is considered. A high percentage of juvenile delinquent girls are in detention homes for being prostitutes.

Since it takes two to perform a sex act, it is a clear Fourteenth Amendment equal protection violation to punish females in any way in which males are not punished. Young people are bombarded with media admonitions to be sexy and to have sex. Yet there are few high schools in this country which give birth control information and equipment to the students; until recently, abortion was a crime in most states.

Marriage, for any woman who cannot support herself and her children, differs little from prostitution: it is a trade of sex for food.

> The wife who married for money, compared with the prostitute, is the true scab. She is paid less, gives much more in return in labor and care, and is absolutely bound to her master. The prostitute never signs away the right over her own person, she retains her freedom and personal rights, nor is she always compelled to submit to man's embrace.[6]

Emma Goldman—who understood the relationship between sex and economics—has written about how the prostitute's plight is that of all women. She herself was slated early in life for domesticity. When she told her father that she did not want to marry—that she wanted to travel, study, and learn—he was enraged. "Girls do not have to learn much," he said, "only how to prepare gefüllte fish, cut noodles fine, and give the man plenty of children."[7] Afraid of her father's plans for her, Emma fled to America, to live with a sister.

A similar circumstance affected the life of Golda Meir. As a high school student, living in Milwaukee, Wisconsin, with her parents, she planned to be a schoolteacher. Her parents forbade this, since at that time schoolteachers in Wisconsin were not allowed to be married, and they could not imagine their daughter an "old maid." Golda also fled (to Colorado) to live with a sister.

> No where is woman treated according to the merit of her work, but rather as a sex. It is therefore almost inevitable that she should pay for her right to exist, to keep a position in whatever line, with sex favors. Thus, it is merely a question of degree whether she sells herself to one man, in or out of marriage, or to many men. Whether our reformers admit it or not, the economic and social inferiority of women is responsible for prostitution.[8]

On March 28, 1915, Emma Goldman addressed six hundred people in New York's Sunrise Club.[9]

> Marriage for monetary considerations is perfectly legitimate, sanctified by law and public opinion, while any other union is condemned and repudiated. Yet a prostitute, if properly defined, means nothing else than "any person for whom sexual relationships are subordinated to gain."

> Marriage and love have nothing in common. Certainly the growing-used to each other is far from the spontaneity, the intensity, and beauty of love, without which the intimacy of marriage must prove degrading to both the woman and the man. Marriage is primarily an economic arrangement, an insurance pact.

> . . . It is like that other paternal arrangement—capitalism.

. . . The institution of marriage makes a parasite of woman, an absolute dependent. It incapacitates her for life's struggles, annihilates her social consciousness, paralyzes her imagination, and then imposes its gracious protection, which is in reality a snare, a travesty on human character.[10]

The similarities between the married woman and the prostitute are many. In prostitution "circles," a prostitute who is related to one or more other prostitutes by association with the same pimp, is called a "wife-in-law."[11] It is well documented in the women's liberation movement that upper-middle-class housewives who join the movement identify with two groups: domestic workers and prostitutes. This is, obviously, because they have much the same work to perform.

The wife generally can only be excused from her domestic-worker duties if she is physically or mentally ill. "A wife's neglect of her home and her husband have been listed among indignities recognized in Pennsylvania, but if she fails to cook her husband's meals, and wash his clothes and clean his house, and if she neglects him generally because she is physically or mentally unable to do otherwise, of course, the neglect does not constitute an indignity. She is excused . . . on the theory that such conduct lacks the spirit of hate, estrangement and malevolence which is the heart of the charge of indignities."[12]

In like manner, particularly since the so-called sexual revolution, wives must not only have sex with their husbands, they must now enjoy it. A California conciliation agreement states: "The wife agrees to respond to the husband's efforts in lovemaking and not to act like a patient undergoing a physical examination."[13] And no wonder many women feel etherized upon the table.

One type of interference with the husband's interests is variously called abduction, enticement, or harboring of the wife. There was an early writ of ravishment, which listed the wife with the husband's chattels, and was available to him when she was taken away forcibly or eloped with another man. In time, this was replaced by the action of trespass for depriving him of a servant. Since there is an obvious loss of consortium when a wife is either compelled or induced to live apart from her husband, all courts are agreed that he may maintain a tort action against anyone who, without justification and for an improper purpose, influences or advises her to do so, or assists her to depart.

The medieval law was so strict that "if one's wife missed her way upon the road, it was not lawful for another man to take her into his house, unless she was benighted and in danger of being lost or drowned"; this gentle rule for the encouragement of chivalry is a thing of the past. It may still be a tort against the husband to harbor the wife, if it is coupled with persuasion or encouragement not to return to him; but a mere reception in good faith upon grounds of friendship, hospitality, or common humanity will not result in liability.[14]

Though in 1973 there is no liability against the man who shows friendship or hospitality to another man's wife, social law is doing an adequate job of replacing the statutes. Rare is the married woman who will dare, for example, to be seen eating lunch in a restaurant with a man who is not her husband. This is apparently a carryover from the chattel days, but engenders strict obedience despite the present lack of a potential tort action.

In the previously mentioned Pennsylvania case in which a wife was convicted of drunken driving despite her reliance upon the "presumption of compulsion" resulting from her husband's presence in the car, the trial judge denied the defendant's motion for a new trial even though he held that she was entitled to take advantage of a rebuttable presumption of compulsion:[15]

> . . . human experience of the wife's tendency to follow her husband's bidding. The rule is not founded on . . . public policy to promote domestic tranquility. The rule is based upon human experience and therefore its continuing validity is not affected by any change in a wife's property or personal rights.

> While . . . instances could possibly be found where a wife may dominate her husband . . . , we have not yet reached the point where we decry the nobility, dignity or grace of a wife's deference to her husband's desires.

The same mentality which punishes women for prostitution, punishes them for sexual behavior outside of marriage. Married men, in many states, who are involved in adultery are not in danger of losing their property rights, but a married woman can lose her share of the property if she has committed adultery.[16] Florida law states "no alimony shall be granted to an adulterous wife," while the adulterous husband suffers no financial loss. A Nebraska divorce law depriving women who commit adultery of all but their personal property is being tested in a federal lawsuit by the Nebraska Civil Liberties Union. Since men are not similarly penalized, the case is being tried on the Equal Protection Clause of the Fourteenth Amendment.[17]

The husband may recover damages—including loss of his wife's services and society (consortium) and his costs for her care—resulting from another's injury to his wife.[18] Several jurisdictions have abolished the husband's right to recover for loss of consortium, either judicially[19] or by statutory interpretation.[20] A few jurisdictions have obtained equality by permitting the wife to recover for loss of her husband's consortium.[21]

Except for the financial necessity which might be plaguing her, the prostitute can always refuse to have sexual intercourse; not so the wife, because the law has always held that coercion of a wife to submit to sexual intercourse is not rape.[22]

English law in 1800 stated:[23]

> By their mutual matrimonial consent and contract the wife hath given up herself in this kind unto her husband, which she cannot retract.

The literature, legal and sociological, is fraught with confusion as to whether innocent men are lured into sexual relations by evil women, or whether weak women need protection from unscrupulous men. The Mann Act rests on a legislative judgment that women need protection:[24]

> It is not an allowable choice for a witness-wife [whose husband has led her into prostitution] "voluntarily" to decide to protect her husband by declining to testify against him. For if a defendant can induce a woman, against her "will," to enter a life of prostitution for his benefit—by the same token it should be considered that he can, at least as easily, persuade one who has already fallen victim to his influence that she must also protect him. To make matters turn upon ad hoc inquiries into the actual state of mind of particular women, thereby encumbering Mann Act trials with a collateral issue of the greatest subtlety, is hardly an acceptable solution.

> Pointing out that in the Mann Act Congress had chosen between the interest in prohibiting the transportation of prostitutes and the interest of women in voluntarily engaging in prostitution, the dissenters said "It is hardly

surprising that Congress passed the Mann Act and made the consent of the female entirely immaterial."

So, in the growing body of law, we see that what women want to do, about having sex or not having sex, is not material to the criminal code. In addition, to be a credible person in the eyes of the court, a woman must have been married at one time, although she need not be married at the present time.[25]

> The mere absence of a man from a group is not what we are talking about. Widows and divorcees need not be considered as unstable because no man is involved in their home . . .

> The minimum acceptable standards in the community for men and women who wish to live together, to have sexual relations . . . is that they be married . . . something less than that is immoral.

Judges have also recognized the necessary connection between marriage and women's economic ability to survive.[26]

> . . . it is impossible for a mother of less than independent wealth to care for three or four or seven or eleven or twelve illegitimate children on the slender means provided her by the welfare department.

> . . . impossible for such a woman to provide the moral training and the spiritual counseling that ought to surround the nurture of children of tender years so they will not themselves fall into the difficulties that she has fallen into.

It is fairly evident that the law is set up to deny a woman sexual pleasure and/or motherhood, unless she is living with and is legally married to one male; it is fairly evident that the law is in full accord with women's obtaining money from men, but only if these women agree to the marriage ceremony. Any deviation from these practices may subject a woman to the loss of her children, the loss of her source of income, or the loss of her liberty.

A wife cohabiting with her husband for money is not only law-abiding, she is law-breaking if she refuses. A nonwife cohabiting with a man for money will, if she is caught and convicted, wind up in jail. Perhaps this is because she is not accompanying her "love-making" with kitchen duties, which many men hold so dear.

In the Soviet Union, there was a law[27] that prostitutes could not be punished as long as there was unemployment that the government could not eradicate. In this country, we must be very careful to make sure that any war against prostitution does not turn into a war against prostitutes.

It should be noted that what we know about female prostitution comes mostly from males—lawyers, sociologists, and psychiatrists. The laws on prostitution have, of course, been written by male legislators; they have been enforced by male police forces. Female prostitutes are defended by male lawyers, and sentenced by male judges. If jailed, they are dealt with by female wardens, under the direction of male prison administrators.

Prostitution is one of the few ways in which women, especially uneducated women, have been able to earn money. Today, for example, only 60 percent of American women have some source of income (wages, inheritance, welfare payments). This 60 percent has an average income of $1,600 per year. The other 40 percent has no source of income, and is dependent totally on a husband for support.

To prostitute means to set oneself up for sale, or to devote to infamous purposes what is in one's power; as in the prostitution of talents or abilities; the prostitution of the press.[28] Despite the existence of male prostitutes, when we say prostitute we usually mean a woman. The law dictionary definition of prostitution does not mention men.

> Common lewdness of a woman for gain; whoredom; the act or practice of a woman who permits any man who will pay her price to have sexual intercourse with her.[29]

> The act or practice of a female of prostituting or offering her body to an indiscriminate intercourse with men for money or its equivalent.[30]

The definitions of prostitute similarly apply only to women.

> A woman who indiscriminately consorts with men for hire.[31]

> A woman who has given herself up to indiscriminate lewdness.[32]

> A woman submitting to indiscriminate sexual intercourse, which she solicits.[33]

The major federal law controlling prostitution is the Mann Act.[34]

> Whoever knowingly transports in interstate or foreign commerce . . . any woman or girl for the purpose of prostitution or debauchery, or for any other immoral purpose . . . shall be fined not more than $5,000, or imprisoned not more than 5 years, or both.

The formal title of the Mann Act is the White Slave Act. The term "white slave" connotes a (white?) female held for the purpose of commercial prostitution against her will. The term was apparently coined when black slavery was still in existence, to distinguish the slavery of white women for prostitution from that of the involuntary servitude of blacks, which of course included free sex for the white master.

State laws on prostitution appear in alcoholic beverage control laws, correction laws, criminal laws, executive laws, judicial acts, penal laws, and public health laws. The New York penal law, for example, defines prostitution:[35]

> A person is guilty of prostitution when such person engages or offers to engage in sexual conduct with another person in return for a fee.

Prostitution in New York is a violation. Prior to September 1, 1967, it was a form of vagrancy, with emphasis placed on loitering in public places. The revised section disregards the loitering aspects, and defines it as an individual substantive offense. The law makes no reference to the sex of the parties, but the cases do. For example:

> Prostitution consists of common, indiscriminate, meretricious commerce with men, and not a mere meretricious relation with a single individual.[36]

The New York state law on patronizing a prostitute is rumored not to be heavily enforced. It states:[37]

> A person is guilty of patronizing a prostitute when:
>
> 1. Pursuant to a prior understanding, he pays a fee to another person as compensation for such person or a 3rd person having engaged in sexual conduct with him; or

2. He pays or agrees to pay a fee to another person pursuant to an understanding that in return thereof such person or a third person will engage in sexual conduct with him; or

3. He solicits or requests another person to engage in sexual conduct with him in return for a fee.

Similar statutes are in the codes of Illinois, Wisconsin, and Colorado, and in the American Law Institute Model Penal Code.

In the New York law,[38] the sex of the parties makes no difference.

In any prosecution for prostitution or patronizing a prostitute, the sex of the two parties or prospective parties to the sexual conduct engaged in, contemplated or solicited is immaterial, and it is no defense that:

1) Such persons were of the same sex; or

2) Person who received fee is a male, and the person who paid is a female.

The New York Penal Law provides the sentence for those convicted of prostitution to be from fifteen days to six months.[39]

Other countries, for example, Austria, have laws to protect the individual working prostitute from having her earnings cut into by others. The Vienna Regulations[40] provide that a prostitute may live in a house, or have an apartment, on condition that the landlady has no share or percentage in the proceeds of the trade. Swedish prostitutes have formed their own trade union "to protect their rights in business and social matters."[41]

It is interesting to note the legislative intent of the U.S. prostitution statutes. They could almost be called "male protective" laws:[42]

And it must be entirely obvious that the purpose of the Legislature was not to place in the hands of two or more prostitutes, voluntarily accompanying one or more men upon a night's debauch, the power to blackmail these erring brothers, under threat of a term in state prison, but rather to reach and punish those conscienceless vampires who make merchandise of the passions of men.

In New York, a person is guilty of promoting prostitution in the first degree when he knowingly[43] (1) advances prostitution by compelling a person by force or intimidation to engage in prostitution, or profits from such coercive conduct by another, or (2) advances or profits from the prostitution of a person under the age of sixteen.

A famous case is that of oleomargarine heir Mickey Jelke,[44] who was prosecuted for inducing and attempting to induce certain women to live a life of prostitution. The stated purpose of the statute which prohibits attempts to entice women into prostitution is to "get" the tycoons of organized vice, not to reach the pimps. In the Jelke case, the prosecution conceded that the defendant was no vice lord, but rather a shallow and irresponsible youth who managed to live for some months according to the style he wanted to become accustomed to, with a comparatively small amount of financial aid from a prostitute, Pat Ward.

Jelke evidently enjoyed the tinsel of New York cafe society. Although he had some $27,000 at his disposal during these 6 or 7 months from bank loans, gifts or loans from relatives, and income from trust funds in addition to anything which he received from Pat Ward, he nevertheless spent some of her earnings in their fast, short life together.[45]

The court "pointed out" that Pat Ward had been "depraved" at age sixteen; at the time of the trial she was eighteen. Apparently, a rich man does not get convicted of pimping for a depraved woman of eighteen.

Although women are considered to be romantics, our economic position does not allow us that luxury. We must be dependent upon one man, or perhaps upon many. As Eleanor Antin expressed it: [46] "Anna Karenina doesn't leave her up-tight husband to become commissioner of railroads. She leaves only when she finds another host to live off. Tolstoi calls that bizarre practicality a romantic nature."

Prostitution is an inherent part of American business, both within organized crime and on a small-time basis. In 1913, Lenin wrote an analysis critical of the way the bourgeoisie combats prostitution. [47]

> Recently the fifth international congress for combatting the white slave traffic was held in London. Duchesses, countesses, bishops, parsons, rabbis, police officials and all sorts of bourgeois philanthropists displayed themselves at this congress . . . There was no end of solemn speeches on the harm and shame of prostitution.

> But what were the means of struggle which the elegant bourgeois delegates demanded at the congress? The two means were: religion and the police. These, they said, were the surest and safest means against prostitution. According to a report by the London correspondent of the *Leipziger Volkszektung*, an English delegate boasted of the fact that he had introduced into Parliament a bill providing for the *corporal punishment* for pandering.

> . . . When the Austrian delegate Gertner ventured to mention the social causes of prostitution, the want and misery of working class families, the exploitation of

child labor, the unbearable housing conditions, etc., the speaker was silenced by hostile shouts! On the other hand, instructive and solemn stories were told among the delegates concerning various high personages. For instance, that when the German empress is about to visit a lying-in hospital in Berlin the mothers of "illegitimate" children have *rings put on their fingers*, so as to spare the high personage the shocking sight of unwedded mothers!

There has been some attempt in British and American statutes to equalize the sanctions for male and female prostitutes. The 1956 British Sexual Offenses Act[48] was clearly restricted to female prostitutes. The object of the 1969 British Street Offenses Bill was to remove legal discrimination between men and women, between prostitute and client, and between heterosexual and homosexual conduct. The Wolfenden Report, on the role of law in relation to street activities connected with prostitution, concluded that what the law can and should do is to ensure that the streets of London and other cities are freed from what is offensive and injurious, and made tolerable for the ordinary citizen. Even with the attempts to equalize, however, the situation is not the same for men and women.

The social objections to prostitutes, a convenient device for keeping all women out of certain places of public accommodation, apply strictly to female prostitutes. The defenders of the male-only bar or restaurant staunchly defend their discrimination on the grounds that they are protecting their (male) customers from loose women.

The most flagrant example of duplicity is the male attitude toward prostitution. As Simone de Beauvoir points out, it is his demand that creates the supply:[49]

I have told with what disgusted skepticism prostitutes regard the respectable gentlemen who condemn vice in general but view their own personal whims with indulgence; yet they regard the girls who live off their bodies as perverted and debauched, not the males who use them.

De Beauvoir relates an incident to illustrate the point. Around the turn of the century the police found two little girls of twelve and thirteen in a brothel. Testifying at the trial, the girls referred to their clients, who were men of importance. As one of the girls was about to give a name, the judge stopped her. "You must not befoul the name of a respectable man!"

A gentleman decorated by the Legion of Honor is still a respectable man when deflowering a little girl; he has his weaknesses, as who does not? Whereas the little girl who has no aspirations toward the ethical realm of the universal—who is not a magistrate, or a general, or a great Frenchman, nothing but a little girl—stakes her moral value in the contingent realm of sexuality: she is perverse, corrupted, vicious, fit only for the reformatory.[50]

The laws in both England and America present a fascinating contradiction with regard to women. On the one hand, women are regarded as evil, preying on the uncontrollable passions of the male. On the other hand, women are regarded as children—"protected" from jobs which require overtime hours, prohibited from doing "men's" work, and prevented from earning money.

Sir Reginald Manningham-Buller, attorney general of Great Britain at the time of the passage of the Street Offenses Act, was satisfied that "no honest constable" would have any difficulty in identifying a prostitute.[51]

One of the standard ways to discredit women fighting for equality—political, economic, or social—is to discredit them sexually, calling them "prostitute," "lesbian," or "frigid." Apparently each of the three classifications poses some kind of threat to the American family, but more significant, since women have been defined in strictly sexual terms for thousands of years, it is only appropriate that this is the "best" way to discredit a woman.

The pimp is an affront to the American way of life. *He lives off a woman.* But is that really why he is so abhorred? I think not. Corporation profits, made by men, are created in good part because of the large cadre of women workers who do office and factory labor for low wages. The president of General Motors lives off women. And one of the most cherished of American traditions is marrying the boss's daughter. In American success literature, the young clerk doesn't make it because he goes to church and works overtime without pay. He becomes president of the company by marrying the right woman.

The pimp is distinguished from these men because in his relationship to a woman economic roles are truly reversed, whereas marrying the boss's daughter is still within the accepted traditional pattern.

Robert Seidenberg, a psychoanalyst, explores the idea that the traditional arrangement, in which men "give" and women and children "receive," may not be an ideal one for women and children:[52]

Generally it is the male's great pride that he can "give" his wife and children more than the next fellow does. Yet there is always an overhanging terror in reserve— the potential for the male's self-righteous nastiness about being ruined or being run into bankruptcy. And the wife, with her children, all euphemisms aside, is placed in the role of recipient and dependent.

Perhaps some women would enjoy having recipients and dependents. This pleasure, in addition to the obvious advantages of having power, may be sensual. Magazine and television ads pay homage to the concept that any man worth his salt loves to buy beautiful trinkets—furs, jewels, perfume, life insurance—for a beautiful woman. A woman might indeed get equal pleasure from buying beautiful trinkets to adorn a beautiful man—and hence gain his devotion, similar to the devotion a rich older man buys from women.

As he sentenced a pimp to seven years at the Nottingham Assizes, the trial judge said:[53]

> It is a loathsome thing for a man to batten on the earnings of women . . . It is very difficult to trace men who have done what you have, but when the crime is brought home the duty of the court is to emphasize the disgust people feel for men like you.

In *The Taming of the Shrew*, Petruchio gives the wife's traditional definition:[54]

> She is my goods, my chattels, she is my house,
> My household stuff, my field, my bard,
> My horse, my ox, my ass, my anything.

Pollack and Maitland[55] explain how the law served to make women dependent, both financially and psychologically.

> We can not be certain that for long centuries the presiding tendency (underlying the husband's right to his wife's property) was not one which was separating the

wife from her blood kinsmen, teaching her to forget her own people and her father's house and bringing her and her goods more completely under her husband's dominion.

The domestic relations laws in the various states show that legislatures and courts also frown on a man and a woman deciding to reverse financial roles.

A Michigan case[56] invalidates a contract in which the husband was to be paid a retainer fee by the wife to act as her theatrical agent:

I am convinced that . . . the contract was not a competent one for married persons to enter into. In the first place, it is highly doubtful if the alleged contract is within the capacity of a married woman to make under Michigan law . . . a married woman has no general power to contract, but can contract only in relation to her separate property.

However, I do not rest my decision on this ground, but rather upon the broader ground that even if the contract is otherwise within the contractual power of the parties it is void because it contravenes public policy. As a result of the marriage . . . the husband has a duty to support and to live with his wife and the wife must contribute her services and society to the husband and follow him in his choice of domicile. The law is well settled that a private agreement between persons married or about to be married which attempts to change the essential obligations of the marriage contract as defined by the law is contrary to public policy and unenforceable.

. . . Thus, it has been repeatedly held that a provision releasing the husband from his duty to support his wife . . . makes the contract void . . . Even in the states with the most liberal emancipation statutes with respect to married persons, the law has not gone to the extent of permitting husbands and wives by agreement to change the essential incidents of the marriage contract.

Under [the contract's] terms, the husband becomes obligated to accompany his wife upon her travels; while under the law of marriage the wife is obliged to follow the husband's choice of domicile . . . The contract, furthermore, would seem to suffer a second defect by impliedly releasing the husband from his duty to support his wife.

Unemployment laws in many of the states reinforce the dependence of the wife. For example, there are provisions specifying that any nonworking wife may be a dependent, but that a nonworking husband can be a dependent only if totally and permanently disabled.

The whole subject of laws on prostitution is very much in need of a feminist analysis. The National Conference of NOW, in February 1973, passed the following resolutions concerning prostitution:

1. WHEREAS the existence of prostitution in this society is a reflection that women in the society are considered not to be the equals of men, and are valued, almost without exception, for their sexuality first, and their humanness second, and

2. WHEREAS the society maintains a double standard with regard to the sexual activities of women and men, and under this standard, women are harshly categorized, to wit, the woman who is loved and cherished is protected from any sexual deviation, but any kind of sexual deviation is permissible with a woman who prostitutes herself, and

3. WHEREAS research has shown that a woman becomes a prostitute for several reasons, among these

being a breakdown in positive reinforcement for her early creative and constructive efforts, an overemphasis on her sexuality as a vehicle for male attraction, and finally on her *economic distress*, which in instances where she has defied the racial or sexual mores of the society is combined with social recrimination and is particularly overt, and

4. WHEREAS coercion has been reported, first in the reports of some welfare workers, encouraging women to supplement welfare checks by prostitution, and secondly, in reports in some cities of women being kidnapped and, through torture and drugs, being made dependent on earnings from the "fast life," and

5. WHEREAS a practicing prostitute must ally herself with a pimp in order to achieve status in the sub-culture, but also for protection and to supply legal support when she is arrested, and then surrenders her earnings in exchange for his economic and psychological support, and

6. WHEREAS the prostitute is often a victim of customer brutality but under prohibitive laws and discriminatory enforcement practices found throughout the United States cannot seek police protection, and

7. WHEREAS prostitutes enter into an agreement, contractural in nature, with a consenting adult, to perform a service in private, and

8. WHEREAS while the act of prostituting is almost always illegal in this society, consorting with a prostitute and using coercion to influence a woman to prostitute herself are often also illegal, and

9. WHEREAS statistics in the areas where all acts involved in prostitution (being a prostitute, consorting with a prostitute, or coercing a woman to prostitute herself) show that only the prostitute is arrested and convicted, and that customers are almost never arrested, let alone charged or convicted, and

10. WHEREAS a prostitute, having been imprisoned for an act she considers essentially a service, can be exposed to persons who may have committed heinous crimes, with the possible result of this internment teaching her perpetration of genuine crime, such as theft, against further clients, and

11. WHEREAS enforcement of existing laws serves to make prostitution a crime only in the lower echelons of society (for example, the streetwalker) and at the same time virtually ignores prostitution in the middle and upper classes, and

12. WHEREAS the entrapment of prostitutes requires an exorbitant outlay of police time, effort, and expense, and thus contributes to a situation in which public morality is regulated at the possible expense of the public safety, and

13. WHEREAS policemen who volunteer for such activities as entrapping and arresting prostitutes often manifest verbal and physical abuse against these women and may as well suffer, because of these activities, a deterioration in their personal and professional self-images, and

14. WHEREAS in the instances of crimes such as prostitution, which have no complainants, the police become the complaining party, a practice which lends itself to payoff and other corruption, and in turn prompts disrespect for the law, and

15. WHEREAS there is no evidence to indicate that liberalization of such prohibitive laws will encourage women to become prostitutes;

BE IT THEREFORE RESOLVED,

1. that NOW condemns first the social and economic structure which limits women's alternatives and thus contributes directly to the decision of many women to

turn to prostitution in hopes that it will provide adequate earnings and remove them from the mindlessness of low-skill, low-paying jobs, and secondly condemns the legal structure which persecutes women prostitutes while ignoring the participation of men.

2. that NOW opposes continued prohibitive laws regarding prostitution, believing them to be punitive, especially where women are concerned, and unenforceable, and furthermore, believing they do not deter women who must become prostitutes but rather that the laws encourage the prostitute to become involved in serious crime.

3. that NOW strongly opposes the licensing of prostitutes, believing that (a) such licensing will result in ongoing persecution of women who will not register because they do not wish publicly to proclaim themselves prostitutes, perhaps in the belief that they will one day seek an alternative life, and (b) such licensing would serve to place governmental bodies in the business of making money off the sale of women's sexual services, and further place government in the role of regulating public morality, when in fact we believe those to be ill-advised roles for government.

4. that NOW supports full prosecution of any acts of coercion by any person, public agency, or group to influence women to become prostitutes.

5. that NOW seeks to remove the inequities against prostitutes who are, on the one hand, brutalized without having legal recourse, and on the other, are by their singular arrests, the subjects of flagrantly selective law enforcement, realizing that to repeal the laws prohibiting prostitution is not to make a judgment that prostitution is "good," but rather, that it is instead a judgment about the appropriate use of the criminal justice system.

6. that NOW therefore favors removal of all laws relat-

ing to the act of prostitution per se, and as an interim measure, favors the decriminalization of prostitution.

At the first National Convention of El Partido de la Raza Unida (the Party of the United People), in September 1972, Spanish-surnamed women pledged "support to Latina women in their struggle for equal rights in all spheres of life."[57] The platform included a resolution on prostitution:

> Whereas prostitution is used by a corrupt few to reap profits for themselves with no human consideration for all the needs of *mujeres* [women], and whereas prostitutes are victims of an exploitative economic system and are not criminals, and whereas legalized prostitution is used as a means of employing poor women who are on welfare, be it resolved that:
>
> (1) those who reap profits from prostitution be given heavy prison sentences and be made to pay large fines;
>
> (2) *mujeres* who are forced to prostitution not be condemned to serve prison sentences;
>
> (3) prostitution not be legalized.

In late 1972, the police in New York City made an attempt to pick up "the johns." Policewomen were sent to Times Square; any man who propositioned them was charged with patronizing a prostitute. The maximum penalty was fifteen days in jail. The point was to scare off potential customers. Previously, the police had concentrated on arresting prostitutes only.

The New York City campaign to harass prostitutes began in the summer of 1971. Police took photos of women in the Times Square area, supposedly to use as evidence in court. The judges kept demanding higher and higher bail from the women. Some of the women were denied bail entirely—although it is legal to deny bail on a misdemeanor charge such as soliciting—apparently to make examples of them.

One of the women held without bail, a former addict and prostitute, had held a job and been in a drug program for over two years at the time she was busted. The next day, fifty demonstrators from the women's movement picketed the courthouse.[58]

It is time—for women, especially—to cease condemning prostitutes; to band together and force legislatures and judges to stop harassing our sisters. The Seattle-King County Chapter of NOW, building on the work of Dr. Jennifer James of the University of Washington, did an extensive study of prostitutes in Seattle. It was found, for example, that the pimp-prostitute relationship often resembles a marriage. Much as the doctor's wife acquires status from her husband's position in the community, the prostitute, to gain "respect" and have protection in her culture—which is also obviously a product of male chauvinism—must have a pimp.

Dr. James, who studied a hundred and forty prostitutes for three years, concluded:

> There's no more force involved in prostitution than, I think, in the average husband-wife relationship. There are some cases of pimps beating prostitutes; there has been a rare case of a pimp shooting a prostitute, but there have been just as many cases of husbands beating wives and husbands shooting wives. I want to emphasize that the force is not out of proportion to the kind of force you find between men and women in other kinds of relationships.

The aspect of the pimp-prostitute relationship that is most difficult for traditionalists to comprehend is that the prostitute earns money which she then turns over to the pimp. Most of the money will go toward her care and keeping. Her situation is analogous to that of the husband whose salary goes for the support of his wife and children, but whose earnings are nevertheless *his*. Dr. James has pointed out that the prostitute's slapping two hundred dollars down on the dresser is an exhibition of *her* power, not the pimp's.

Insofar as the sexual nature of her work is concerned, studies have shown that generally the prostitute does not consider sex to be the degrading aspect of her profession.[59] Rather, what she finds degrading is the constant threat of arrest and the treatment she receives from the police. Policemen are not simply enforcers of the law. More realistically, they are oppressors with attitudes toward the oppressed, and men with attitudes toward women. Arresting prostitutes—as well as arresting other victimless crime offenders—can become a game to policemen, especially those men who have little gratification from their jobs and other aspects of their lives.

The criminal justice section of the New York State Bar Association recommended in January 1973 that all criminal sanctions be removed from a variety of victimless crimes.[60] The group recommended repeal of the existing law on prostitution, and adoption of measures similar to the British Streetwalkers Act, which is directed principally against public solicitation.

The criminal code sections on rape are as sexist as those on prostitution. Rape is the only violent crime in which a victim is required to convince the jury that she vigorously tried to fight off her attacker.

The pervasive community feeling about women who are raped seems to be that somehow they must have been "asking for it." Our laws do not require a victim of robbery to show that she or he offered physical resistance, screamed, or tried to run away before "consenting" to part with property. We do, however, require this type of showing from a woman who cooperates with prosecutors attempting to obtain a conviction of rape.

The Model Penal Code still suggests that corroboration is a proper requirement. The corroboration requirement makes conviction of a rapist practically impossible. Additionally, because of the way women reporting rapes are treated (like criminals themselves), because often their names are listed in the newspapers, and because they know the man is not likely to be convicted anyway, only a small percentage of women who have been raped even bother to report the crime. Yet even so, FBI statistics reveal that 37,270 rapes were reported in 1970—one every fourteen minutes.

For women, the term "crime in the streets" refers to rape. Between 1960 and 1967, the number of forcible rapes known to law enforcement officials increased 61 percent. In contrast, the proportion of forcible rapes followed by arrest of the offender decreased annually.[61] Psychologist Dr. Jo-Ann Evans Gardner explains:[62]

> Rapists perform for sexist males the same function that the Ku Klux Klan performed for racist whites; they keep women in their "place" through fear. The threat of rape is used to keep women out of jobs—for example, the *Pittsburgh Post Gazette* has used this as a reason not to hire women reporters; it is used to keep women off the streets at night (unless they are telephone operators or nurses); it keeps women passive and modest for fear they will be thought provocative.

The threat of rape indeed gives employers a splendid excuse for not hiring women—we must be kept from this neighborhood or that, we must be kept from working at this time of day or that—all for our own good. The most disastrous result of the threat of rape is what it does to women, in our own heads.

While every woman is affected by the threat of rape, it is a crime that is most common among low-income women who must work late at night clerking in department stores, cleaning in hotels, and waiting on tables.

If indeed the only "safe" place is at home, no wonder we are all afraid to leave home—whether to go to work, or to go to political meetings, or to just meet some friends at night for coffee. If we have to call someone to meet us at the subway station, does not that reinforce the idea that women are like eight-year-old children?

And when a woman reports that she was raped or attacked, and the police question her about whether *she* was being provocative, does not that put in her head at least the germ of an idea that it was really her fault? Anyone who walks in the park is asking for it; why else walk in the park? Anyone who wears a short skirt is asking for it; why else wear a short skirt?

We have been so brainwashed about it's being our fault that when I, for example, am explaining the humiliation and fury I experienced in not being able to walk in midmorning from my hotel to the art museum in Mexico City, without being pawed and slurped at by the men of Mexico City, *I find myself saying that I wasn't wearing sexy clothes, that I wasn't giving provocative looks*.

Women indeed are treated like criminals, rather than the victims. For practical purposes we are all under house arrest. The title of an article by Martha Weinman Lear: "Q: If you rape a woman and steal her TV, what can they get you for in New York? A: Stealing her TV,"[63] suggests the problem.

Margaret Mead has described societies in which rape is as unheard of as cannibalism is in ours. In contrast, in male-dominated and competitive modern society, men who cannot assert their dominance otherwise turn to brutality against women, who have been cast in submissive and inferior roles.

The rape victim is made to feel guilty, shamed, and tainted. One of the most incredible facets of the horrible war in Bangladesh was that the women (the youngest of whom were ten) who had been raped by invading Pakistani soldiers were thrown out, not only by their husbands but by their parents.

Novels and movies glorify rape. Some "romantic" novels actually suggest that both men and women prefer a sex act that has overtones of rape.

The three local NOW chapters in the national capital area studied rape around Washington, D.C. They found that only about one-third of the rapes are actually reported; a five-year study revealed that of the reported rapes, only about one-half were investigated.[64] The F.B.I. shows 5 percent of all rapes solved, but 86 percent of all aggravated assaults solved.[65]

When Golda Meir was asked if she felt there should be a curfew for women because of the rape problem, she replied that since men did the raping, there should be a curfew for men.

In some states, a man's previous rape convictions are not admissible evidence, but the sexual experience of the victim is admissible. There is actually a prevailing view that if a woman will have sex with *any* man she is not married to, she therefore wants to have sex with *every* man she is not married to. Sex performed outside of marriage by a woman automatically puts her in a category—shameless hussy—where it is assumed she cannot be raped (she asked for it). Rape victims have been subjected in the courtroom to endless questions about the intimate details of their sexual behavior.

In New York State in 1969, 1,840 rapes were reported. There was one conviction.[66] To safeguard men against women's "unfounded accusations," the law provides that a woman's testimony is not sufficient to convict him of rape, as it would be to convict him of assault. She must produce additional evidence, usually a witness.

In 1972, New York State lessened, but did not eliminate, its corroboration requirements. In the *Linzy* case,[67] upon prosecution for rape no independent evidence was offered to support the charge that the defendant was the assailant.

When a defendant is charged with the crime of rape, the New York law requires that the victim's testimony be corroborated and that there be some independent showing that it was the defendant who committed the crime. No independent testimony was introduced to corroborate the identity of the alleged rapist in the *Linzy* case. The state offered no proof which would have placed the defendant or the defendant's car in the vicinity where the alleged rape occurred on the night in question. In the absence of independent corroboration, the conviction failed, and a new trial was ordered.

The court approved of the legislation amending the Penal Law,[68] which no longer requires corroboration of the complaining witness's testimony regarding penetration or, in most instances, the perpetrator's identity. The court recommended that the requirement of corroboration be eliminated entirely, and that instead there be a requirement of especially convincing and satisfying evidence.

The *Linzy* case is an appeal, by permission of a justice of the Appellate Division of the Supreme Court in the Third Judicial Department, rendered upon a verdict convicting the defendant of rape in the first degree.

The complainant, a seventeen-year-old school girl, willingly, but apparently unwittingly, accepted a ride from a male stranger in the early evening on October 13, 1968. By her own testimony she refers to a two-hour stay with her assailant before and after an act of forcible intercourse at a secluded spot near her home. When she was released, she ran home and reported the incident to her mother, who in turn notified the state police.

The court agreed that there was no real doubt that the record afforded sufficient corroboration that intercourse was committed by forcible compulsion. The girl's mother testified to her daughter's bloodied mouth, bruised lips, disheveled appearance, and apparent emotional distress. Independent medical proof of her condition shortly after the incident occurred, verified that intercourse had taken place, and that she had been physically abused.

Judge Scileppi explains the weaknesses of the corroboration rules:[69]

> First, and perhaps foremost, is the fact that in imposing an evidentiary standard more befitting a public event, the law necessarily frustrates the prosecution of an inherently furtive act. Secondly, it establishes a system of false distinctions between offenses committed most often against the person of a woman and other equally serious charges where "the motivation for falsehood or occasion for inaccuracy is . . . [as] great, and the disproof difficult.

New York law now no longer requires corroboration of the complaining witness's testimony regarding penetration or, in most instances, the perpetrator's identity. Proof of force or lack of consent, however, still requires corroboration. Judge Scileppi comments on the new law:[70]

This amended version represents an improvement over the present law, but retains crude vestiges of the former evidentiary standard: the element of force, and in certain cases, identity, still requires corroboration. Consistency, as well as a quest for greater justice suggests instead a proposal to eliminate corroboration entirely.

. . . A better principle . . . variously phrased, [would require] especially convincing and satisfying evidence, within the rubrics of proof beyond a reasonable doubt and the preponderance of evidence.

Because the laws on rape are so blatantly unfair to the women victims, and because the whole issue requires much additional investigation—both legal and sociological—the National Organization for Women at its Sixth Annual Conference in February 1973 created a national task force on rape. The guidelines for the task force include

1. To define the crime of rape.
2. To research existing laws covering rape and related crimes against women and children.
3. To propose a model guide for state legislatures, for adoption into their criminal codes.
4. To research and recommend follow-up procedures, i.e., psychological assistance, to help victims of rape.
5. To explore effective forms of resistance.

In May 1973, Florida's First District Court of Appeals ruled that rape laws must protect men as well as women. The 3-to-0 opinion, written by Chief Judge Sam Spector, reversed the convictions of two men accused of sexually assaulting a fellow inmate at Raiford State Prison, under an antisodomy law that has been overruled.

But the judge ordered a new trial on charges of rape and forcible carnal knowledge under a statute previously used only to prosecute men for raping women.

"It is no longer consonant with constitutional principles of equal protection to continue a criminal sanction against sexual assaults on females and not provide the same criminal sanction where such assaults are made on males," the judge ruled.

The case is the first time in the United States that men were given protection under a rape law.

The persecution of prostitutes, the persecution of rape victims, and the totally inadequate rape laws, are part of the total picture of discrimination against women in the administration of criminal justice. These areas of the law have received much press attention, because (of course) they deal with sex. But other areas of criminal justice also deal with sex—the denial of justice to women because of their sex.

Female juvenile offenders are subjected to a double standard. In New York State, for example, they could be declared to be "persons in need of supervision" for noncriminal acts until age eighteen, while boys were covered by the statute only until age sixteen.[71] The New York Court of Appeals held, in a case decided in July 1972, that there is no justification for the differentiation of that statute. The court said:

> Lurking behind the discrimination is the imputation that girls who engage in sexual misconduct ought more to be censured, and their conduct subjected to greater control and regulation than boys.[72]

Despite that enlightened decision, many girls all over the country are sent to reform school because they engage in sexual activity, while boys who do so are considered healthy and normal.

In Texas and Utah, the defense of "passion killing" is allowed to the "wronged" husband, but not to the "wronged" wife.[73]

Longer prison terms for women than for men convicted of the same crime have been declared unconstitutional under the Fourteenth Amendment. A federal court held that "differential sentencing laws for men and women constitute invidious discrimination against women in violation of the Equal Protection of the laws guaranteed by the Fourteenth Amendment."[74]

A Pennsylvania court, in the now famous *Commonwealth v. Daniel* case,[75] struck down a state statute imposing heavier criminal penalties on women than on men for the same crime. In a Connecticut case,[76] differential sentencing laws were also overturned.

In New Mexico, a complaint has been filed to equalize facilities and educational opportunities afforded women inmates.[77]

The poor woman suffers most from inequities in criminal justice. Statistics show[78] that one-half of all girls appearing before juvenile courts are referred there for noncriminal behavioral problems, while that is true of only one-fifth of the cases involving boys. The family of a poor girl cannot afford tuition in a private school should she get "into trouble"; therefore she is committed to a reformatory.

Hearings were held in the summer of 1972 in New Jersey on the state's policy of differential sentencing treatment for males and females convicted of similar crimes. Under this system, only men can receive credit for "continuous orderly deportment" and only men are eligible for parole consideration by the state parole board. Females, on the other hand, receive indeterminate terms at the Correctional Institution for Women. The women are generally imprisoned for a longer period of time under this system. The New Jersey State Supreme Court then ordered a full lower court hearing to determine whether the law governing the sentencing of criminals discriminates against women. In a 7-to-0 ruling, the court noted that the question has never been decided before in the New Jersey courts, nor by the U.S. Supreme Court. The court acted in an appeal by Mary A. Costello, who pleaded guilty in Camden County Court to gambling offenses, including bookmaking and running a gambling resort. She was sentenced to an indeterminate term not to exceed five years.

Ms. Costello contended her constitutional right of equal protection under the law was violated because she would have received a shorter sentence for the same crime if she had been a man. Based on New Jersey sentencing patterns, a man convicted of the same offense would likely receive a state prison sentence of not less than one nor more than two years.

The court declined to overturn the law on sentencing because it said the state should have the opportunity to present its arguments in support of the statute. In his opinion for the court, Justice Frederick W. Hall said[79] it could be argued that women should be treated differently from men because they "were more amenable and responsive to rehabilitation and reform which might, however, require a longer period of confinement in a different type of institution." Justice Hall said that the high court wanted a complete record on the case before it decided the constitutional issue, and consequently he remanded the case to the lower court. He said the state should have the opportunity to present formal proof in support of its thesis that the statutory scheme rests on a solid basis from the standpoint of both societal benefit and the welfare of the affected women themselves.

(As we go to press, we read in the Trenton *Times* of June 27, 1973, that the 124 women serving indefinite state prison sentences have been given a chance to seek more specific and shorter fixed terms by the New Jersey

State Supreme Court, which says men and women must be treated equally when being sentenced. In a unanimous 7-to-0 decision, the court said the old system that differentiated between men and women violated the Equal Protection guarantee of the Fourteenth Amendment to the U.S. Constitution. The ruling could give the 124 women an opportunity for earlier parole. The ruling represented a decision in the appeals of six women who had been sentenced to the New Jersey Correctional Institution for Women at Clinton, on indeterminate sentences.)

The question has not been decided by the U.S. Supreme Court, although it has been ruled in Pennsylvania, Connecticut and now New Jersey, that there are no reasonable grounds to differentiate between the sexes in sentencing for the same crime.

Dr. Jo-Ann Evans Gardner draws the connection between discrimination in sentencing and discrimination in the prevention of crime:[80]

> It is well known that often the length of sentence is longer and rehabilitation less available for women than for men convicted of the same crime. This, of course, must end. However, it is apparently less well known and certainly more commonly accepted, that the prevention of delinquency should show more concern for boys than for girls. The United Fund, through its participating agencies, funnels twice as much money into Boy Scouts and the YMCA than into Girl Scouts and the YWCA. Boys Clubs receive generous funds; but there are no Girls Clubs, but only homes for the unwed mother. Boys are taken care of before they get in trouble, girls after. We must end this bias and treat all children as worthy of equal treatment.

The Women's Bureau of the U.S. Department of Labor calls the women in jails and prisons across this country "the forgotten offenders."[81] There are 15,000 of them, about 4 percent of the total state and federal prisoners.

Women are more enforced against, than enforcers. Across the country, women make up an estimated 1.5 percent of police forces, maintaining low-ranking positions. When Gertrude Schimmel, deputy inspector on the police force in New York City, was asked if she ever expected to see a woman police commissioner appointed, she answered: "Only by the first woman mayor."[82]

In fall 1971, after months of making regular visits to the female inmates at the Dade County (Florida) Jail, members of the Dade County Women's Committee of 100 issued a report highly critical of jail conditions. They particularly cited such things as lack of proper exercise, insect control, and telephone privileges, inadequate medical attention, and discrimination against those women prisoners who wished to attend worship services held for the men.

There is generally a more negative attitude toward women in prison than toward men. Many agencies are at work to convince employers, and the society at large, that a man can be rehabilitated once he gets out of prison. A "fallen" woman, however, has a very difficult time, and little help from social agencies, in convincing employers and social contacts that she too is a good risk.

An eloquent account of life for women in prison is given in an open letter from the Women in the House of Detention, New York City, to the concerned people of New York:[83]

We the prisoners of the Women's House of Detention wish to inform you of the barbaric conditions we are subjected to by the correction officials here in the House of Detention. The system breeds mental degradation and physical deterioration. The majority of us are Black and Puerto Rican. We cannot afford the ransom the courts call bail. It is apparent to us that you, the public, are not aware of the barbaric conditions that exist here.

Our grievances are:

1. We do not receive adequate medical attention. We do not have a doctor on duty twenty-four hours a day although there are seven hundred and fifty-four women in here. The doctors we do have are old and senile.

a. We ask that all doctors practicing medicine here be required to take a medical Board examination at least once a year.

b. We ask for a doctor to be on duty twenty-four hours a day.

c. We ask that it be a requirement that any inmate suffering from any medical problem be permitted to see a doctor at any time day or night, and that it not be left to the discretion of the officer on duty or the nurse in attendance.

d. We ask for first-rate medicine. That it be labeled properly and after it has lost its potency, it be thrown out.

2. We do not receive an adequate diet. We do not get any fresh vegetables or any fresh fruits. Our diet consists of beans, rice, potatoes, and powdered milk. We get hot cereal twice a week, one boiled egg once a week. The rest of the days we get cold cereal and powdered milk. The meats that we eat are as old as the building we must live in.

a. We ask for our meats to be inspected.

b. We ask for at least one glass of fresh milk daily.

c. We ask for fresh vegetables and at least one piece of fruit a day.

3. The House of Detention is infested with mice and roaches. They roam the building freely, carrying filth and disease. We are often bitten by these germ-carrying rodents. There is no extermination system.

a. We ask that an exterminating company be allowed to come in twice a month to eliminate these health hazards.

4. There are four punishment strip cells where we are put if we receive an "infraction." The cells do not have any toilets, sinks, or mattresses. In them we are stripped of all our clothing. We do not receive any bedding for the cold tile floor. We are allowed to shower only every five days. We ask that these cells be shut down immediately.

5. We are beaten by the male guards. We ask that male guard brutality be stopped immediately. We are harassed and threatened with an infraction by the female guards. We ask for the harassment to be stopped.

6. Our funds which are sent and brought to us are misappropriated. We ask for an investigation.

7. We are unable to purchase in the commissary bras, panties, socks, or stockings. None of these are given to us by the state as long as we are being held in detention. We ask that we be allowed to purchase bras, panties, socks, stockings, bobby pins for our hair, hair rollers, makeup, large rubber combs for the sisters in here who cannot comb their hair with the very small combs we can now buy, creams for our faces, lotions for our bodies so that we can care for ourselves as women.

8. We are two in a cell. The cells are 5′ by 9′. Out of a fifteen-hour day, we are locked up eleven of these hours. We ask for longer recreation periods.

9. The adolescents are separated from the adults as long as they are on detention floors. Once they have been sentenced, they are put in the same corridors as the adults. We ask that the adolescents be kept separate from the adults after sentencing.

10. When we are appointed a legal representative by the courts, they do not come to us to discuss the facts of our cases. We ask that the courts require a visit to be made by the court-appointed legal representative to us, the accused, before we go to court.

11. We are often brought to court and required to wait in the bull pen five or six hours in order to see a judge only to be told our cases have been adjourned. We ask that when we are brought to court that we see the judge.

12. There are some of us who have been here twenty months and still have not gone to trial. We ask for speedier court dates. We ask that our court dates be made known to us.

13. We have been raided at five-thirty in the morning, made to strip off all our clothing and to squat down, our personal belongings being thrown on the floor. The adolescents have been made to go into the kitchen and strip off their clothing in front of everyone.

a. We ask that the stripping of inmates be stopped immediately.

We have refused to lock ourselves in our cells to protest this inhuman treatment and have been met with water hoses turned on us by the prison officials. We are locked in our cells for eight to ten days as punishment for protesting. All of our privileges are taken away.

We the oppressed women of the New York House of Detention humbly seek your support and help. We who are your fellow human beings need you, the public, to help us in our struggle to eliminate these injustices.

Captive sisters in the House of D.

Chapter Ten
Motherhood and Abortion:
Women and Children Last

Led Eve, our credulous mother, to the Tree of Prohibition, root of all our woe.
 —JOHN MILTON, *Paradise Lost, Book IX, Line 644*

Men have broad and large chests and small narrow hips and are more understanding than women who have but small and narrow chests and broad hips, and to the end they should remain at home, sit still, keep house, and bear and bring up children.
 —MARTIN LUTHER, *Table Talk*, P. 725.

Miamian Joan Neu [was] the first woman in the state to try to become a fireman. Mrs. Neu passed the written Civil Service exam and two swimming tests but failed when she tried to climb a rope 10 feet using only her hands. She has now passed the age limit for Miami Fire Department recruits and is home taking care of her newly-adopted child.
 —Miami *Herald*, DECEMBER 31, 1972

When a little girl takes a good look at her mommy, she may notice a person who appears less than relaxed and happy. Nonetheless, every little girl is carefully prepared for the career of mother—by her toys, her parents, her teachers, her psychiatrist, her newspaper, and her religious leader.

Even in this day of Zero Population Growth, women into their fourth pregnancies proudly tell their friends,

"We're the kind of people who should have a lot of kids. We have so much to give them. Our kids will contribute so much to the world."

Any woman who says "no way" to the idea of having children is either considered neurotic or else must have a "sound" reason, such as "Our marriage will be stronger if we just have the two of us to concentrate on." In the final analysis, anything in the world that we women cannot accomplish can always be "excused" by the fact that we were taking care of our children.

I believe that the process really operates in reverse. It is not that we are looking for an excuse not to accomplish very much. It is that a young woman, observing the impossibility of making it in a man's world, simply resigns herself to failing, and in so failing, calls it success. She gets pregnant, and then the whole world loves her. Or does it?

Children who go far are a credit to their fathers. Children who get into trouble—become drug addicts, drop out of school, boys who can't get a good job—are usually credited to their mothers.

Modern fiction writers have been dumping on their mothers for decades. Barbra Streisand knocked the audiences dead in *Up the Sandbox* when she (a) slammed the door in her mother's face, and (b) slammed her mother's face into a decorated cake.

A woman can't get a mortgage for a house, because she might become a mother. The foreman doesn't want to hire women, because they either are mothers, or they might become mothers. Governor Cahill of New Jersey explained why New Jersey's delegation to the Republican convention did not have more women (they occupied 12½ percent of the state's seats, while in the convention as a whole 34 percent of the delegates were women):[1]

Most women want to stay home and take care of their home and their family. To ask them to do more is to ask them to do more than they are able. Our women have the conviction that they want to do more at home. They're interested in politics, but they don't want to do more than they are doing.

The mystique of motherhood prevails, despite the enormous penalties that women pay for its pleasures. These penalties come whether the woman is married or not.

And they often come from unexpected sources. The "enlightened" Horace Greeley, for example, fired Margaret Fuller as a writer for his *Tribune* when he learned that she had had a child, and had not married the father. She had counted on the five dollars she received for her weekly column to support her and the child; her greater problem was that Greeley's defection left her without a publisher for her two-volume manuscript on the Italian Revolution.[2] She had been living in Italy. When she lost her job and her publisher, she, her child, and his father (whether Margaret and Giovanni Angelo Ossoli ever married is open to question) took a ship for America. The ship sank, and they all died at sea.

She had anticipated, ironically, how motherhood would "do her in" when she wrote:[3] "Too much is said of women being better educated that they may become better companions and mothers *for men*."

The patriarchal system has always found it very threatening when unmarried women have children on their own. The punishment which is meted out (to mother and to child) seems to exceed (even) the crime of confusing the lines of descent and devise which had been codified in the English common law.

Kate Millett describes the attitude in this country

toward so-called illegitimacy (I say "so-called" because I firmly believe that any person who is born is clearly "legitimate"):[4]

> To insure that its crucial functions of reproduction and socialization of the young take place only within its confines, the patriarchal family insists on legitimacy. Bronislaw Malinowski describes this as "the principle of legitimacy," formulating it as an insistence that "no child should be brought into the world without a man— and one man at that—assuming the role of sociological father."[5] By this apparently consistent and universal prohibition (whose penalties vary by class and in accord with the expected operations of the double standard) patriarchy decrees that the status of both child and mother is primarily or ultimately dependent upon the male. And since it is not only his social status, but even his economic power upon which his dependents generally rely, the position of the masculine figure within the family—as without—is materially, as well as ideologically, extremely strong.

Malinowski had said earlier:[6] "In all human societies moral traditon and the law decree that the group consisting of a woman and her offspring is not a sociologically complete unit."

Apparently, the male chauvinism which shows itself in laws and customs surrounding illegitimacy is not restricted to capitalist societies, or to those which derive their rules of property from the English common law. Aleta Wallach[7] has analyzed the legal mother/father/child relationship in the United States and in the Soviet Union. Apparently the Bolshevik Revolution had as one of its goals the complete removal of the stigma against illegitimacy. The main concern was to protect the child from this cruel injustice. In additon, the revolutionaries were determined to sweep away the double standard which punished the woman who had a child outside marriage, but allowed the man to evade censure.

Therefore, blood relation, and not legal marriage, became the basis of the legal relationship, and a man was under an obligation to provide equally for all his children. This step was considered necessary to establish true equality among the class of children, and to ensure an unmarried mother and her child complete legal identity and rights, independent of any relationship to a man.

Those children born within and without marriage had an equal claim to be supported by the state and to inherit from their mother and their father. During the Stalin era the concept of illegitimacy was reintroduced in the decree of the Presidium of the U.S.S.R. Supreme Soviet of July 8, 1944. This decree provided that only a legal marriage gave rise to the rights and responsibilities of spouses and abolished the mother's right to sue to establish paternity and to claim child support payments from a father to whom she was not legally married.[8]

The mother was not left without support, since the state became surrogate-father for the support of all children born to single women and provided mothers with monthly support. However,

> Soviet women resented bitterly the dual standard of sexual morality, which the Bolsheviks had for years been condemning as an outrageous by-product of capitalist civilization, and which the Soviet State was practically legalizing. A man might father all the children he wished out of wedlock without incurring any responsibilities other than those his conscience might impel him to assume. Russians openly spoke of it as a "law for men."[9]

In 1968, the U.S.S.R. reinvoked the right to establish a child's paternity by joint application of the unmarried parents or by court action. A mother whose child's paternity has not been established can receive a state allowance for the support and upbringing of the child. She also has the right to place it in a child-care institution for support and upbringing at the state's expense. Soviet law expressly provides for imposition of liability on anyone who attempts to insult an unwed mother or lower her dignity.[10]

Wallach points out that no comprehensive attempt has ever been made in the United States to obliterate the stigma attached to the illegitimate child and its mother, and replace it with ideological equalitarianism.

Obviously, this is in part an attempt to punish women who have sexual relations outside of marriage. Underlying the arguments of the "right to life" abortion opponents is a heavy disapproval of the woman who enjoys free sexual relationships, and refuses to bear any resultant children. In our culture, we forbid women to separate sex from motherhood, or motherhood from marriage.

Illegitmate children in the United States have gained certain rights, such as the right to sue for the wrongful death of their mother[11] and the right of their mothers to sue for their wrongful death.[12] However, in *Labine v. Vincent*,[13] the Supreme Court upheld a Louisiana statute which allows an illegitimate child to be an intestate heir only *after* it is ascertained that the father has no ascendants, descendants, spouse, or collateral relatives.

The original Soviet plan was to achieve a collectivized social arrangement wherein the family would cease to exist as an individual unit, and parental authority over children would be transferred to the state. This was supposed to liberate women from patriarchal family life, while at the same time removing children from the reactionary influence of parents whose tradition was prerevolutionary. This trend was reversed in the thirties. While legislative enactments were important in strengthening family ties, the 1945 amendments[14] to the Family Code of 1944 also considerably advanced state protection of mother and child. With this act the Soviet state assumed a considerable share of the financial burden of childbearing and rearing. This legal recognition of motherhood as a service rendered by Soviet women provides them with meticulous care during pregnancy: preferential treatment when waiting in lines, reduced fees at kindergarten,[15] special labor laws (after four months' pregnancy, women are not to be given overtime work, and women with infants are to be exempted from night work throughout the period of nursing), and maternity leave (during which a pregnant woman's tenure in her job is retained) with pay four weeks before and four weeks after a birth.[16] A pregnant woman cannot be fired because of her pregnancy; the Criminal Code[17] punishes the refusal to employ or the dismissal from work for reasons of pregnancy or breast-feeding, with correctional tasks for terms of up to one year, or dismissal from the position of authority. A husband may not divorce his pregnant wife without her consent during and one year subsequent to her pregnancy. (It is unclear whether a woman can institute divorce proceedings against her husband without his consent during her pregnancy and for one year after the birth.)[18] All medical services in connection with pregnancy and childbirth are free, and the state provides increased subsidies to mothers of one child or more.[19]

Engels said: "The first conditon for the liberation of the wife is to bring the whole female sex back into public industry . . . and this in fact demands the abolition of the monogamous family as the economic unit of society."[20]

Lenin de-emphasized separate households:[21]

> We are establishing communal kitchens and public eating houses, laundries, and repairing shops, infant asylums, kindergartens, children's homes, educational institutes of all kinds. In short, we are seriously carrying out the demand in our programme for the transference of the economic and educational functions of the separate household to society.

That the Russians have made a good start in the direction of freeing women is not doubted. However, the Russian wife/mother is at present complaining of the same work load as her American sister. Any woman who works, in Russia or in the United States, has two jobs. Although the women in Russia do have child-care facilities, and more communal facilities, the Russian man still objects to doing "women's work." As a result, she must do the shopping, cleaning, and caring for the children when they are at home. Therefore, she cannot achieve as much on her job because she simply cannot put in the overtime demanded.

In addition, it should be pointed out that for most Russian women, motherhood is a highly lauded profession in itself. Valentina Tereshkova, the first woman cosmonaut, said in a speech in 1969[22] that her greatest achievement was giving birth to her children.

The Russian woman may suffer in her career, as the Russian man does not when he becomes a father. But she does not have the incredible financial struggle that American women face, trying to raise children on their own.

According to the Department of Labor, there are 3.5 million single mothers in this country (divorced, widowed, never married).[23] These women are in severe trouble—economic and social.

For example, the California State Social Welfare Board recently issued a position paper calling illegitimacy "one of society's tragic dilemmas." Couched in the terminology of concern for the children, the paper asked that the mother be considered morally depraved upon the birth of the third out-of-wedlock child, and that the third and subsequent illegitimate children be placed for adoption. As Pat McCormick[24] points out, from a feminist perspective the problem of illegitimacy can indeed be a tragic dilemma—but for reasons very different from those cited by the Social Welfare Board. The need to establish paternity recognizes implicitly that women are not able to support a family on what they themselves can earn.

Mothers should not be bound by law to divulge the name of the unwed father to the welfare department, if they choose not to. This is discrimination against a man, who after a casual sexual encounter with a woman (who often has no access to birth control) finds himself in court, being sued by the welfare department, and faced with eighteen years of supporting a child he didn't plan for or want. He should have no right, of course, to force the woman to have an abortion; but if he is willing to share the financial responsibility of an abortion and the woman refuses to have one, then he should not be forced to support the child.

It is obvious that both men and women must take responsibility for birth control, and that it should be made easily and freely available. It is, of course, fair that both single men and single women be able to adopt children. Nevertheless, it is the woman who must (for obvious biological reasons) be given the choice of whether or not to bear a child. And, if she chooses to bear a child, there is no reason why paternity must be established if she chooses not to establish it.

The reasoning of the California State Social Welfare Board implies that the factor preventing women from providing adequate economic support for their illegitimate children is to be found in not knowing the identity of the father. Such reasoning supports a way of life which imposes hideous discrimination on women and children without men to support them.

Illegitimacy is a problem only in a patriarchal system which requires the dependence of women and children upon men. The solution to this lies in restructuring economic, political, and social institutions so that women have an opportunity to become economically independent.

As McCormick expresses it:[25]

> It should be remembered that the *poverty* of mothers is not the result of children, born in or out of wedlock. Nor is it the result of unknown or absent fathers. It *is the result of massive and pervasive discriminatory practices in banks, telephone companies, stores, universities, offices, and governments.*

> . . . If the State Social Welfare Board needs material for a future position paper, let it begin to tackle how the State can provide equal opportunity for women; the lives of the children will surely be improved.

The case law is slowly beginning to improve in this area. U.S. District Judge Sarah T. Hughes has ruled[26] that a bank that refuses to hire a woman because she has had illegitimate children is guilty of sex discrimination.

The decision came down in a suit by Phyllis A. Davis, twenty-four, and ordered the American National Bank of Terrell, Texas, to change its recruitment policy. Testimony showed that Ms. Davis, now married, is the mother of three illegitimate children, but stated in a 1969 application for a job as a proof-machine operator that she was single and childless.

Bank officials told the court that they regarded any "sexually immoral" person as dishonest, and therefore a poor risk as an employee. Judge Hughes ruled that such a policy discriminates against women because "it is common knowledge that it is easier to determine if a woman has illegitimate children than a man." Judge Hughes also claimed the bank's behavior constituted an "unlawful employment practice," under the National Labor Relations Act.

A major problem faced by mothers, married and unmarried, is that although one out of every three women with preschool children works, there are fewer than 700,000 spaces in licensed child-care centers to serve their more than 5,000,000 preschool children. In 1972, a comprehensive child-care bill was passed in both houses of Congress, but vetoed by President Nixon. It has been reintroduced in the 1973 Congress.

Our society can't seem to make up its mind about motherhood. Women have been persecuted, and have died, for generations, in trying to terminate unwanted pregnancies. Women who do have their babies are also punished. Most private businesses have no qualms about firing women who get pregnant. Women who work for government agencies are forced to take unpaid maternity leave at arbitrary states of pregnancy, sometimes as early as the fourth month, which means that their incomes are cut off just when they are most likely to need them.

The New York Civil Liberties Union is lobbying for a change in the New York State labor law, which specifically excludes pregnancy from disability coverage.[27] Under the present law, one can get paid while recovering from a broken arm, but not while having a baby.

A real runaround takes place when women who are suddenly out of work because they have become pregnant try to get unemployment compensaton. The states enforce special unwritten standards on pregnant women by expecting them to take work outside their field, almost any work—this is not required by any other class of applicant.

As Barbara Shack, of the Civil Liberties Union, expresses it:[28]

> As a matter of course, women chase around from employer to employer, searching for any job, only to find that almost nobody will hire a woman expecting a baby. Eventually, defeated in the whipsaw, many women have given up trying to satisfy the requirements for unemployment compensation. They just go away broke.

South Carolina welfare regulations requiring mothers of illegitimate children to prosecute the supposed fathers for support before receiving federal welfare funds were recently struck down by a three-judge federal court.[29] The court called the regulation an "unauthorized barrier" to the benefits of the Social Security Act. The state had argued that it had a responsibility "to ultimately seek out and locate support for the child." The court held that the regulations denied the mother the equal protection of the law, privacy, and other constitutional guarantees.

Women in poverty are not adequately subsisting either on monies they collect from welfare departments or from "deserting fathers." In New York State, for example, it is estmated that about $35 million in dependent support has remained uncollected. The State Assembly's Committee on Child Abuse estimates that in addition to the $35 million in support orders already processed by the court, but as yet uncollected, there was an estimated total of $13 million in pending orders on which court action was not yet complete.[30]

Women are not able to support themselves and their children. While 6.3 percent of families headed by white males and 18.9 percent of families headed by nonwhite males are in poverty, 25.2 percent of families headed by white females, and 52.9 percent of families headed by nonwhite females are in poverty, as defined by U.S. government poverty standards.[31]

Women are severely punished by the culture if they do not live with and raise their children; they are unable to earn enough money to support their children; although men are legally responsible for support, it is often impossible to collect.

Men are getting increasingly interested in custody, however, and (male) judges are having trouble with the concept of (male) parenthood. In a recent California divorce action—involving a contest for the custody of two young children—the judge awarded the youngsters to the mother. When the father's lawyer objected, pointing out that both parents were working and the father would in fact be able to spend more time with the children, the judge said: "Fathers don't make good mothers."[32]

Judges have trouble picturing a man feeding the baby, or changing a diaper. However, there is some legislative and judicial progress toward equalizing parenthood. Many state legislatures have passed laws eliminating any preference for the mother. Last year California ended a provision in its code which specified that children of "tender years" should be given to the mother. Colorado and Minnesota have specified statutes requiring that neither parent should be preferred merely on the basis of gender.

Many court decisions have recognized the right of the father to raise his children. Last year, the Supreme Court held unconstitutional an Illinois law wherein the state automatically took custody of the children of an unwed father after the death of the mother, saying: "All unmarried fathers are not unsuitable and neglectful: some are wholly suited to have custody of their children."[33]

A California court has held that the mother of an illegitimate child could not put him up for adoption without the consent of the father, who could obtain custody if he showed he could provide adequately for his son.

In January 1973, the Equal Employment Opportunity Commission ruled that male teachers in the New York City school system must be given the same opportunity to take paternity leaves as female teachers are to take maternity leaves, in order to be with and take care of newborn children. In 1969, mothers and fathers in Finland fought for and obtained paid paternity leave. The rationale is that fathers are parents, with the same rights and responsibilities as mothers, *and* that until fathers have the same duties to their children, employers will be able to continue to discriminate against women in employment, using their motherhood against them.

The original City University of New York proposal included up to twenty days of paid leave, and up to eighteen months' unpaid leave for both men and women. Only the unpaid leave was sanctioned by EEOC. While the leave is without pay, tenure continues at the conclusion of the leave, and includes service prior to the leave.

In July 1973, the Labor Department became the first federal agency to grant paternity leave to male employees "so that the home and family are taken care of" after their wives give birth.

The new benefit—previously restricted to women—allows up to thirty days' leave either without pay or charged to annual leave. This was included under a new two-year contract signed by Labor Secretary Peter J. Brennan and Local 12 of the American Federation of Government Employees. Some 5,000 workers in the Washington, D.C., area are covered under the contract, which also doubles from 90 to 180 days the maximum time women can take for maternity leave.

I consider it unlikely that many men—given their conditioning to be achievers, not nurturers—will ask for paternity leave.

The Supreme Court, as recently as January 1973, has declined to review the policy of the Texas Employment Commission that requires a pregnant woman to be laid off two months before the expected date of delivery of her child.[34] In many states, still, only the father's signature is acceptable on the driver's license application of a minor child. In some states, only the father has the right of guardianship and control of a child's earnings and property. And, in seven states, boys have a right to parental support up to age twenty-one, while girls have that right only to age eighteen (Arkansas, Idaho, Nevada, North Dakota, Oklahoma, South Dakota, and Utah).[35]

An appeal is currently pending with the New York Court of Appeals in the case of a woman employee of the City University of New York who was wrongfully barred from work following the birth of her child.[36]

Admitting during the grievance procedure that management had erred, the Chancellor of the University agreed to reinstate her with back pay for lost time. The city's comptroller, however, refused to authorize pay for the time not worked, claiming that the settlement was an "unlawful gift of public monies."

The Alaska Human Rights Commission awarded a nurse's aide several weeks' back pay for the time she was forced to refrain from working due to pregnancy rules.[37] The commission ruled, in the case of Shirley Dick, that a woman has the right to work up to the final day of her pregnancy if she chooses, and can return to work as soon as her physician permits.

As of March 31, 1972, the Equal Employment Opportunity Commission has ruled on Employment Policies Relating to Pregnancy and Childbirth:[38]

Section 1604.10

(a) A written or unwritten employment policy or practice which excludes from employment applicants or employees because of pregnancy is in *prima facie* violation of Title VII.

(b) Disabilities caused or contributed to by pregnancy, miscarriage, abortion, childbirth, and recovery therefrom are, for all job-related purposes, temporary disabilities and should be treated as such under any health or temporary disability insurance or sick leave plan available in connection with employment. Written and unwritten employment policies and practices involving matters such as the commencement and duration of leave, the availability of extensions, the accrual of seniority and other benefits and privileges, reinstatement, and payment under any health or temporary disability insurance or sick leave plan, formal or informal, shall be applied to disability due to pregnancy or childbirth on the same terms and conditions as they are applied to other temporary disabilities.

(c) Where the termination of an employee who is temporarily disabled is caused by an employment policy under which insufficient or no leave is available, such a termination violates the Act if it has a disparate impact on employees of one sex and is not justified by business necessity.

Possibly one of the greatest displays of misogyny is directed toward the pregnant teen-ager. Her condition brings out all the hatreds of the (usually married, old, male) determiners of her fate. These men include school principals, school administrators, judges, doctors, state legislators, and psychologists. They combine, having previously denied her information about and access to birth control, to make her feel shame and guilt—about having sex, and about being a fertile *female* (a fertile male is not so punished).

Although the pleasures of sex will quickly become apparent to young people, it cannot be denied that this may be accentuated in our culture by the bombardment of the media. Almost every television commercial tells you, you are not OK if you aren't having sex.

Even young female students who get pregnant while they are married (presumably a more socially acceptable procedure) are severely punished. An Ohio case deals with a sixteen-year-old woman, who was forced to leave high school because she was pregnant. Her husband, also age sixteen, was permitted to continue.[39]

The Trenton (Ohio) Board of Education had a regulation that all pregnant students must withdraw from school immediately upon the knowledge of their pregnancy. The plaintiff attacked both the power of the board to adopt such regulations, and the reasonableness thereof. The court upheld the right of the school board to keep her out of school.

> The evidence here shows that the relator's further school attendance was denied in the interest of her physical well-being and not as a punitive measure. Furthermore, is it unreasonable for a Board, having in mind that it serves the entire student body, to consider the effect upon the other students the continued presence in the classroom of a pregnant fellow student might have? May it not calculate that such presence might adversely affect the morale of the student body, cause disruption to the orderly operation of the school's daily activities and to some extent, interfere with the discipline and government of the students?

It is interesting to note what the "friends" of young pregnant students have to say. A member of the ACLU secondary school pamphlet subcommittee writes:[40]

> . . . I can see where the presence of an obviously pregnant girl in a classroom could have a rather disruptive effect upon the maintenance of order and discipline. On the other hand, the fact of pregnancy should not deny the girl the right to continue her education. I would therefore make the following recommendation: That a girl be permitted to continue to attend class and to take part in other activities in the school until such time *as her pregnancy actually affects the maintenance of order and discipline, at which time she should be transferred to a special school or to a special class within the same school, where she should continue for as long as she can. At that point, however, I would exclude the girl from participation in extra-curricular activities.* [emphasis mine] After the child is born, the girl should be permitted to return to class and to participate in school activities to the same extent as she partook in

such activities prior to her pregnancy. The school officials and teachers should make no special note of the pregnancy in her school records, nor should she be punished or disciplined in any way for the fact that she became pregnant.

As to the father, I believe that the school has no right to take any disciplinary action against him or to restrict his class activity or his extra-curricular activities in any manner.

A decision more favorable to women was handed down in a Mississippi case.[41] Here the issue was whether the policy of the school board of denying admission to unwed mothers violates the Equal Protection Clause of the Fourteenth Amendment.

The plaintiffs introduced evidence in the case which showed that unwed mothers who are allowed to continue their education are less likely to have a second illegitimate child. In effect, the opportunity to pursue their education gives them a hope for the future, so that they are less likely "to fall into the snare of repeat illegitimate births." (Such language, of course, indicates that even the girl's lawyer thinks she should be feeling guilt and shame about her behavior.)

The school board argued, predictably, that they feared that the presence of unwed mothers in the schools would be a "bad influence on the other students vis-à-vis their presence indicating society's approval or acquiescence in the illegitimate births or vis-à-vis the association of the unwed mother with the other students."

The court, deciding for the female student, nonetheless used language reminiscent of Nathaniel Hawthorne's *The Scarlet Letter*.[42]

The Court would like to make manifestly clear that lack of moral character is certainly a reason for excluding a child from public education. But the fact that a girl has one child out of wedlock does not forever brand her as a scarlet woman undeserving of any chance for rehabilitation or the opportunity for future education. . . . the school is free to take reasonable and adequate steps to determine the moral character of a girl before she is readmitted to the school. If the board is convinced that a *girl's presence will taint the education of the other students* [emphasis mine], then exclusion is justified.

. . . In sum, the Court holds that plaintiffs may not be excluded from the schools of the district for the sole reason that they are unwed mothers; and that plaintiffs are entitled to readmission unless in a fair hearing before the school authorities they are found to be so lacking in moral character that their presence in the schools will taint the education of the other students.

After holding that, in fact, an unwed mother might be admitted to high school (if she would not "taint" her fellow students), the court refused to grant a preliminary injunction in the case.[43] The explanation:

Obviously, the policy not to admit unwed mothers as students in this school system is based upon what this court judicially knows to be a belief held by a large segment of the people in this area (perhaps, by a majority) that it is sinful, or immoral for unwed people to engage in sexual intercourse and that an unwed mother is not a fit associate for teenage children in a public school or elsewhere. The fact of such motherhood demonstrates such sinful, or immoral conduct.

The superintendent of schools testified that no effort was made to learn the identity of unwed fathers. But, he also said, there was no evidence that any effort was made to discover pregnant female students or unwed mothers of school age. The court noticed "that natural differences between male and female make obvious the case of discovery of the erring female, without any special effort so to do." No unwed father had ever been expelled or denied admission to the Grenada, Mississippi, public schools because of such status.

The court explained why the unwed mother should be excluded:[44]

> By analogy, plaintiff's situation could well be likened to that of a typhoid carrier who otherwise is an acceptable student in every way. The only real difference is that the carrier is one who acquired that status without fault, while plaintiff's status is the result of her own wrongdoing. Medical opinion and enlightened public opinion agree that the presence of a typhoid carrier as a student in a public school would present a threat to the health of all other students, the faculty and staff. Public opinion, enlightened or not, in the Grenada School territory, identifies an unwed mother of school age as a threat to the moral health, particularly of all other teenage school girls.

> By comparison, the typhoid carrier would have the stronger case for admission as a student to a public school system, because of the absence of fault.

The court apparently did not take judicial notice of the fact that typhoid fever is contagious; pregnancy is not.

Unmarried pregnant students may now attend high school in Boston and in New York. The pregnant-woman-as-a-taint-to-the-environment battle is now being fought also, believe it or not, for teachers.

In an historic court decision in favor of a pregnant

teacher, a federal court judge in Richmond, Virginia,[45] ruled that Susan Cohen's dismissal from her teaching job in the Chesterfield County (Virginia) school district, because of her pregnancy, was unconstitutional. She became the nation's first educator who challenged and won the right to be pregnant and to continue teaching in a public classroom beyond the fifth month of pregnancy. That ruling will directly or indirectly affect nearly 70 percent of the women teachers in the public elementary and secondary schools in the country.

A male teacher could go into the hospital for an operation, take leave time, and return to the school system, retaining his salary, tenure, and other benefits. A woman teacher, on the other hand, was forced to take unpaid maternity leave, as well as losing her employment rights and benefits. The court ruled that the maternity leave provision violated Ms. Cohen's constitutional rights in that it deprived her of equal protection of the laws. The court also ruled that she would receive all rights and benefits to which she should have been entitled, including full salary for the three months in which she would have worked prior to the birth of her baby, seniority credit, and other benefits.

The U.S. Supreme Court, in December 1972, sent back to the lower appeals court the case of Air Force Captain Susan Struck, who fought being discharged from the Air Force when she became pregnant. The Court said the appeals court should consider whether any legal dispute is still involved, since the Air Force now allows retention of pregnant women.

Captain Struck, a nurse, had a baby in 1970. She was not, and is not, married. Formerly, the Air Force had required that any woman officer who became pregnant or bore a live child must be given an immediate honorable discharge.

As a Catholic, Captain Struck refused an abortion, and gave the child up for adoption to a friend. The American Civil Liberties Union, which handled her appeals, charged that the former Air Force discharge regulations discriminated against women, because a serviceman's paternity was not grounds for discharge.

In an attempt to avert Supreme Court review of the doctrine of sexual equality, the U.S. Solicitor General reminded the Court that pregnancy "is a physical condition which happens to be peculiar to women."[46] He argued that the armed forces were not practicing sex discrimination when they automatically discharged pregnant servicewomen because "persons similarly circumstanced" were not treated differently. There was a good reason for the rule, he said, because "pregnancy diverts personnel from the primary function of fighting or support."

Captain Struck lost at every turn in the lower courts, but she did have a court stay granted by Justice William O. Douglas, to keep her on duty pending settlement of her suit. Her case obviously "raised the consciousness of the Air Force," which changed its regulation on dismissal seventeen days before the Supreme Court handed down its ruling.

The Victorian instinct to ignore reproduction, and to consider sex a shameful activity, obviously is coming into direct conflict with the 21 million women of childbearing age who are in the work force: more than one million of them get pregnant each year.

Why men, from ancient times right up to today, seem to fear pregnant women would be an interesting subject for study. Their fears are being, if not put to rest, at least put underground by court decisions. In *Matter of Murphy*,[47] for example, the Commissioner of the City of New York struck down the practice of excluding pregnant female students from graduation ceremonies.

Fear of sexuality and pregnancy has led to a terrible double bind for women: Pregnancy is considered to be the "price" of sexual activity; abortion was considered to be a crime (until the January 1973 Supreme Court decision) and is still considered to be a sin by many Americans. And, women are systematically punished—economically and socially—for fulfilling their "destinies" as mothers.

For example, women who want to be sterilized still run into trouble in New York State. The New York Civil Liberties Union has gone into court four times since 1970 to put pressure on hospitals that have turned them away.[48] The assumption that underlay the refusals was that an anonymous hospital bureaucracy was better qualified than the woman herself to make the decision about her reproductive life. In all four cases, the women won. In one case where the delay was substantial, the Federal Appeals Court ruled that the hospital can be sued for money damages for violating the woman's constitutional rights.

On January 22, 1973, women in the United States won what can best be characterized as an "emancipation proclamation." The Supreme Court ruled, 7 to 2, that forced motherhood will no longer be required of women, that unsafe, illegal abortions will no longer be a cause of death for women; all state laws that prohibit or restrict a woman's right to obtain an abortion during the first three months of pregnancy were overruled.

The Court ruled[49] that states cannot prohibit voluntary abortions during the first three months of pregnancy, during which time the decision should be left to the woman and her doctor. During the remaining six months, however, states may regulate abortion procedures in ways reasonably related to maternal health, and for the final ten weeks, may prohibit abortion except where doctors find the life of the mother endangered.

In addition, it held[50] that the state's limitations on abortion may not unduly restrict the patients' rights by such provisions as prohibiting treatment for nonresidents, or requiring involved screening procedures.

Having sat through heated debate when the National Conference of the National Organization for Women, held in Washington, D.C., in November 1967, became the first women's organization to support abortion repeal, and having in the years that followed picketed, demonstrated, debated, made speeches, lobbied, and otherwise begged for the right to determine the fate of my own body, I consider this decision to be a—perhaps *the*—major victory of the women's movement. The decision certainly should have been stronger and more absolute, but life for women in this country will never be as dangerous or as humiliating again.

The practical effect of the decision is wholesale repeal of most anti-abortion laws in the forty-six out of fifty states where they now exist. Four states, with legalized abortion laws, were not affected directly by the decision (Alaska, Hawaii, New York, and Washington). However, even they will be indirectly affected. In New York, for example, the anti-abortion (so-called "right to life") forces were gearing up for a battle to eliminate the abortion repeal law. This they had succeeded in doing in the 1972 legislative session, and only the veto from Governor Rockefeller had saved the law.

Fifteen states, which have relatively modern abortion laws, will be able to conform to the Supreme Court decision if they do considerable rewriting. They are: Alabama, Arkansas, California, Colorado, Delaware, Florida, Georgia, Kansas, Maryland, Mississippi, New

Mexico, North Carolina, Oregon, South Carolina, and Virginia.

States which have older anti-abortion laws must write entirely new laws; their statutes have been entirely invalidated. These include: Arizona, Connecticut, Idaho, Illinois, Indiana, Iowa, Kentucky, Louisiana, Maine, Massachusetts, Michigan, Minnesota, Missouri, Montana, Nebraska, Nevada, New Hampshire, New Jersey, North Dakota, Ohio, Oklahoma, Pennsylvania, Rhode Island, South Dakota, Tennessee, Texas, Utah, Vermont, West Virginia, and Wyoming.

States may prohibit abortions only during the last ten weeks of pregnancy, after the fetus has become "viable," or likely to survive on its own if prematurely delivered. Prior to these final two months, a state may only attach such regulations to a legalized abortion plan as are designated to protect the health of the mother. During the first three months, the patient and her doctor are free to determine without regulation by the state that an abortion should take place and that determination "may be effectuated . . . free of interference by the state."[51]

It goes without saying that it seems almost preposterous that an all-male Supreme Court was called upon to overrule male state courts and male legislatures in an issue as personal to women as the right to control their own bodies. In addition, since persons are, for example, entitled by law to have open heart surgery, which is clearly dangerous, it seems unnecessary to place any restrictions on the right of a woman to get an abortion.

New York's experience with legal abortion shows that it can have an important effect on health statistics. Maternity mortality—to which criminal abortion once contributed heavily—has fallen markedly since the state law took effect, with a 28 percent drop in pregnancy-associated deaths during the first two years.[52]

Infant deaths dropped as births to "high-risk" women —the unmarried, the poor, the older mothers—declined through legalized abortion to 20.3 per 100,000 live births in the first six months of 1972—an all-time low.[53]

The day following the abortion decision, *The New York Times* of course ran the story on the front page, even though Lyndon Johnson's death was occupying most of the news coverage. The *Times* interviewed persons on both sides of the issue—abortion repeal supporters and Catholics who oppose any form of abortion. *Those interviewed were all male*: William Baird, Alan F. Guttmacher, Cardinal Cooke, Cardinal Krol, et al.

Sarah Weddington, attorney in the Roe case, argued on the Ninth Amendment—the so-called right to privacy—and concretely demonstrated many ways in which women suffer irreparable damage as a result of compulsory pregnancy. Marjorie Pitts Hames, attorney in the Doe case, challenged the Georgia law on the grounds that to deny women, physicians, and nurses the right to seek and administer medical aid deprives them of liberty without due process of law. It had been assumed that the Court would decide the cases on procedural grounds, without deciding the far-reaching constitutional issues involved. However, at the hearing the Justices asked numerous questions about the basic objections to anti-abortion statutes; it became apparent they would write a long, and important, decision.

Perhaps the most crucial aspect of the opinion is that it concludes that a fetus is not a "person" under the Constitution and, once and for all, the rights of a grown woman are established as superior to the rights of a fertilized egg.

The Court wrote:[54]

The appellee and certain amici argue that the fetus is a "person" within the language and meaning of the 14th Amendment. In support of this they outline at length and in detail the well-known facts of fetal development. If this suggestion of personhood is established, the appellant's case, of course, collapses, for the fetus' right to life is then guaranteed specifically by the amendment.

The Constitution does not define "person" in so many words. The use of the word is such that it has application only postnatally.

All this, together with our observation that throughout the major portion of the 19th century prevailing legal abortion practices were far freer than they are today, persuades us that the word "person," as used in the 14th Amendment, does not include unborn.

. . . We need not resolve the difficult question of when life begins. When those trained in the respective disciplines of medicine, philosophy and theology are unable to arrive at any consensus, the judiciary, at this point in the development of man's knowledge, is not in a position to speculate as to the answer.

Justice Blackmun summarized the decision:[55]

To summarize and to repeat:

1. A state criminal abortion statute of the current Texas type, that excepts from criminality only a *life saving* procedure on behalf of the mother, without regard to pregnancy stage and without recognition of the other interests involved, is violative of the Due Process Clause of the Fourteenth Amendment.

(a) For the stage prior to approximately the end of the first trimester, the abortion decision and its effectuation must be left to the medical judgment of the pregnant woman's attending physician.

(b) For the stage subsequent to approximately the end of the first trimester, the State, in promoting its interest in the health of the mother, may, if it chooses, regulate the abortion procedure in ways that are reasonably related to maternal health.

(c) For the stage subsequent to viability the State, in promoting its interest in the potentiality of human life, may, if it chooses, regulate, and even proscribe, abortion except where it is necessary, in appropriate medical judgment, for the preservation of the life or the health of the mother.

2. The State may define the term "physician" to mean only a physician currently licensed by the State, and may proscribe any abortion by a person who is not a physician as so defined.

. . . The decision leaves the State free to place increasing restrictions on abortion as the period of pregnancy lengthens, so long as those restrictions are tailored to the recognized state interests. The decision vindicates the right of the physician to administer medical treatment according to his professional judgment up to the points where important state interests provide compelling justifications for intervention.

The Court ruling may force even the New York law to be further liberalized. Gordon Chase of the Health Services Administration of New York City said that the health code must be changed in line with the ruling.[56] Until now the New York City Health Code said that a woman could not seek an abortion in a doctor's office. Chase said this would have to be changed.

On the day after the Supreme Court decision, thirty

New York legislators sponsored a bill that would repeal the abortion laws in New York. This bill would take the present abortion law out of the penal code and make abortion strictly a medical matter. Representative Bella Abzug (D.-New York) is trying to get the Abortion Rights Act of 1973 passed as a federal law. It would eliminate all abortion laws all over the country.

Human Rights for Women, Inc., expressed why January 22, 1973, is indeed a day of triumph for American women:[57]

> The Court's decision sets a new moral tone for the Nation: Affording the protection of the Constitution of the United States to a woman's right to decide whether she wants to terminate a pregnancy or have a child recognizes the dignity of women as people. This is now constitutional doctrine. It is the law of the land.

> No longer may we be subjected to legal restrictions that implicitly regard women as reproductive instruments of the State. No longer need the enjoyment of sex be tainted with guilt and fear of pregnancy, which often results in resentment and hostility to men, embitters our hearts and damages our personalities. No longer are we prisoners of the State and of men.

> No longer need we bear unwanted, unloved children. We can choose not to have any children or plan childbirth so that it does not destroy our careers. We need not be condemned to dependency on men.

> With our new constitutionally protected right to self-determination, no longer can sex be a tool for the oppression of women. It has lost the power to control our lives. Sex is thereby deemphasized and placed in proper and healthier perspective.

Sex can now serve women, instead of women serving sex. With a bow in the direction of Norman Mailer, we women can say, as of January 22, 1973, we are no longer prisoners of sex.

Chapter Eleven
The Law of Names:
Frailty, Thy Name Is Woman![1]

When I got divorced for the second time, I thought I should get back "my own name."

What was that? My first husband's last name wasn't my name. My late father's last name wasn't my name. I thought of taking my mother's maiden name, but realized that wasn't her name, but her late father's.

I came to the conclusion that a woman has no name.
—KAREN (ABT LIPSCHULTZ KOLBEN DE CROW)

✤✤✤ Even the U.S. Supreme Court has ruled that a state has the authority to require a wife to assume her husband's surname at the time of their marriage. The ruling was made in a one-sentence order affirming a decision by a three-judge federal court in Alabama.[2] Wendy Forbush married Ronald P. Carver of Anniston, Alabama, in 1970; they agreed she would continue to use her maiden name in her personal and business dealings in an effort "to demonstrate the equality of contract and commitment that they felt in their marriage." But when she applied for a driver's license, Calhoun County officials told Ms. Forbush that the license must be issued in her married name, citing a thirty-five-year-old Alabama policy. The courts upheld the county authorities.

In those cases where women have petitioned to legally retain their maiden names after marriage, the courts have almost uniformly rejected the effort. In twenty-one states, there are statutory restrictions which impede a woman's choice to retain her maiden name for legal purposes after marriage.[3]

Many states have statutes which expressly deny a married woman the right to change her surname to one other than her husband's. No comparable restriction is imposed on men. When a married man changes his surname, his wife's surname is automatically changed, regardless of her personal wishes.

Not only does a woman automatically lose her name upon marriage; children of the marriage also acquire the husband's surname. The law on naming children highlights the basis of Western culture—patriarchy. This is particularly ironic, since the raising of children has been "women's work." The American woman, therefore, spends the greater portion of her lifetime raising children who do not even have her name.

Under current laws, a husband may intervene by injunctive proceedings to prevent his wife's attempt to change her name informally.[4] Statutes which prescribe formal procedures for changing one's name often expressly[5] or impliedly[6] exempt married women. Some states permit a woman to reassume her maiden name only if she is the successful complainant in a divorce action, and not the defendant. (A strange "punishment" for being the defendant in a divorce action—to be forced legally to keep one's ex-husband's name.)

A practical side of the name changing that goes on for women (most women marry once; many women marry more than once) is that one is lost to one's old friends. To raise consciousness, think what it would be like to arrive in the city thinking, "I'd like to find Bill Smith, my old friend from college. I wonder what his wife's name is, so I can find him in the telephone directory."

The telephone company refuses to list both the husband and the wife in its directory, claiming this will take up too much space. Many NOW chapters have been arguing this point, offering to help the telephone company find abbreviations, and so forth. But that fight is only for the wife's first name. Her last name is her husband's.

The senior judge of the Arlington (Virginia) County Circuit Court ruled in summer 1972 that women in Virginia may not change their married names unless they divorce their husbands.[7] Barbara Ann Aiello, who is married to Dennis Osterman, forced the court ruling after a two-month struggle *to please her father* and regain legally her maiden name. Clerks in Virginia, Maryland, and Washington, D.C., courts, when interviewed by the Washington *Post*,[8] said petitions for legal name changes are almost always approved for men and for single and divorced women. The clerks could recall no other case in which a married woman sought to regain her maiden name and still stay married.

The Virginia case is on appeal to the Virginia Supreme Court. The attorney, Elise B. Heinz, is calling attention to the Virginia Constitution, which forbids governmental discrimination on the basis of sex. In Virginia, however, a married woman can vote only when using her husband's name.

Two married women in Washington, D.C., sued the U.S. Passport Office to have their maiden names placed on their passports, rather than their husbands' names preceded by "Mrs." Karla Simone and Nancy Hermann filed suit under the First, Fifth, Ninth, Thirteenth, and Fourteenth Amendments to the U.S. Constitution, claiming that "the practice of forcing a woman to be known by her husband's name is a principal indicia of a patriarchal society."[9]

The women are married, respectively to Richard D. Hobbet and Theodoros Karrikolas. Since marriage, according to the suit filed in U. S. District Court, both had used their maiden names for all purposes. That worked, until they tried to get passports. Nancy Hermann applied, and was told that the passport could be issued only in the name of Nancy Karrikolas.

Two Connecticut women who use the title "Ms." and their maiden names have sued the Secretary of State for the right to register under their maiden names. Margo Custer and Jane Holdsworth say they were refused the right to register under their maiden names, which they have each used since they were married. In their suit, filed by the Connecticut Civil Liberties Union, the women contended that there is no Connecticut law that requires a married woman to use her husband's name, and that a married woman has the right to use whatever name she likes so long as she uses it consistently.[10] The Attorney General cited tradition and a shortened election timetable for the married name requirement.

Apparently it is legal to retain your father's surname in Louisiana. State law holds:[11]

Under the civil law, a woman does not lose her patronymic name through marriage; and her legal name never varies with a change of her marital status. Socially, a wife is known by the name of her husband, but under the civil law she never acquires his name. In the legal and judicial acts which concern a woman who is married, divorced, judicially separated, or a widow, the name of her husband or former husband is shown to establish her marital status.

While a judgment of divorce or separation from bed and board affects the rights of the wife, and her marital status, it does not change her legal name.

In Dublin, Werner Braun was awarded the equivalent of $31,000 in damages from Stanley Roche, *for taking* Braun's fifty-year-old wife Heide.[12] Since Roman Catholic Ireland has no divorce law, a civil action for damages is the only recourse for a "wronged spouse." Braun accused Roche of having debauched and carnally known his wife. A wife in Ireland is "regarded as a chattel, just as a thoroughbred mare or cow," a High Court judge told a Dublin jury.[13]

In this period when women are demanding their own identities, there have been several victories in the law of names. Maryland is one of twenty-eight states which carried on its books: A woman who has undergone a change of name by marriage must register to vote under her married name if she would cast a ballot.

In October 1972, the Maryland Court of Appeals ordered the name of Mary Emily Stuart to be put back on the voter rolls. Ms. Stuart had married, and refused to reregister. She and her husband-to-be had entered into an agreement that she would continue to use her maiden name after their marriage. The court held that "under the common law of Maryland, her surname had not been changed solely by reason of her marriage."

Apparently, a woman may so register if she can show that she has continued to use her maiden name since her marriage. The Court of Appeals, in reversing a lower court decision, held:[14]

. . . because of her exclusive, consistent, nonfraudulent use of her maiden name, she is entitled to use the name of Mary Emily Stuart unless there is a statute to the contrary.

The decision stated that, although Maryland law requires a woman to reregister if she has undergone a change of name by marriage, Ms. Stuart had not changed her name under common law.

Ms. Stuart continued her battles through the bureaucracies of the state of Maryland. The Maryland State Motor Vehicle Administration told her that her driver's license will be revoked unless she applies for a new one, in her husband's name.

Apparently, Ms. Stuart had driven undisturbed, using her own name on her driving license, until the Motor Vehicle personnel read about her court case on voting rights. They then sent her a letter, informing her that she had violated the law by holding a driver's license in her maiden name. The letter, however, was returned, with the handwritten notation on the envelope: "No one by this name at this address. Letter opened by mistake."

The Motor Vehicle Administration is one of the few Maryland state agencies to define a "true legal name." Under the definition, a "true legal name" is "the name given at birth or as changed by a court decree or by marriage." The definition was adopted during the period when the late Malcolm X was alive, and many Marylanders informally dropped their surnames and substituted X.

Information on the name practices in Utah comes to us from a letter in *Glamour* magazine.[15]

. . . It rankled me increasingly to be addressed as "Mrs. Ray Wilson" in situations where my husband wasn't involved in the slightest. This spring I stopped brooding and saw a lawyer. Two months and $250 later, I was once again Marcia Greenwold, though still married to Raymond Wilson. The judge said, before issuing the decree, "You know, you'll have a lot of trouble." He was wrong.

When we are introduced as "Marcia Greenwold and her husband, Ray Wilson," nobody seems bothered. Similarly, we use checks with our two surnames and we have no trouble signing for charges on accounts bearing the other's name. The only special notice we have received has been from women who say, "I wish I could do that!" They can.

Marcia D. Greenwold
Salt Lake City, Utah

Marcia Greenwold apparently knows liberated people. In the bourgeois world, the name issue is an extremely sensitive one. Women, not just men, become furious at the idea that Mrs. Bill Smith is not a perfect name. They run up to me at lectures, telling me that they love being Mrs. Bill Smith. One friend, who married but kept her maiden name, received heavy pressure from members of her family; one relative simply refused to send her a wedding check if it could not be sent to "Mrs. Bill Smith."

Why is there all this heat? The answer seems fairly clear to me. From the time a girl is about six years old, talk of her future husband is prevalent. What kind of man does she want to marry? Will he be a lawyer or an engineer; have brown hair or red? When I was in high school, whenever we were "in love" with a boy, we wrote "Mrs. His Name" all over our notebook covers, just to try it out. Not to marry, not to change one's name, is to admit failure, for a woman. And then, having achieved success, what could be more frustrating than to have a group of women telling you that *the winning title* should not be used.

This is about the same as telling a group of doctors who have just finished medical school that they shouldn't be called "Dr."

To force women to pay $250 in legal fees for the "privilege" of retaining their names, when men have to pay no such fee, seems to be a blatant denial of equal protection under the laws. And, one designed to keep women married, and clearly identifiable as married.

For women and men who struggle with the problem of what to call themselves after marriage, assuming they have rejected the old patriarchal methods, a Washington, D.C., couple have a new idea. Susan Sadoff-Lorenzi and Henry Lorenzi changed their names to Susan Hasalo Sojourner and Henry John Sojourner. They explained the new name: "Sojourner, evoking struggle for freedom—Liberation: A black slave woman —Sojourner Truth—strong force for abolition and women's rights, speaking, acting, living out her struggle for human rights."[16]

Many women in the women's movement have concluded that there is something of a nonissue in going through court battles and social pressures in order to change from your husband's to your father's name. Although it has the advantage of at least being "your name" in elementary school and on your birth certificate, being allowed to keep your father's name is certainly not the solution to ending institutionalized patriarchy.

If anything blows the minds and the cool of newspaper reporters and family friends alike, it is a woman taking *her own name*. One woman who did this is Nola Claire, New York State Coordinator for NOW. Nola's name at birth was Nola Claire Dorries, Dorries being her father's name. It later became Nola Szymalak, Szymalak being her husband's name. After years of deliberation, in 1970, Nola decided to drop both surnames, and become Nola Claire. Because her case is almost unique, and may indeed become a model for name changes around the country, I reproduce her legal papers below. Her attorney is Faith A. Seidenberg, of Syracuse, New York.

County Court
County of Onondaga: State of New York
In the Matter of the Application of
NOLA CLAIRE DORRIES SZYMALAK
For Leave to Assume Another Name

Upon reading and filing the petition of NOLA CLAIRE DORRIES SZYMALAK verified the 30th day of October 1970, praying for leave to change the name of petitioner, it being requested that such person be permitted to assume the name of NOLA CLAIRE in place of her present name, and the court being satisfied by said petition that there is no reasonable objection to the change of name proposed and due notice of the presentation of said petition having been given and the said person having been born in the City of Schenectady, County of Schenectady, in the State of New York, on the 19th day of December 1933, and the court being further satisfied that the interest of the said person will be substantially promoted by such change, now, on motion of Faith A. Seidenberg, attorney for the petitioner, it is hereby

ORDERED, that the said Nola Claire Dorries Szymalak be and she hereby is authorized to assume the name of Nola Claire in place of her present name on or after the 3rd day of March, 1971, and it is further

ORDERED, that this order be entered and the papers on which it was granted be filed within ten days after the entry thereof in the office of the County Clerk of the County of Onondaga and that a copy of this order be published within twenty days after the entry thereof in the Syracuse Herald-Journal, a newspaper published in the said County of Onondaga at least once.

Jan. 21, 1971 Albert Orenstein, Judge of County Court

County Court
County of Onondaga
In the Matter of the Application of
NOLA CLAIRE DORRIES SZYMALAK
For Leave to Assume Another Name
Petition on Application for Change of Name

The petition of NOLA CLAIRE DORRIES SZYMALAK, respectfully alleges that:

1. Your petitioner resides at 109 Smith Lane, Apt. 2-b, in the City of Syracuse, County of Onondaga, State of New York, and has so resided for a period of three months.

2. Your petitioner has a home at 69 North Main Street, City of Homer, State of New York, and has resided there, prior to the last few months, for a period of six years.

3. Your petitioner desires to assume another name other than now held by her, and that name which she proposes to assume is "Nola Claire."

4. Your petitioner is married and has two children but is not seeking to have their names changed.

5. The grounds for this application for such change of name are as follows, to wit:

Petitioner is a university student and is registered and enrolled as Nola Claire. Petitioner is generally known to her friends and associates as Nola Claire, and your petitioner has generally used this name. Since it is possible for a woman to sue in the name of which she is generally known (*Treberg v. Vetter*, 12 Abb. N.C. 302.; note, reversed on other grounds 2 Civ. Proc. (11) 391), and your petitioner has a right to contract individually and is individually liable upon her debts and tort actions against her (General Obligation Law 3-301), she wishes to use her own given name and not that of her husband or father who would not be liable for said actions. The name your petitioner wishes to assume has caused no fraud, evasion nor interference with the rights of others.

Petitioner wishes to use her given name and not her married name. Although she has a legal right to use her married name (*Bauman v. Bauman*, 250 N.Y. 382), she has no duty to do so (*Bell v. Sun Printing and Publishing Co.*, 42 Super Ct. (10 Jones & S) 567), and wishes to assume the name "Nola Claire" based upon her own separate identity and founded upon a legally honest purpose.

6. Your petitioner is a citizen of the United States of America.

7. Your petitioner was born at Schenectady, New York, on December 19, 1933, and is now thirty-six years of age. The name of petitioner's father was Herman Dorries, and the name of petitioner's mother is Hilda Dorries.

8. Your petitioner under the name by which she is now known or under any other name she has ever used, has never been convicted of a crime and has never been adjudicated a bankrupt.

9. There are no judgments or liens of record and no actions pending against your petitioner in any court of this state or of the United States, or of any governmental subdivision thereof, or elsewhere, whether the court be

of record or not. There are no bankruptcy or insolvency proceedings, voluntary or involuntary, pending against your petitioner in any court whatsoever or before any officer, person, body or board having jurisdiction thereof and your petitioner has not at any time made any assignments for the benefit of creditors.

10. There are no claims, demands, liabilities or obligations of any kind whatsoever on a written instrument or otherwise against your petitioner under the only name by which she has been known, which is the name sought herein to be abandoned, except for a first mortgage on the above mentioned domicile, and your petitioner has no creditors who may be adversely affected or prejudiced in any way by the proposed change of name.

11. Annexed to this petition and made a part hereof is a birth certificate of your petitioner.

12. No prior application for this or other similar relief has been made.

WHEREFORE your petitioner prays that an order of this court may be entered granting leave to her to assume the name of "Nola Claire" in place of that of "Nola Szymalak" on a day to be specified therein not less than thirty days after the entry of such order, and for such other and further relief as may be proper.

James Baldwin wrote about the problem of being black in America—nobody knows your name, but more important, you don't know your own name. Nola Claire, after proving to the courts in the State of New York that she isn't a criminal, or trying to evade her creditors, is one of the few women in America who knows her name.

Chapter Twelve
The Equal Rights Amendment:
A Beacon to Nine
Rip Van Winkles

Equality of rights under the law shall not be denied or abridged by the United States or by any state on account of sex.

—THE EQUAL RIGHTS AMENDMENT

This amendment, if passed, would be like a beacon which should awaken those nine sleeping Rip Van Winkles to the fact that the 20th century is passing into history. It is a different world and they should speak for justice, not prejudice . . . I seek justice, not in some distant tomorrow, not only in some study commission, but now while I live.

—REP. MARTHA GRIFFITHS

24 words that will lead this nation to the brink of Hell.
—REV. BILLY JAMES HARGIS, CHRISTIAN CRUSADE

In 1948 the Supreme Court of California denied alimony to a wife married thirty-six years who had reared eight children. She had no property or other source of income and no profession. Her husband worked as a laborer. The judge said:[1]

Defendant has no ability to earn more than sufficient for his own support and maintenance . . . and has no ability to pay further for the support and maintenance

of plaintiff or for her attorney's fees or court costs
herein.

Despite the Fourteenth Amendment, many thousands
of state laws throughout the country still discriminate
against women. After surveying a hundred years of court
opinions in women's rights cases, two New York University law professors, in 1971, concluded that ". . . by
and large, the performance of American judges in the
area of sex discrimination can be succinctly described
as ranging from poor to abominable . . . Sexism is as
easily discernible in the contemporary judicial opinion
as racism ever was."[2]

The Fourteenth Amendment was finally extended to
women in 1971. In *Reed v. Reed*,[3] the Supreme Court
held that the Idaho statute which provided that as between persons equally qualified to administer estates,
males must be preferred, is based solely on a discrimination prohibited by, and therefore violative of, the Equal
Protection Clause of the Fourteenth Amendment.

The Court took judicial notice of the fact that in the
United States, presumably due to the greater longevity of
women (seven years), a large proportion of estates, both
intestate and testate, are administered by surviving
widows.

The equal protection clause of the 14th amendment does
not deny to states the power to treat different classes of
persons in different ways; the clause does, however,
deny to states the power to legislate that different treatment be accorded to persons placed by statute into different classes on the basis of criteria wholly unrelated
to the objective of that statute.

In order not to violate the equal protection clause,
statutory classification must be reasonable, not arbitrary,
and must rest on some ground of difference having fair

and substantial relation to the object of legislation, so that all persons similarly circumstanced shall be treated alike.

The Court held that making it easy for the state was not reason enough for arbitrariness. "To give mandatory preference to members of either sex over members of the other, merely to accomplish the elimination of hearings on the merits on application for appointment to administer an estate, violates the equal protection clause of the Fourteenth Amendment; the choice may not lawfully be mandated solely on the basis of sex."[4]

The issue in the case was, Does the difference in sex of competing applicants for letters of administration bear a rational relationship to a state objective? The Court answered no. They overruled the Idaho Supreme Court, which had held that the elimination of females from consideration is "neither an illogical nor arbitrary method derived by the legislature to resolve an issue that would otherwise require a hearing as to the relative merits of the two or more petitioning relatives."[5] The Idaho statute was the first ever declared unconstitutional by the U.S. Supreme Court on grounds of sexual discrimination.

Senator Birch Bayh, in inserting the *Reed* decision into the *Congressional Record*,[6] explained the limited implications of the case:

Furthermore, today's decision by the Supreme Court does not reach every instance of sex discrimination. In adopting the 14th amendment test of reasonableness, the Court has left the burden on the woman plaintiff to prove that State action perpetuating sex discrimination is unreasonable. In my brief [Bayh submitted the amicus brief for the National Federation of Business and Professional Women's Clubs] I urged the Court to adopt the strictest 14th amendment standard, one which would shift the burden to the State to demonstrate a compelling, overriding interest in the discriminatory practice. The Court has adopted the strictest 14th amendment standard in overturning discrimination in voting power, discrimination against aliens, discrimination against the poor, and most importantly, instances of racial discrimination. I believe that women, too, are entitled to the fullest protection of the 14th amendment, and I regret that the Court did not go further in its decision today. The need for an equal rights amendment is underscored by the inherent limitation of the Reed holding.

In *Reed*, appellant, as the mother of an intestate decedent, filed her petition for probate of the estate. Decedent's father also petitioned for letters of administration. Both parties were equally entitled to letters of administration under the Idaho Code.[7] The probate judge ruled in favor of the father on the grounds that §15-314 of the Idaho Code required that males be preferred to females as between persons equally entitled to administer an estate. The probate court order was reversed by the Fourth Judicial District Court of Idaho, which held that that provision of the Idaho Code violates the Equal Protection Clause of the Fourteenth Amendment. The Idaho Supreme Court reversed the district court.

The *Reed* decision actually strengthens the case for the Equal Rights Amendment. If the Court, in 1971, is still using the reasonableness test, we know we cannot win equality in the courts using only the Fourteenth Amendment.

Emanuel Celler, former Brooklyn congressman, had said many times, in his role as head of the Judiciary Committee, that the Equal Rights Amendment would get out of committee over his dead body. It did get out of committee, and it did pass both the Congress and the

Senate. As of August 1973, thirty of the necessary thirty-eight states have ratified it.

California, a state where ratification seemed particularly difficult, ratified the amendment on November 13, 1972, at about 11 P.M. A friend called me from the state house in Sacramento—it was 2 A.M. where I live. I think I may have been one of the first persons on the East Coast to know the good news about California.

Although the Equal Rights Amendment will have enormous influence on court decisions, and on legislation, even before it is passed, its greatest value will be psychological. Not to be constitutionally equal in one's own country is humiliating. During the three years that I lobbied congressmen, and the few months that I lobbied in the New York State legislature, for the ERA, I felt embarrassed every time I had to sit (or stand) in the office of some legislator and *beg* for my own constitutional equality.

As Carolyn Bird expressed it,[8]

> Even if the equal rights amendment did nothing but state the principle, it would be worth it . . . the time has come when this . . . amendment is needed and politically feasible. Women are beginning to see their situation. They can never go back so we must all go forward.

But the Equal Rights Amendment will do much more than state the principle.

The amendment will restrict only governmental action, and will not apply to purely private action. What constitutes state action will be the same under the Fourteenth Amendment, and as developed in Fourteenth Amendment litigation on other subjects.

Under the ERA, special restrictions on the property rights of married women would be unconstitutional. A married woman could engage in business as freely as a member of the male sex. Inheritance rights of widows would be the same as for widowers. This means, for example, that married women in Alabama, Florida, Indiana, North Carolina, and Texas will be able to sell their property without their husbands' permission. Wives will be allowed to start an independent business without the approval of the court or their husbands in California, Florida, Nevada, Pennsylvania, and Texas.

Dower rights will not be nullified. They will simply be extended to men in those few states where men do not have a right in their wives' estates.

Married women will be able to manage their separate property, such as inheritances and earnings.

Lawyers and law professors differ strongly as to the standards judges will use in interpreting the ERA. Those who oppose the amendment say that a court must strike down beneficial laws based on sex, as well as those which deprive one sex of a benefit or opportunity. Those who favor the amendment contend that if a law favors one sex but not the other, courts are free to read it expansively to include both sexes. If a law takes something away from one sex but not the other, courts could simply strike it down totally.

Even though debates about the ERA often end up as a discussion of public bathrooms, it is clear that the major, most important effect of the ERA will be on the *employment* of women.

Restrictive work laws for women will be unconstitutional. There will be no more maximum hours laws, night work laws, or weight-lifting restrictions on women. It is for this reason that the ERA is of vital importance to the women of the country, and it is for this reason that the most formidable opponent to the ERA has been organized labor. It is no secret that there is a shortage of jobs; the white male workers are fighting (in decreasing numbers, fortunately) to keep women out of the good jobs. It has long been a practice in many states to forbid women to take particular jobs—bartender, for example; to enter particular industries—coal mining, for example; to work overtime; to work throughout a day without a specified "break"; to work at night; and to lift objects weighing more than a certain amount.

There seem to be two major objections to the ERA's effect on the employment of women. The first is that if the ERA is law, women will be forced to work overtime or lose their jobs. Because women usually have more home responsibilities, this appears to place a greater burden on them. Obviously, the solution is a series of state laws that mandate that *no one*—male or female—should be forced to work overtime under threat of losing a job.

The second deals with insurance, and other benefits such as retirement. Opponents of the ERA fear that women will lose certain advantages they now have. However, according to HEW guidelines, issued October 1, 1972,[9] "Retirement benefits must be equal for both sexes, *or* the employer's contribution must be equal for both sexes."

As early as 1971, the Supreme Court let stand a lower court ruling that pension plans compelling women employees to retire at an earlier age than men are a violation of federal civil rights law.

The Court acted without comment in a brief order refusing to review the finding of the Seventh U.S. Circuit Court of Appeals on behalf of a woman brewery worker. The appeals decision said that requiring her to retire at age sixty-two while men were allowed to continue working until sixty-five was "tantamount to discharge" on an unfair basis of sex discrimination.

The pension discrimination case was initiated by Ann Bartmess, of South Bend, Indiana, who had been forced to retire from her job in 1967 at age sixty-two under a pension plan agreed to by the brewery and the local union of the United Brewery, Flour, Cereal, Soft Drink and Distillery Workers of America.

Since the greatest impact of the ERA will be on the employment and money-making capacities of women, it is essential that women understand the union objections to ERA, and why they are not valid. First of all, most union opponents of the amendment are men who are afraid for their jobs. Secondly, men who truly understand the labor movement and what it should acomplish for all workers, are for women's equality. Samuel Gompers, in 1913, realized the dangers of separate treatment for women: [10]

> This woman movement is a movement for freedom of action and thought, liberty, tending toward a condition when women shall be accorded equal independence and responsibility with men, equal freedom of work and self-expression, equal legal protection and rights.

> We should view with apprehension present sentiment in favor of setting up public and political agencies for securing industrial benefits for wage-earning women. These agencies would constitute a restriction on freedom of action capable of serious abuses.

> Instead of aiding women in the struggle for industrial betterment and freedom, we should be foisting upon them fetters from which they would have to free themselves, in addition to the problems that now confront them, and we should still leave unsolved the problem essential to real freedom—self-discipline, development of individual responsibility and initiative.

> The industrial problems of women are not isolated, but are inextricably associated with those of men.

From what we can deduce from congressional debate on the ERA, the effect on state protective laws which now only apply to women will be, basically, to apply them to all workers. Minimum wage laws and rest and lunch period laws will be extended to men. There are laws, for example, requiring that wherever a certain number of women are employed, there must be a couch. The theory behind this must be that women—with menstrual periods, with pregnancies—need to lie down more than men. Of course, this is unfair to men, who, in my experience, tend to "rest" at least as much as women.

Laws prohibiting hours of work beyond a specified number, night work, employment in particular occupations, and weight-lifting will be invalidated. Most of these prohibitory laws will have been litigated, by the time the ERA is ratified, by women going to the courts under Title VII of the Civil Rights Act of 1964. This, however, is a terrific burden—of time and of money—on the women litigants, and most women who are treated unequally in employment cannot afford to bring their cases to court.

Also, court cases and even administrative complaints bring up the problem of retaliatory firing. Under the Equal Pay Act, which is administered by the Department of Labor, the identity of the complainant is never revealed. But this is not the case with women who file suit under Title VII. Women are even afraid to make complaints to state human rights commissions (often one must "exhaust all administrative remedies" before going to court) for fear of losing their jobs. As Jack M. Sable, Commissioner of the New York State Human Rights Commission, stated, when people who make complaints are fired, the burden of proof is upon them to show that they were fired for making the complaint.[11]

The ERA would not affect private employment, except insofar as it affected state laws governing private employment. It would prohibit discrimination by government as an employer—federal, state, county, and city—including school boards. One of the largest groups of employees which would be affected is teachers, professors, and other employees of public schools and state institutions of higher education. It would require equal pay for equal work for employees of government.

Basically, ERA would render unconstitutional laws that restrict or deny freedom or opportunity to one sex. Prohibited occupations for women under state laws are basically of two types: working in mines or other specified hazardous occupations, and bartending.[12] When opponents of free choice in occupation call up the specter of women working in mines or digging ditches, the only reasonable response must be that women should have the same opportunity as men to work at (perhaps) less-than-dainty occupations for the same reasons that men do—*because they pay well*.

Laws in a few states still limit the weights which women are permitted to lift. In Utah women are not allowed to take jobs where they might have to lift more than thirty pounds; in Ohio the limit is twenty-five pounds; and women in California are not allowed to carry more than ten pounds up and down stairways. These laws violate the rights of women to equal employment opportunity under Title VII of the Civil Rights Act of 1964. Irrespective of Title VII, such laws also limit the freedom of a woman to choose certain types of work, and would therefore deny women equal rights under the ERA.

Weight-lifting laws should of course not be arbitrary, but should relate to the strength of the persons involved, whether male or female. The way these laws are currently used is to segregate men and women in factories, with men having the higher-paying jobs. Most often, the jobs that require weight-lifting require that it be done once a week or so, and male-run unions are delighted to see women automatically eliminated from those jobs. In addition, if the laws applied to housewives and mothers, they would all have to leave "their jobs."

Senator Sam Ervin's minority views, stated in the *Senate Report on the Equal Rights Amendment*,[13] have been widely used to discredit the ERA by misinterpretation of its meaning. Senator Ervin supports his interpretations by excerpts from the *Yale Law Journal*.[14] Following a detailed comparison by Dr. Virginia J. Cyrus, it was concluded that Senator Ervin has been quoting the journal article out of context by quoting only parts of sentences and sections of paragraphs. The journal article, in fact, is very favorable to the ERA. The *Yale Law Journal* article discusses protective legislation:

> . . . it is difficult to imagine an occupational hazard which is based on a physical characteristic unique to one sex; if the occupation is dangerous, it is dangerous to both sexes. Under the Equal Rights Amendment, courts are thus not likely to find any justification for the continuance of laws which exclude women from certain occupations. Legislatures which are concerned with real hazards in certain jobs will have to enact sex-neutral protections.

> . . . Hence, while a law protecting both men and women from coerced overtime is desirable, the courts are likely to leave the matter to legislative decision, meanwhile equalizing both sexes under the Equal Rights Amendment by invalidating the law. This would seem to be one area, therefore, in which legislative attention between ratification and the effective date of the Amendment would be important.

In general, labor legislation which confers clear benefits upon women would be extended to men. Laws which are plainly exclusionary would be invalidated. Laws which restrict or regulate working conditions would probably be invalidated, leaving the process of general or functional regulation to the legislatures.

The legislatures could regulate, but no matter how male their composition, no matter how much women are on pedestals in the minds of the state leaders, no matter how much lobbying has been done by exclusionist union leaders—women workers will for the first time have the opportunity to earn as much money as men. Women will have the opportunity to work overtime in twenty states, including California, Connecticut, Massachusetts, New Jersey, New York, and Wisconsin. Women will be able to apply for jobs as nighttime elevator operators in North Dakota, bellhops in Washington, gas or electric meter readers in Ohio, moving-machinery cleaners in Missouri.[15] Women will be allowed to sell alcoholic beverages for on-the-premises consumption in California, Connecticut, Illinois, Pennsylvania, and five other states.

Since the "job" for which the greatest number of women prepare and train is marriage, it is important to analyze the effect of the ERA on laws governing marriage and motherhood. One of the primary objections to the ERA cited by opponents is that it would weaken men's obligation to support the family and therefore weaken the family. This objection is based largely on erroneous assumptions about application and enforcement of support laws, and lack of knowledge of the legislative history of the ERA.

The rights to support of women and children are much more limited than is generally known, and enforcement is very inadequate.[16] A married woman living with her husband can in practice get only what he chooses to give her. The legal obligation to support can generally be enforced only through an action for separation or divorce; alimony is granted in only a small percentage of cases; and alimony and child support awards are very difficult to collect. Where the divorce will result in economic hardship—as is almost inevitably the case, except among the wealthy—greater hardship is placed on the wife and children than on the husband. The welfare of the husband and his prospects for remarriage are given much greater weight than the wife's and children's welfare.

It is true that a married woman legally has a right to be furnished "necessaries" and to charge purchases of "necessaries," but this is an empty right, since merchants will not give her credit if her husband asks them not to.

A *Yale Law Journal* article[17] explains how the ERA will have little effect on the marriage relationship.

> The reluctance of courts to interfere directly in an ongoing marriage relationship is a standard tenet of American jurisprudence. As a result, legal elaboration of the duties husbands and wives owe one another has taken place almost entirely in the context of the breakdown of marriage—either voluntary breakdown through separation, desertion, or divorce, or involuntary breakdown through incapacitation or death. Any legal changes required by the equal rights amendment are thus unlikely to have a direct impact on day-to-day relationships within a marriage, because the law does not currently operate as an enforcer of a particular code of relationships between husband and wife.

One recent trend among "liberated couples" is the drawing up of a marriage contract, specifying the duties and responsibilities of each partner. However beneficial the psychological effects of such a "contract" might be, it is no contract at all, and totally unenforceable in the courts.

Since the state does indeed step in when a marriage is dissolved, one must look to judges' views on alimony, in order to determine the possible effects of the ERA. The only nationwide study of alimony and child support was made by the Support Committee of the Family Law Section, American Bar Association, in 1965, when Una Rita Quenstedt, then chairwoman of the support committee, and Carl E. Winkler, former chairman of the support committee, made a survey of 575 domestic relations court judges, friends of the court, and commissioners of domestic relations. Here are some typical responses:[18]

> In this country permanent alimony is given in less than 2% of all divorces, and then only where the marriage has been of long duration, and the wife is too old to be employable, the wife is ill, particularly if the husband's behavior was a contributing cause, or other highly unusual factors exist. Temporary alimony is given, *pendente lite*, or for some portion of the interlocutory period in less than 10% of all divorces, chiefly to give the wife a breathing space to find employment.

> A healthy young woman should not be permitted to go on indefinitely living on alimony. Her outlook is more healthy and her life a good deal more full as an active member of the community and not as a kept woman.

It is interesting to observe that the Nevada judge responding considers a woman living on alimony to be a kept woman, whereas women who are full-time housewives are encouraged and supported not only by the mores of society, but by the income tax and Social Security laws.

Alimony is awarded with regard to the wife's ability to support herself. The wife's capacity to earn was taken into account by 98 percent of the judges in the Quenstedt-Winkler study. "In determining the amount of permanent alimony the court should consider the earning capacity of the wife and the extent of her opportunity to work."[19]

For example, a 1966 case in the District of Columbia Court of Appeals reversed a grant of fifty dollars alimony made by the lower court, solely on finding that the wife was not likely to become a public charge.[20]

As early as 1926 a California court gave great weight to a wife's capacity to earn, even though the wife had phlebitis and could not be on her feet. The court said:[21]

> . . . where the ex-husband is earning wages by daily labor, a trial court, in awarding alimony, should not do so in a sum inducing idleness on the part of the ex-wife.

The status of wives is not very secure before ratification of the ERA. After ratification, however, certain aspects of their status would improve abruptly.

Laws or legal customs which deny them equal share in property and in debts—because they are not employed outside the home—would fall. Laws which force the woman to have her legal residence where her husband's is would be void. Legal bars to a woman's right to go into debt or into business would not stand.

Different ages specified for men and women or boys and girls in the same law would be equalized under the ERA. Where the two different ages specified in the law are ages at which a right terminates, the *higher* age would apply to both sexes. This would be consistent with the rationale of extending the rights, benefits, and privileges accorded to one sex under the law to the other sex.[22] Where the ages are those at which limitations or disabilities are terminated, the limitations are nullified with respect to persons between the two ages by applying the lower age to both sexes.

In a few Western states the age at which a child's right to parental support terminates is eighteen for girls and twenty-one for boys.[23] Under such laws, boys between the ages of eighteen and twenty-one have a right which girls do not have, and the effect of the amendment would be to extend that right to girls and make the cut-off age twenty-one for all children.

Some laws provide that juvenile court jurisdiction may extend to girls at a higher age than boys.[24] Under the amendment the advantages accorded to one sex would be extended to the other by applying the higher age of juvenile court jurisdiction to both sexes.

In some states the age at which marriage can be contracted with parental consent and the age below which parental consent is required for marriage is higher for boys than for girls.[25] By contrast, some child labor laws provide a higher age for girls than for boys. In New York, for example, boys between ages sixteen and eighteen can work later into the night than can girls of the same age. The clear implication of such legislation is that it is more appropriate for girls to get married than for boys; it is more appropriate for boys to work than for girls.

The right to marry and the right to engage in labor are restricted for persons between the two ages. Under the ERA, the restriction would be removed, and the lower age applied in both cases.

With respect to child support—and with regard to the myth that all fathers support their children—the data available indicate that payments generally are less than enough to furnish half of the support of the children.[26] A Pennsylvania judge commented: "The Support Court usually sets the amount of a support order at the highest figure the defendant seems capable of paying. Even then the amount is usually not enough to support the wife and children on a minimal basis."

With the earnings of women averaging 60 percent those of men, women who work to support their children are contributing more than their proportionate share, even when fathers comply fully with awards. The effect of the ERA would be to make the duty a joint, or parallel, duty of both parents, not just of the father. But, in reality, this would not change the practice of what is currently happening.

The ages at which children would no longer be guaranteed support would be the same for girls as for boys. In addition, ancient rules which assume that the husband is the proper legal guardian of the children probably could not remain in legal use. The custom that mothers are to be preferred in child custody cases, when the child is born out of marriage, or when there is a divorce, would fall. However, as we have seen in the family law chapter, the preference for the mother in custody suits is today not as prevalent as rumor has it—particularly where older or male children are involved, and specifically when the father desires custody.

According to a 1971 report,[27] collection of alimony and child support is even more difficult than obtaining the awards. One year after the divorce decree, only 38 percent of fathers were in full compliance with the support order. By the tenth year, 79 percent of the fathers were in total noncompliance. Although in practically all states husbands can be held criminally liable for nonsupport of wife and children, most states require that the wife or children be in "destitute or necessitous circumstances" or without adequate, sufficient, or reasonable means of support.

The Uniform Desertion and Non-Support Act provides that the refusal to support must be without lawful excuse and willful and that the wife or children under sixteen must be in "destitute or necessitous circumstances." At present, the Uniform Act and most state laws are applicable also to mothers who refuse to support children under sixteen. As in other criminal proceedings, guilt must be established beyond a reasonable doubt and the burden of proof is on the state. The defendant father is entitled to a jury trial.

The prevalence of mistaken ideas about a husband's responsibility for support of wife and children, which have been reinforced by opponents of the ERA, are a great disservice to the nation, particularly to its women and young girls.[28] Whereas young boys are asked what they are going to do when they grow up, young girls are asked whom they are going to marry. The clear presumption, apparently not backed up by statistics on support, is that the girl will marry and be supported. Many young women, relying on the belief that marriage means financial security, do not prepare themselves vocationally. In addition, girls who announce their aspirations to high-paying vocations (doctor, lawyer, executive)—and presumably would be self-supporting throughout life— are discouraged in these ambitions by parents, friends, and vocational guidance counselors.

A U.S. Department of Commerce survey[29] shows that 27 percent of the women who entered into teen-age marriages more than twenty years before the survey was conducted are divorced, as compared with 14 percent of the women who were older when they married. The chances of getting alimony and child support in teen-age divorces is of course minimal.

The major reason for the nonenforcement of support orders is the difficulty of getting money out of a person (the father) who has little. However, an additional reason why criminal non-support statutes are not pressed may indeed be a feeling on the part of male judges that they are somehow "brothers" to the noncomplying father. The woman who must press her claims monthly in family court is considered a *pest* by the court system, and often by her own lawyer, who dreads her monthly (or weekly) phone call to announce the nonarrival of the support check.

Far from resulting in diminution of support rights for women and children, the ERA could very well result in greater rights. A case could be made under the ERA that courts must require divorced spouses to contribute in a fashion that would not leave the spouse with the children in a worse financial situation than the other spouse. Since most men do not want custody, and since practically every man earns more than his wife, this would be to the betterment of women.

The suggestion that alimony laws permitting alimony to wives would be invalidated by the courts rather than extended to men is not supported by any legal authority or the legislative history. The legislative history clearly indicates the intent of the proponents in Congress to extend alimony to men in those states now limiting alimony to women. Furthermore, in view of judges' preoccupation with keeping women from becoming public charges, it seems almost certain, should a state legislature fail to extend to men a law limiting alimony to women, that a judge would extend the law to men rather than invalidate it. If any judge should invalidate the law, it is clear that legislatures' concern for keeping women from becoming public charges would be sufficient to enact a new law applying equally to women and men.

The best answer to a man who asked how he can eliminate alimony and child support from his life, is that he should support the women's liberation movement. Only if women have equal employment opportunity, preceded by equal educational opportunity, will we be able to support ourselves.

The ERA would not deprive women of any enforceable rights of support and it would not weaken the father's obligation to support the family. Because it would require complete equality of treatment of the sexes, it might be used to require that the spouses in divided families contribute equally *within their means* to the support of children so that the spouse with the children is not bearing a larger share of the responsibility for support than the other spouse.

Since men do not bear children, a law which applies to pregnancy and childbirth and which refers only to women is not making a sex classification. Despite its terminology, the law would apply in the same way and have the same effect if it referred to "people." These laws must be distinguished from laws which refer to motherhood, which should be changed to parenthood, as in the case of Ms. Phillips in the Martin Marietta case.

If a law provides for cash benefits for the birth of a child, it would not be violative of the ERA. It should be observed, however, that special maternity benefits laws are almost non-existent.[30]

The Citizens' Advisory Council on the Status of Women has adopted the following statement on "Job-Related Maternity Benefits":

Childbirth and complications of pregnancy are, for *all job-related purposes*, temporary disabilities and should be treated as such under any health insurance, temporary disability insurance, or sick leave plan of an employer, union, or fraternal society.

Of the six jurisdictions which have government-sponsored temporary disability insurance programs, only New Jersey and Rhode Island require that the benefits under these laws be available for temporary absence from work for a normal delivery. The ERA would nullify requirements that women take a specific time off for maternity leave, that they lose their seniority while doing so, that they lose time allotments for unemployment compensation while on leave, and similar disadvantages.

As Mary Eastwood summarizes:

> . . . singling out childbirth for special treatment does not discriminate on the basis of sex even though the law refers only to women because men cannot give birth. But if in referring to childbirth the law goes beyond to spheres other than the reproductive difference between men and women (*e.g.*, employment), the law must treat women who give birth the same as men are treated in respect to the area of regulated employment (*e.g.*, absence from work for temporary disability).

> Similarly, women and girls could not be discriminated against in pursuing education because of childbirth. The expulsion or segregation of girls in public schools who have become mothers, but not boys who have become fathers, would be inconsistent with the Equal Rights Amendment. Just as laws prohibiting women from working for certain periods before (or after) childbirth regulate women's employment, not the childbirth, exclusion of pregnant girls from public schools regulates their education, not their pregnancy.

As we have seen in the chapter on motherhood and abortion, there is much discrimination against girls who become pregnant in high school. Although these practices are ending as they are challenged, state-by-state, in the courts, there are often rules (made by the Boards of Education) which require that a pregnant girl leave school entirely, or attend a special school. The punitive aspects of this are more sexist than puritanical. When, during a class in law school where we were studying the "problem" of unwed mothers, I asked what happens to the unwed father, the class broke up. Apparently the concept of the unwed father is a foreign one.

The ERA would not prohibit special maternity benefits. Only Puerto Rico gives any special benefit, and its terms often discourage employers from hiring women.[31] Laws in several states *prohibit* employment of women during specified periods before and after childbirth but do not require reemployment or any of the benefits given for other forms of temporary disability. Two states have temporary disability insurance plans that include benefits for loss of employment due to childbirth along with other types of temporary disability.

It can be asserted, then, that the ERA will not have a very critical effect on domestic relations laws. And, in those places where it will effect change, that change will be for the benefit of women. As the *Yale Law Journal* article states:[32]

> The present legal structure of domestic relations represents the incorporation into law of social and religious views of the proper roles for men and women with respect to family life. Changing social attitudes and economic experiences are already breaking down these rigid stereotypes. The Equal Rights Amendment, continuing this trend, would prohibit dictating different roles for men and women within the family on the basis of their sex. Most of the legal changes required by the Amendment would leave couples free to allocate privileges and

responsibilities between themselves according to their own individual preferences and capacities.

Although there is a common view that in the community property states women fare well, this is far from the case. The husband is favored as manager of property; he can often sell property without so much as the wife's signature. Community property does protect the wife who has stayed at home during the marriage from being left penniless—which can happen in common law states —but it is still a male-oriented arrangement of law. Under the ERA, laws which vest management of the community property in the husband alone, or favor the husband as manager in any way, would not be valid. In the absence of new legislation, the courts would leave decisions about the disposition of the community property to be made jointly by the husband and wife.

In the past many grounds for divorce were highly discriminatory to women; today there are still laws which apply solely to one sex or the other. These are nonage (legal minority), pregnancy by a man other than the husband at time of marriage, non-support, alcoholism of husband if and only if accompanied by wasting of his estate to the detriment of his wife and children, wife's "unchaste" behavior (without actual proof of adultery), wife's absence from the state for ten years without her husband's consent, wife a prostitute before marriage, and willful neglect by the husband. Under the pressure of the impending ERA, these provisions are being dropped from the state books, or extended to the opposite sex in the course of divorce law reform. However, the judges' attitudes toward the double sexual standard remain, and the ERA will be useful to women in forcing a single sexual standard.

The ERA will also change the laws on retirement and Social Security. The differing ages at which persons are permitted to retire—usually younger for women than for men—would violate ERA, at least if they are provided by law or by tax-supported pension plans. Many of the Social Security provisions which favor working men, and penalize working women, will be changed.

The extremely important laws governing name and domicile would be changed. Women would no longer be required to change their names when they married. States could, however, pass laws giving either sprouse the option of choosing the name of the other, or a new name.

Under present state laws, if a husband moves to a new state (or city) and the wife does not follow him, she is guilty of desertion. Under the ERA, a husband would no longer have grounds for divorce if a wife refuses to follow him to a new home, unless the state also permitted the wife to sue for divorce if her husband refuses to accompany her in a move. A person's domicile or legal residence can determine where to vote, where to run for public office, where to serve on juries, pay taxes, or have one's estate administered. In most states, a married woman's domicile is where her husband lives, and is determined by him regardless of her intentions or *where she lives*. In five states married women have the right to establish their own domicile.[33] Three additional states allow a married woman to establish her own domicile for purposes of running for public office, two for purposes of jury service, three for probate purposes, and thirteen for voting.[34]

The ERA would prohibit restriction of public schools to one sex, and it would prohibit public institutions from requiring higher admission standards for women (or men, should such a case exist). Universities traditionally have higher admission standards for women. The reason that was given to me on why the State University of New York has higher admission standards for women, is that women do so well in high school, and on the College Boards, that if they were let in on merit, the state university system would be *overrun with women.*

Any publicly supported school would be forbidden to have different course offerings for men and women, and different career promotion programs. Any private school with such variations would risk loss of its tax-exempt status, and any public funds it gets.

Women would also automatically gain the right to equal pay and equal advancement as teachers and professors, at least in publicly supported institutions.

Many people have the mistaken idea that the ERA will be of greatest benefit to middle-class professional women. This is far from the truth. Perhaps the women who have most to gain are the "disadvantaged" ones. Women and girls have systematically been excluded from vocational education courses for the high-paying vocations—automotives, aircraft mechanics, electronics, and the like. More than half the women and girls in public vocational education programs are being trained in home economics, and a third are studying office practice. The ERA will require that all vocational education be open to both sexes. Young women from poor families will benefit at the college level, too. Many depend on scholarships for tuition and other expenses, but often women are restricted by a quota system, and men are given preference in the awarding of scholarships and fellowships.

There is disagreement as to how far courts would go to nullify laws against sex crimes. Probably, any crime based on a woman's unique physical characteristics would still be punishable. Even before ratification of the

ERA, however, there are suggestions, for example, for changing the crime of rape to felonious assault. (Assault, unlike rape, requires no corroboration.) Any law which levies a heavier penalty on a woman than a man, or vice versa, would no longer be valid. For example, Arkansas sends women to prison for up to three years for habitual intoxication. The maximum in Arkansas for men is thirty days for drunkenness.

The Women's Bureau has summarized the state laws on jury service:[35]

> In 28 states women serve under the same terms and conditions as men, with the same qualifications, disqualifications, and exemptions. In 22 states and the District of Columbia, women may be excused on grounds not available to men. Of these, 11 states permit a woman to be excused solely on the basis of her sex. An additional 10 states . . . and Puerto Rico permit her to claim an exemption because of child care or family responsibilities. Rhode Island further provides that women shall be included for jury service only when court house facilities permit. In 1967 Florida and New Hampshire removed their requirement that women register before they may be considered for jury service. Louisiana is now the only state with this requirement.

Since jury service is a right and obligation of citizenship, the obligation to serve imposed on men would be extended to women.[36] Excuses from jury service, such as for hardship, child care or family responsibilities, should be regarded as an individual privilege and extended to men.

Although the most significant effect of the ERA is the financial benefits which will accrue to women, the most controversial aspect is the draft. Women in the movement are accused of being "man haters," but I can think of nothing more man-hating than the idea that a man's getting killed in war is any less offensive than a woman's getting killed in war. To lose a son could not possibly be less horrible than losing a daughter. Cynics believe that the reason for the heavy opposition to women in the military is because of the benefits and advantages which accrue. Obviously, getting killed in war is not one of them. And perhaps the masculine mystique prefers to think of men as the only killers. Nonetheless, women, who do not get drafted, also do not share in the following benefits:[37]

> Valuable in-service training, even for high school dropouts
> Correction of physical problems
> Opportunity to travel
> Opportunity to learn leadership
> Educational opportunities and scholarships
> Veterans' bonuses
> Veterans' loans
> Continuation of G.I. insurance
> Medical treatment in V.A. hospitals
> Veterans' preference in federal and state employment
> Civil service listing
> Extra points on the civil service tests
> Less likelihood of losing government jobs during work reductions

If the ERA is ratified, it seems likely that it will require Congress to treat men and women equally with respect to the draft. This means that, if there is a draft at all, both men and women who meet the physical and other requirements, and who are not exempt or deferred by law, will be subject to conscription.[38]

Women who have moral objections to bearing arms will be able to seek a classification to serve in noncombat service, just as men now do, serving as medics and in other fields. Women who have ethical objections to any kind of military service could seek a classification to perform community service instead of military service, also as men do now. Not so incidentally, Congress has always had the power to draft women. During World War II there was a critical shortage of nurses—so critical that a bill drafting nurses was passed by the House and reported favorably by the Senate; however the war ended before it reached a final vote in the Senate.

The Military Selective Service Act of 1967, as amended, makes only men liable for compulsive military service.[39] In the House debate on the ERA,[40] Martha Griffiths pointed out that women would be equally subject to the draft but "would not be required to serve—in the Armed Forces—where they are not fitted any more than men are required to so serve. The real effect . . . would probably be to permit both sexes to volunteer on an equal basis, which is not now the case."

Women have served in the armed forces for thirty years. At present there are more than 40,000 women in military service.[41] In 1967 special restrictions placing a ceiling on the rank to which women in military service could be promoted were removed. It was not until September 1972 that every type of job (except combat) was opened to women in the military. Until then women could fill only 139 of 484 Army jobs. At present, only 48 positions are denied women. (All involve carrying a rifle.)

Despite the nonsexist attitudes of persons like Admiral Zumwalt, the chauvinism in the military sounds like a repetition of what happens in the academe, the professions, and in business. In the Marines, for example, the worst insult one can give another is "You're acting like a woman!" And KP and latrine duty (women's work), are the traditional army punishments. Recently, the Army tried to make Army life more attractive by eliminating KP. They hired *neighborhood women* to do the work.

> Military women have generally fallen into the same patterns of employment that prevail in the private sector—that is, a concentration in the jobs traditionally classified as "women's work" and in the lower skill/grade levels. To date, top level management and executive positions are, for all practical purposes, closed to military women except those directly involved with women's programs.[42]

Women are now accepted in college R.O.T.C. programs and serve on draft boards. As early as 1967, the National Advisory Commission on Selective Service recommended recruiting women volunteers into the armed services to hold down draft calls. Yet women at present comprise only 1.6 percent of the military personnel.[43]

Women today cannot even volunteer for military service unless they are high school graduates or equivalent, and must meet higher standards than men in other respects. They must provide character references, and WACS must have a personal interview.

As important as is exclusion from various educational, financial, and medical benefits, there is an even more crucial discrimination. Law Professor Norman Dorsen explained to House Judiciary hearings:[44]

> . . . when women are excluded from the draft—the most serious and onerous duty of citizenship—their status is greatly reduced. The social stereotype is that women should be less concerned with the affairs of the world than men. Our political choices and our political debate often reflect a belief that men who have fought for

their country have a special qualification or right to wield political power and make political decisions. Women are in no position to meet this qualification.

Even if one disagrees with Professor Dorsen about the draft's being the most serious duty of citizenship, it is clear that a volunteer army can come into being much faster if women could volunteer and be admitted on an equal basis with men. It is also clear that most arguments used against women in combat are ridiculous. The opponents of ERA conjure up visions of mothers putting down infants and picking up rifles. Another image is that of a pregnant woman crawling under barbed wire in Marine training. Perhaps a brief history of Dependency Deferment legislation is in order.

When it was difficult to get manpower for the services during 1942–43, and while public opinion remained strongly in support of protecting the home and family, legislation was passed to provide financial protection of men with dependents who were facing induction. The Dependent Allowance Act of 1942[45] provided deferment for men who had persons dependent upon them for support, which rendered their deferment advisable. The President was authorized to provide for deferment of any or all men with wives and/or children, with whom they "maintain a bona fide family relationship in their homes."

The fear that mothers will be conscripted from their children into military service if the ERA is ratified is totally and completely unfounded. Congress will retain ample power to create legitimate sex-neutral exemptions from compulsory service. "For example, Congress might well decide to exempt all parents of children under 18 from the draft."[46]

The history of the Selective Service System shows that

Congress has the power to exempt certain groups of people at will. At various times, all fathers have been deferred, just as have all married men. With a larger pool to draw from, the likelihood of any parents being drafted is that much less.

Women in the military could be assigned to serve wherever their skills or talents were applicable and needed, in the discretion of the command, as men are at present. As former Representative Louise Day Hicks stated during the House debate on the ERA:

> ... it is an absurd scare tactic to summon up images of girls slogging through rice paddies with M-16's and full 60-pound packs strapped to their backs.

Anyone who likes men would agree that images of them doing these things are also absurd.

Hicks continued:

> Even in Vietnam, the number of men involved in active combat is a small percentage of our forces. There are any number of roles in all branches of the Armed Forces which could very well be carried out by women —in personnel, supply, intelligence, communications, and other fields as well as secretarial and nursing jobs to which they have been traditionally limited.

Since the ERA would require that publicly supported educational institutions accept women on an equal basis, the military academies would all be open to women. These schools are now starting to accept token women; probably under ERA no quota limiting the number of women would be allowed.

Finally, there is the question of how many women want to be drafted. The George Washington University

Women's Liberation Group answered the question, at House hearings in 1972:

> Just as many as the number of men who want to be drafted. We question the members of Congress who use the issue of the draft to impede passage of the Equal Rights Amendment at the same time they are considering abolishment of the draft.

Discussions about the ERA get very heavy. When one discusses the hundreds of laws in each state which discriminate against women (totaling thousands in the country), one should bear in mind that while many of them are oppressive and cruel, some are frivolous, often hilarious, statutes. In Maryland, for example,[47] there is a law prohibiting any female from using a musical instrument to solicit money. Another permits a slander suit against a person who questions a woman's chastity. A Maryland law exempts women and persons over the age of sixty-four from paying the oyster tonging fee.

Senator Sam J. Ervin, Jr. (D.-N.C.) has said, in fighting the ERA:[48] "I am trying to protect women and their fool friends from themselves."

Senator Ervin and his friends might well take note that women and their friends are ready, very ready, to take on constitutional equality.

Chapter Thirteen
Sexism in Education:
To Bow Down No Longer

*American working women have learned the lesson that
the black people have learned. There is no such thing
as separate but equal. We do not want separate little
unequal, unfair laws and separate little unequal, low
paid jobs. We want equality.*

— GEORGIANNA SELLERS, ONE OF THE PLAINTIFFS
IN THE *Colgate* CASE

*We're tired of studying our status. We mean to have
some of it.*

— LIZ CARPENTER

*In education, in marriage, in everything, disappoint-
ment is the lot of woman. It shall be the business of
my life to deepen this disappointment in every
woman's heart until she bows down to it no longer.*

— LUCY STONE, 1855

❧❧❧ St. Bonaventure University in New York
State was all-male until a few years ago, when it was
integrated because of falling enrollment. The men students have some unusual customs, such as pelting the
women's dorm (which they call the Cow Palace) with
so many snowballs that St. Bonaventure's women were
forced to study in the hallways to avoid flying glass.

Each year the men have "gross-out" contests in which
a prize is awarded to he who can disgust or embarrass a
female in a "new and creative" way. Men take women

students to the "shrines" around campus, and then take off their pants to see how fast the women run. One of the all-time gross-out kings won his title by defecating on the floor of the women's dorm at a nearby college.[1]

The boys at St. Bonaventure are carefully taught by the men. One friar who teaches history starts the class by ordering all the women to sit in the front of the room with their legs crossed. Once the legs are crossed, he winks at the boys and says, "Now that the gates of hell are closed, we can proceed."[2]

Sexism is not limited to religious educational institutions. The campus security department at Syracuse University has just issued a poster—five hundred were printed—urging students to "Lock Up Your Valuables." The illustration for this message is the midsection of a woman, wearing hip-clinger jeans and no top. The jeans zipper is padlocked.

The nation's schools and colleges are riddled with sex bias, according to a study by the U. S. Office of Education.[3] The current federal budget provides outlays of $15.7 billion for education. The Office of Education itself is dispensing federal money to support illegal discriminatory practices against students, teachers, and other employees.

The unusually candid report (still unpublished) *A Look at Women in Education* was compiled by a task force at the Office of Education in spring 1972. The 141-page, closely documented report concludes, "Our educational institutions everywhere have been denying females their right to equal opportunities." It charges that HEW aid has contributed to sex discrimination and that U.S. schools and colleges are still imparting concepts of male superiority, while women are still primarily educated to be housewives.

The report charges that as an employer the educational system is equally guilty.

> Women working in education can generally expect lower pay, less responsibility and far less chance for advancement than men at the same level.

> As a girl progresses through the educational system, she confronts serious biases and restrictions at each level, simply because she is female.[4]

The study also charges that programs under the Vocational Education Act and the Manpower Development and Training Act "wittingly or unwittingly" help to channel most female workers into low-paying jobs. Noting that the professional and policy-making echelons of the Office of Education, and of the Department of Health, Education, and Welfare's Office of Civil Rights are dominated by men, it recommended "cleaning our own house."

Among other things, the Office of Education is accused of funding an extremely sex-biased career guidance test, and perpetrating the bias in its workbooks and public information materials. The report recommends speedy implementation of a law passed by Congress in June 1972 that cuts off all federal educational aid to institutions discriminating on the basis of sex. The Education Amendments Act of 1972, Title IX, prohibits sex discrimination in schools receiving federal funds.

The report recommends new legislation that would expand the law to cover admissions to elementary and secondary schools, military academies, single-sex public undergraduate colleges, and private coeducational undergraduate colleges. It demands tougher enforcement of Executive Order 11246, as amended by Executive

Order 11375, which bans sex bias by recipients of federal grants and contracts. The definition of "contract" is very broad, and is interpreted to cover all government contracts, even if nominally entitled "grants," which involve a benefit to the federal government.

The report recommends a stepped-up effort by the Civil Rights Office of the Department of Health, Education, and Welfare to end sex discrimination. Its record thus far is called "disappointing."

Disappointing is scarcely the term I would use. At a meeting in central New York,[5] where representatives of the Civil Rights Office had come to the area from Washington, D.C., and New York City specifically to instruct local civil rights leaders on how to file complaints, on how to make sure affirmative action was indeed going to be both affirmative and action, the invited guests were exclusively those connected with race discrimination agencies. Members of NOW were invited—by others who had been invited, not by the planners of the meeting.

After the meeting had proceeded for some time, dealing strictly with the issue of race, I asked what steps could be taken to end certain kinds of sex discrimination in education, which I categorized and elaborated upon. The representatives from the Office of Civil Rights were courteous, but approached my question as if I had mentioned something totally unrelated, and something totally out of their province. Their concern was for black males; they made it clear they had not come to central New York to help any women, black or white.

A Look at Women in Education recommended more sex equality in the Office of Education itself, which employs 3,200 women and men, and in the Office of Civil Rights.

The report says that no one should be denied an education simply because she—or he—has chosen to raise a family. To implement that, action is also recommended to expand child-care facilities, opportunities for adult education, part-time study, and assistance for school-aged parents.

The Equal Employment Opportunity Commission and the Office of Federal Contract Compliance now have a memorandum of understanding that all individual complaints against educational institutions and public employers of fifteen or more employees will be referred to, reviewed, and investigated by the EEOC. The Equal Employment Opportunity Act of 1972 gave jurisdiction over educational institutions and agencies of state and local governments.

There are powerful laws now to end discrimination in education; there is a myriad of agencies to administer these laws. The major problem in achieving justice for women in education is that we have all, women and men, been conditioned for so long to believe that women are inferior intellectually that we find it difficult to train our women equally. And, significantly, although women do most of the *teaching* of the young—women are the parents who are at home with little children; most elementary school teachers are women—men perhaps do not want to admit that they can *learn* something from women.

When cataloging the tools (laws, administrative agencies) to use in our fight, it would be less than honest not to mention *how long it takes*. One case, which began in March 1969, is still in the courts. It has gone through an incredible welter of administrative reviews, jurisdictional challenges, formal and informal delays. Fortunately, the women involved do not depend on their judgment monies to eat. The case is important, not for the amount of money involved, but because of the principle involved.

That principle is equality for women in sports. In school systems throughout the country, supported by taxes from parents of both daughters and sons, there are huge amounts spent on boys' athletics, teams, equipment, and practically nothing spent on the girls. Not only does this deprive young women of the opportunity to develop their bodies, it has enormous image consequences.

The cheerleader cheers, while the players play. Girls learn, at a very early age, that their role is to sit on the sidelines or, at best, to cheer for the boys. This pattern is continued into adult life. Women in professional athletics receive unequal pay, unequal prize money, unequal status, unequal promotional opportunities—and, worst of all, they receive the most biased media coverage of any women, except perhaps women in the women's liberation movement.

I worked as an editor on a golf magazine. The magazine was naturally staffed by golf addicts. They were all male, and not one of them had anything decent to say about any of the women golf pros. I myself, conditioned by male values, joined in the office banter about how "unfeminine" the women golfers were, about how "bad their legs were." The main detriment from the negative image of women in sports, I believe, is not suffered by the women players themselves, but by the young girls growing up who hear the attacks.

Two Syracuse teachers, Carolyn S. Bratt and Marilyn J. Patrick, began an action against the Board of Education of the Syracuse City School District, in 1969, because they were not paid for coaching girls' basketball, while men teachers, under similar circumstances, were paid for coaching boys' basketball.[6]

The New York State Division of Human Rights found probable cause, and appealed from a judgment of the State Supreme Court, prohibiting the Division from proceeding with a public hearing on two verified complaints filed under the Human Rights Law by Marilyn Patrick and Carolyn Bratt.

Complainants were employed by the Board of Education as teachers of academic subjects. On April 7, 1969, they filed with the Board, pursuant to a collective bargaining agreement between the Board and the Syracuse Teachers Association, written grievances alleging that "payment for junior high school basketball coaching was not received on March 4, 1969," and seeking as redress "payment of the junior high school basketball coaching salary immediately."

The collective bargaining agreement included a grievance procedure for disputes involving interpretation or application of the terms of the agreement; it provided that employees may seek alternative statutory relief under certain conditions.

On June 13, 1969, two months after filing their grievances with the Board, the women filed with the Division of Human Rights verified complaints under the Human Rights Law, charging the Board, and the Syracuse Teachers Association, Inc., with sex-based discrimination in compensation, terms, and conditions of employment. The complaints allege, in substance, that complainants agreed in December 1968 to coach the girls' basketball team for the season; that thereafter they practiced approximately twice a week (when they could use the gym, which was usually in use by the boys); that on or about May 14, male coaches received three hundred dollars for coaching basketball; that subsequently they learned that money had not been appropriated for coaches for female basketball teams; that at the end of the season the Parent-Teachers Association awarded members of complainants' team certificates and a trophy for outstanding achievement during the season; and that complainants are female.

After investigation of the complaints, the Division's regional director negotiated a conciliation agreement with the Board. Subsequently, complainants filed counterproposals. Thereafter, on August 10 and August 19, 1970, the Division's regional director issued and served written determinations finding probable cause to credit the allegations of the complaints. On October 23, 1970, the Division issued a written notice of hearing, requiring the Board to answer the complaints at a public hearing to be held in November 1970. This proceeding was begun by an order to show cause, which stayed the Division from conducting its hearing.

Carolyn Bratt and Marilyn Patrick think that there are only two questions at issue: whether only male coaches are paid and only female coaches are unpaid; and whether male and female coaches have equal terms, conditions, and privileges of employment, including access to gymnasiums and practice space.

As of summer 1973, the women have not received their money. They are waiting for argument at the New York Court of Appeals, to determine whether the Division of Human Rights has jurisdiction over the Syracuse School District. Carolyn Bratt is no longer teaching or coaching; she is a third-year law student at Syracuse University, College of Law. Marilyn Patrick is still teaching, but she does not coach athletics.

Today women coaches receive fifty dollars a year. Men coaches receive more, for example, six hundred dollars a year to coach football. And the girl students in Syracuse still have practically no access to the tax monies for their sports programs, while the boys, even in a period of budget troubles, have a well-funded sports program. (The most recent budgets available allocated $200 for girls' after-school sports, and $98,000 for boys.)

Discrimination against women—as faculty members, as coaches, as administrators—creates a disadvantage for both male and female students. Females are denied the presence of healthy female role models; males are denied the presence of healthy female role models.

Women continue to be discriminated against in admissions to public colleges. In the fall of 1968, only 18 percent of the men entering public four-year colleges had received high school grade averages of B-plus, or better. Forty-one percent of the freshman women had attained such grades.[7]

A Western state university published an admissions brochure stating: "Admission of women on the freshman level will be restricted to those who are especially well qualified." No such requirement exists for men.

During the Renaissance, women were not allowed to attend art school. Everyone asks, where are the great women painters of the Renaissance? Today, the public, tax-supported school systems still don't pay women equally for coaching girls' sports. Everyone asks, where are the great women athletes?

On February 16, 1973, nine women from the National Organization for Women, dressed appropriately in black robes, held an action across the street from the U. S. Supreme Court. We read a script, here reproduced, to show how ludicrous and totally unjust it would be if only women made the laws, enforced the laws, and interpreted the laws—concerning the lives of men.

The "Justices" in the action were Dorothy Haener, Jacqueline Michot Ceballos, Jo-Ann Evans Gardner,

Karen DeCrow, Muriel Fox, Nola Claire, Roberta Benjamin, Toni Carabillo, and Wilma Scott Heide.

We sat in nine chairs, with a bench before us. Props and police permits were obtained by Gerald Gardner, Hortense Boutelle, and Virginia Mills.

This judicial sexism action was repeated in front of federal and state court houses throughout the United States on September 28, 1973. There are over six hundred chapters of NOW; many of them participated in this national action.

---

*In the Matter of the Application of
Adam, et al. (and his brothers)*

against *the United States*.

Justice 1. The sole issue in this case is whether men are subject to the laws which are made by women. Petitioners, in a class action, bring before us the constitutional issue that the laws of the United States are made entirely by women, with a few token men sitting in the State Legislatures and in Congress; the laws are enforced entirely by women, with men having great difficulty securing positions on local, state, and federal police forces; the laws are interpreted by women, who sit on all the courts, including this, the highest Court in the land.

Justice 2. The attorney for the men here represented made a motion in the lower federal court, where the case was first litigated, for a male judge for her clients. She pointed out that only .2 percent of the judges sitting on the federal bench are men, and that a woman judge could not properly adjudicate the issues facing her clients, since such person could not have had any male experience, and thereby could not understand any of the personal or social aspects involved. The motion was denied, not on its merits, but because no male judge could be brought conveniently to the trial, the nearest one being 930 miles away.

Justice 3. The attorney for the plaintiffs submits that her clients cannot be held accountable to the laws passed without their consent, and that it is contrary to the U.S. Constitution that an entire class of persons, herein the 48.7 percent of the population which is male, be totally excluded from the exercise of power. She submits that whereas her clients are not suggesting a quota system of representation in the executive, legislative, and judicial branches of government—that being un-American— they are submitting that the present token system excludes them so effectively from the governmental process that they should not be subjected to it. They feel, in addition, since they pay taxes to support these and other governmental services, that such taxation without representation is tyranny.

Justice 4. In the lower federal court, our worthy sister Justice pointed out that these men, while protesting government process, *are using the very system against which they protest*, and expecting it to protect them. The attorney for Adam and his brothers instructs the Court to take judicial notice of the fact that they have no other means available to them for their redress of grievances. She also instructs the Court to take judicial notice of some of the reasons why these men are not present in greater numbers on the various benches in the U.S.: they are encouraged at a very young age to concentrate heavily on their appearance, keeping flat stomachs and luxuriant hair; they are taught to be pleasing at all times to women, and apparently, many women do not feel that being a judge is one of the things a manly man should do; they are pressured to marry at a young age, to a successful woman, and often this liaison is dominated by a concentration on the wife and her career needs, with moves across the country to improve the wife's professional status, and use of the family resources to aid the wife in her success, with the result being that the man frequently finds, upon reaching his thirties, that he has very few opportunities to strike out on his own, in general, and in specific, to enter such occupations as politics or government.

Justice 5. Attorney for the plaintiffs urges the Court to notice the kinds of state laws which are in existence concerning the work lives of men; she urges us to strike them down on the grounds that no compelling state interest has been shown to thusly deprive the men of their rights of due process, and particularly their right of equal protection of the laws under the Fourteenth Amendment. For example, she cites the weight-lifting laws, which are in existence in almost every state. Because noted female physicians have found men better able to lift weights of over twenty-five pounds, they are now legally responsible for the lifting of all such weights. This has the result of forcing men to stay at home to take care of all children who weigh more than twenty-five pounds, thus limiting their opportunities to seek other employment. In addition, in order that the men be available in great enough numbers for the jobs which require lifting the children, they have been restricted from various other occupations.

Justice 6. Attorney for the men urges us to strike down the federal laws on money-making, which apply solely to men, and thus provide a denial of equal protection under the Fourteenth Amendment. Many famous sociologists and social psychologists have noted the intense drive which men often possess, often bordering on an insane proclivity to accumulate cash, stock, and other material goods. In order to protect them from this unfortunate personal and social trait, laws have been passed to protect them from themselves. These laws place a strict limit on the amount of money which a man can earn or accumulate. Attorney for the plaintiffs argues that this consists of a denial of the right to property without due process of law.

Justice 7. Further, attorney for the plaintiffs asks us today to strike down a variety of state escort laws. Our highly qualified sisters who are psychoanalysts assure us that men have a natural tendency for lechery. Based on that medical testimony, laws have been passed in many states, prohibiting men from patronizing bars, restaurants, and other places where they might be attracted to women, unless they are escorted by women. For example, the law in New York State which prohibits men from walking in Times Square unless accompanied by a woman. Attorney for the men urges us to note a) that the medical testimony on lechery is at best anecdotal; and b) that passage of such laws constitutes a denial of equal protection under the Fourteenth Amendment.

Justice 8. Attorney for the men urges us today to strike down the football blackout laws. She urges that a federal government agency which is controlled entirely by women has no right to in any way control, regulate, or prohibit an activity such as football, which is played entirely by men, owned by men and, for the most part, watched by men on TV. For a female governmental agency to make laws determining such matters is just as unreasonable and illogical as, for example, any legislative or judicial determination made by men with regard to conception, abortion, or pregnancy, functions we note which are performed exclusively by women. Even if a female-dominated agency made a superb law concerning football TV blackouts, attorney for the plaintiffs submits it is a subject which should in no way be in our domain.

Justice 9. Lastly, the attorney for the plaintiffs has urged us to strike down the federal laws which restrict men from any participation in diplomacy or international affairs. In addition, we are requested to use the power of the Court to urge the World Court to use its influence to change these manner of laws in other countries. It has been noted by female experts throughout the world, in fields ranging from social science to the literary, that men seem to exhibit aggressive tendencies. This is shown by their moving around their cribs with greater vigor as infants; by their engaging as young boys in excessive punching and socking (much, much more than their sisters); by their preference for games such as hockey, football, and wrestling as they grow older, as contrasted with the seeming natural proclivity of their sisters for reading, writing, and speaking. Because of such sex differences, men have been totally excluded from politics and diplomacy—from any profession which might endanger the planet. They have been kept out by federal law from any occupation which might involve the country in any way—declared or undeclared —in a war or military action. Attorney for the men argues that because many men are aggressive, it cannot be said that all men are aggressive; it is a denial of due process and equal protection to arbitrarily exclude all members of the class, in this case men, from such an important occupation. Such determinations, it is argued, must be made on a case by case basis.

The Court will adjourn to consider the issues raised by this case.

We ain't what we oughta be,
we ain't what we wanta be,
we ain't what we gonna be,
but thank God we ain't what we was.

—Dr. Martin Luther King, Jr.

Notes

CHAPTER ONE: WOMEN AND THE LAW

[1] Keeton, Robert E., *Trial Tactics and Methods*, Boston, Mass.: Little, Brown and Company, 1954.

[2] *Ibid.*, p. 92.

[3] Schubert, Glendon, *Judicial Behavior*, Chapters 3, 4, 5.

[4] Berger, C., *Land Ownership and Use* (1968).

[5] Ginsburg, Ruth Bader, "Treatment of Women by the Law: Awakening Consciousness in the Law Schools," *Valparaiso University Law Review*, Vol. 5, No. 2, 1971, pp. 480–88.

[6] *Muller v. Oregon*, 208 U.S. 412 (1908).

[7] *Op. cit.*, see footnote 5.

[8] 335 U.S. 464 (1948). But *cf.* notes 43–48 *infra* and accompanying text.

[9] *Commonwealth v. Welosky*, Supreme Judicial Court of Massachusetts, 276 Mass. 398, 177 N.E. 656 (1931).

[10] *Ibid.*

[11] *Nairn v. University of St. Andrews* [1909], A.C. 147, 161.

[12] Viscountess Rhondda's Claim [1922], 2A.C. 339.

[13] *Op. cit.*, see footnote 9.

[14] *Robinson's Case*, 131 Mass. 376, at 380, 381, 41 Am. Rep. 239.

[15] Mishkin, Paul J., and Clarence Morris, *On Law In Courts: An Introduction to Judicial Development of Case and Statute Law*, Brooklyn, New York: The Foundation Press, Inc., 1965.

[16] *Ibid.*, pp. 360–61.

[17] *Ibid.*, pp. 364–66.

[18] *Op. cit.*, see footnote 5, p. 486.

[19] *Casey v. Manson Construction & Engineering Co.*, 247 Ore. 274, 428 P.2d 898 (1967).

[20] *Op. cit.*, see footnote 18.

[21] Compare *Casey v. Manson Construction & Engineer-*

ing Co., 247 Ore 274, 289 n.7, 428 P.2d 898, 906 n.7 (1967), with *Owen v. Illinois Baking Corp.*, 260 F. Supp. 820 (W.D. Mich. 1966); *Millington v. Southeastern Elevator Co.*, 22 N.Y.S. 2d 498, 508, 239 N.E. 2d 897, 903, 293 N.Y.S. 2d 305, 312 (1968). *Contra, Miskunas v. Union Carbide Corp.*, 399 F.2d 847 (7th Cir. 1968), *cert. denied*, 393 U.S. 1066 (1969).

[22] *Hoyt v. Florida*, 368 U.S. 57 (1961).

[23] Testimony of Wilma Scott Heide, National President of NOW (The National Organization for Women), to the Senate Judiciary Committee, Nov. 1971. Subject: Presidential Nominations to the U.S. Supreme Court.

[24] *White v. Crook*, 251 F. Supp. 401 (M.D. Ala. 1966).

[25] *Id.*, at 408.

[26] See 116 *Cong. Rec.* S17352–53 (daily ed. October 7, 1970) for a compilation of jury statutes.

[27] The previous federal statute determined competence to serve as a juror by the law of the state in which the district court is held but was amended in 1957. *See* 28 U.S.C. §1861 (1964).

[28] *De Kosenko v. Brandt*, 63 misc. 2d 895, 313 N.Y.S. 2d 827 (Sup. Ct. 1970).

[29] *Ibid.*, at 830.

[30] Sophy Burnham and Janet Knight, "The United States of America v. Susan B. Anthony," *Ms.*, November 1972, pp. 99 ff.

[31] *Ibid.*

[32] *Ibid.*

[33] "The Mother of Us All" by Gertrude Stein and Virgil Thomson. Copyright © 1947 by Virgil Thomson.

[34] *Minor v. Happersett*, 88 U.S. 162 (1874).

[35] *Ibid.*

[36] *Ibid.*

[37] *Plessy v. Ferguson*, 163 U.S. 537, 41 L.Ed. 256, 16 S. Ct. 1138 (1896).

[38] *Ibid.*

[39] *Roberts v. City of Boston*, 5 Cush. 198 (1849).

[40] *State v. Gibson* 36 Ind. 389.

[41] *Op. cit.*, see footnote 37.

[42] *Ibid.*

[43] *Strauder v. West Virginia*, 100 U.S. 303, 25 L.Ed. 664 (1880).

CHAPTER TWO: THE FOURTEENTH AMENDMENT

[1] *Bradwell v. The State*, 83 U.S. 130 (December 1872).

[2] *Ibid.*

[3] *Ibid.*

[4] *Ibid.*

[5] *Ibid.*

[6] *Women's Rights Law Reporter*, July/August 1971, Vol. I, No. 1, p. 5.

[7] *Ibid.*

[8] *In re Goodell*, 48 Wisc. 693, 81 NW 551 (1879).

[9] Carolyn Bird, *Born Female: The High Cost of Keeping Women Down*, New York: David McKay Company, Inc., 1968.

[10] *Time*, March 20, 1972, p. 68.

[11] *Women's Rights Law Reporter*, July/August 1971, Vol. I, No. 1, pp. 61–64.

[12] Miami *News*, September 13, 1972.

[13] Lengyel, *Four Days in July* 123 (1958).

[14] The Fifth Amendment Due Process Clause was brought to the States under the Fourteenth Amendment.

[15] *Reed v. Reed*, 92 S. Ct. 251 (1971).

[16] Eastwood, Mary, "The Double Standard of Justice: Women's Rights Under the Constitution," *Valparaiso University Law Review*, Vol. 5, No. 2, 1971.

[17] For an analysis of constitutional standards under the Equal Protection Clause see "Developments in the Law— Equal Protection," 82 *Harv. L. Rev.* 1065 (1969).

[18] *Op. cit.*, see footnote 16, pp. 283–84.

[19] *Gulf, C. & S. Ry. v. Ellis*, 165 U.S. 150, 165–66 (1897). See also *McGowan v. Maryland*, 366 U.S. 420, 426 (1961); *Hernandez v. Texas*, 347 U.S. 475, 478 (1954); *Royster Guano Co. v. Virginia*, 253 U.S. 412, 415, (1920).

[20] *Korematsu v. United States*, 323 U.S. 214, 216 (1944).

[21] *Loving v. Virginia*, 388 U.S. 1, 11 (1967). See also *McLaughlin v. Florida*, 379 U.S. 184, 192 (1964).

[22] *Sherbert v. Verner*, 374 U.S. 398, 406 (1963).

[23] *Bates v. City of Little Rock*, 361 U.S. 516, 524 (1960).

[24] *Shapiro v. Thompson*, 394 U.S. 618, 634 (1969).

[25] *Harper v. Virginia State Board of Elections*, 383

U.S. 663, 670 (1960); *Reynolds v. Sims*, 377 U.S. 533, 561–62 (1964).

26 *Skinner v. Oklahoma*, 316 U.S. 535, 541 (1962).

27 *Levy v. Louisiana*, 391 U.S. 68, 71 (1968).

28 *Muller v. Oregon*, 208 U.S. 412 (1908).

29 *Ibid*.

30 Freeman, Jo, "The Legal Basis of the Sexual Caste System," *Valparaiso University Law Review*, Vol. 5, No. 2, 1971.

31 *Commonwealth v. Welosky*, 276 Mass. 398, 414, 177 N.E. 656, 664 (1931).

32 *Quong Wing v. Kirkendall*, 233 U.S. 59, 63 (1912); *People v. Case* 153 Mich. 98, 101, 116 N.W. 558, 560 (1908); *State v. Hunter*, 208 Ore. 282, 285, 300 P.2d 455, 458 (1956).

33 *Allred v. Heston*, 336 S.W.2d 251 (Tex. Civ. App. 1960).

34 *Ida Phillips v. Martin Marietta Corporation*, 91 S. Ct. 496, 411.

35 F2d 1, 16 F2d 1257.

36 42 USC 2000e–2 (a) (1).

37 *Op. cit.*, see footnote 34.

38 The Miami *Herald*, January 26, 1971.

39 411 F2d 1257.

40 H0001 Motion of Human Rights for Women, Inc., for Leave to File Amicus Curiae Brief (a–4p); Amicus Brief (b–8p), Sylvia Ellison for HRW, P.O. Box 7402, Ben Franklin Station, Washington, D.C.

CHAPTER THREE: THE FEDERAL GOVERNMENT

1 The Miami *Herald*, October 12, 1970.

2 *Time*, March 20, 1972.

3 U.S. Bureau of the Census, *Statistical Abstract of the U.S.: 1970*, Table 325, p. 218.

4 Syracuse *Post-Standard*, December 12, 1972.

5 Women's Bureau, U.S. Dept. of Labor.

6 *Virginia Woolfolk et al. v. Otis L. Brown et al.* ED Va., Civil Action #225–70–R, opinion April 22, 1971. 39 LW 2649.

[7] *Michele O'Donnell v. Employment Security Department*, State of Washington, Work Incentive Program, Seattle, Washington (EEOC, San Francisco Regional Office #45 FI-066, charge filed August 1, 1970).

[8] *Shelley G. Thorn v. Elliot L. Richardson*, U.S. District Court, WD Washington, N. Div., #9577, filed March 16, 1971.

[9] *Mary Elizabeth Trull v. District of Columbia Department of Public Welfare*, 298, A2d 859 (D.C. Court of Appeals). Reported in the *Women's Rights Law Reporter*, Vol. I, No. 1.

[10] *Joyce Buchanan et al. v. Essex County Welfare Board*, 272 A2d 768 (N.J. Superior Court).

[11] *Elsie A. Dorsey v. State Department of Social Service*, Baltimore City Court, 1970/81/0-085608, December 8, 1970.

[12] *Cleo Johnson v. John Harder*, 438 F2d 7 (U.S. Court of Appeals 2nd Circuit).

[13] *Ibid.*

[14] Boyer, Gene, *Are Women Equal Under the Law?* Beaver Dam, Wisconsin, June 1971.

[15] *Ibid.*

[16] Women's Bureau, U.S. Dept. of Labor.

[17] Syracuse *Post-Standard*, November 11, 1972.

[18] Jack Anderson's column, Syracuse *Post-Standard*, November 1, 1972.

[19] *Ibid.*

[20] The Miami *Herald*, August 25, 1972.

[21] Wire services story, October 9, 1972.

[22] December 12, 1972.

[23] Reported in the Washington, D.C. *NOW newsletter.*

[24] Testimony of William H. Rehnquist, April 1, 1971, on Equal Rights for Women and Men, Subcommittee No. 4 of the House of Representatives Committee of the Judiciary, p. 323.

[25] *Ibid.* p. 324.

[26] Letter from Marilyn Hall Patel, Legal Vice-President of NOW, August 4, 1972, to the Chairman of the House Appropriations Committee, and the Chairman of the Senate Appropriations Committee.

[27] *Ridinger v. General Motors Corp.* and *Johnson v.*

General Motors Corp. 325 F. Supp. 1089 (Ohio 1971), and *Rosenfeld v. Southern Pacific Co.*, 293 F. Supp. 1219 (Calif. 1968).

28 *Op. cit.*, see footnote 8.

29 The Miami *Herald*, September 17, 1972.

30 *Gruenwald v. Gardner*, 390 F.2d 591 (2d cir.) *cert. denied*, 393 U.S. 982 (1968).

CHAPTER FOUR: MONEY AND EMPLOYMENT (I)

1 *The New York Times*, January 13, 1971.

2 Women's Bureau, U.S. Dept. of Labor.

3 The Miami *Herald*, October 29, 1972.

4 The Civil Service Commission.

5 *Op. cit.*, see footnote 2.

6 *Ibid.*

7 *Op. cit.*, see footnote 3.

8 *The Participant*, Teachers Insurance and Annuity Association, November 1972, p. 4.

9 "The Working Women: Can Counselors Take the Heat?" A Conversation with Dorothy Haener.

10 *Ibid.*

11 Pogrebin, Letty Cottin, "Women and Organized Labor," *Ladies' Home Journal*, March 1972.

12 *Lochner v. New York*, 198 U.S. 45, 49 L.Ed. 937, 25 S. Ct. 539 (1905).

13 *Ibid.*

14 *Adair v. United States*, 208 U.S. 161, 52 L.Ed. 436, 28 S. Ct. 277 (1908).

15 *Ibid.*

16 *Adkins v. Children's Hospital*, 261 U.S. 525, 67 L.Ed. 785, 43 S. Ct. 394 (1923).

17 *West Coast Hotel Company v. Parrish*, 300 U.S. 379, 81 L.Ed. 703, 57 S. Ct. 578 (1937).

18 42 USC §2000, 35 seq.

19 Syracuse *Post-Standard*, November 17, 1971.

20 Sec. 703 (h).

21 Gould, William B., "Employment Security, Seniority and Race: The Role of Title VII of the Civil Rights Act of 1964," 13 *How. L.J.* 1 (1967), pp. 781–977.

22 Slichter, Healy, and Livernash, "The Impact of Collective Bargaining on Management," No. 114 (1960).

23 Aaron, "Reflections on the Legal Nature and Enforceability of Seniority Rights," 72 *Harv. L. Rev.* 1532, 1535 (1965).

24 *Steele v. Louisville & Nashville Railroad*, 323 U.S. 192, 65 S. Ct. 226, 89 L.Ed. 173 (1944).

25 *Ibid.*

26 140 National Labor Relations Board, at 185.

27 *N.L.R.B. v. Miranda Fuel Co., Inc.*, United States Court of Appeals. Second Circuit, 326 F.2d 172 (1963).

28 *Kaiser Aluminum Company*, Case No. 246–1345 (EEOC, 1966).

29 29 USC §206.

30 *Bowe v. Colgate-Palmolive Co.*, 416 F.2d 711 (7th Cir. 1969).

31 *Ibid.*

32 *Quarles v. Philip Morris*, United States District Court, E.D. Virginia, 1968. 279 F. Supp. 505.

33 *Commission for Human Rights v. Farrell*, 43 Misc. 2d 958, 252 N.Y.S.2d 649 (Sup. Ct. 1964).

34 CCH ¶17, 252.21 (1966).

35 Civil Rights Act of 1964, Title VII, Section 703 (j).

36 *Contractors Ass'n of Eastern Pennsylvania v. Schultz*, 62 CCH Lab. Cas. ¶ 9421, 2 FEP Cas. 472 (E.D. Pa. 1970).

37 *Packinghouse Workers v. N.L.R.B.* (Farmers' Cooperative Compress), 416 F.2d 1126 (D.C. Cir. 1969), *cert. denied*, 396 U.S. 903 (1969).

38 *Civil Liberties*, December 1971, p. 11.

39 *Local 189, United Papermakers and Paperworkers v. United States*, United States Court of Appeals, Fifth Circuit, 416 F.2d 980 (1969), *cert. denied*, 397 U.S. 919 (1970).

40 *Ibid.*

41 *Ibid.*

42 Conciliation agreement between EEOC and Federal Paper Board Co., July 22, 1966 (1965–68 Transfer Bender) CCH Empl. Prac. Guide ¶ 8100.

43 Brief for EEOC as Amicus Curiae at 30, *Quarles v. Philip Morris, Inc.*, 279 F. Supp. 505 (E.D. Va. 1968);

Brief for EEOC as Amicus Curiae at 20–23, *Hicks v. Crown Zellerbach Corp.*, 58 CCH Lab. Cas. ¶ 9145 (E.D. La. 1968).

CHAPTER FIVE: MONEY AND EMPLOYMENT (2)

[1] *The New York Times*, January 7, 1973.
[2] *Ibid.*
[3] *Ibid.*
[4] *Diaz v. Pan American World Airways, Inc.*, 311 F. Supp. 559 (S.D. Fla. 1970). Reversed, 442 F.2d 385.
[5] 42 *U.S.C.A.* §2000e–5 (f).
[6] *Op. cit.*, see footnote 1.
[7] *Op. cit.*, see footnote 4.
[8] *Ibid.*
[9] 110 *Cong. Rec.* 7213.
[10] The Miami *Herald*, November 11, 1971.
[11] *Weeks v. Southern Bell Telephone & Telegraph Company*, 408 F.2d 228 (5th Cir. 1969).
[12] *Weeks v. Southern Bell Telephone & Telegraph Company*, 277 F. Supp. 177 (S.D. Ga. 1967).
[13] 29 C.F.R. §1604.1 (3) (b) (1968).
[14] 29 C.F.R. §1604.1 (b) (2) (1970).
[15] *Bowe v. Colgate-Palmolive Co.*, 272 F. Supp. 332 (S.D. Ind. 1967).
[16] *Op. cit.*, see footnote 12.
[17] *Griggs v. Duke Power Co.*, 420 F.2d 1225 (4th Cir.), 91 S. Ct. 849, 39 L.W. 4317 (1971).
[18] *Ibid.*
[19] U.S. Equal Employment Opportunity Commission, Washington, D.C., *Toward Job Equality for Women*, 1969, pp. 5 ff. Section 713 (b), 78 Stat. 265, 42 U.S.C., Sec. 2000e–12.
[20] 29 U.S.C. §206(d) (1965).
[21] *Wirtz v. Wheaton Glass Co.*, 284 F. Supp. 23 (D.N.J. 1968), rev'd sub nom; *Schultz v. Wheaton Glass Co.*, 421 F.2d 259 (3rd Cir. 1970), *cert. denied* 398 U.S. 905 (1970).
[22] Memo from the U.S. Department of Labor, August 10, 1971.

[23] Syracuse *Post-Standard*, December 1, 1971.

[24] Memo from the U.S. Department of Labor, July 23, 1971.

[25] *Ibid*.

[26] The Miami *Herald*, October 22, 1971.

[27] *The New York Times*, December 17, 1972.

[28] Memo from the U.S. Department of Labor, June 23, 1972.

[29] *Ibid*.

[30] 42 U.S.C. §2000e–6 (a) (1964).

[31] 42 U.S.C. §2000e–5 (e).

[32] Bird, Carolyn, *Born Female: The High Cost of Keeping Women Down*, New York: David McKay Company, Inc., 1968, pp. 4 ff.

[33] *Ibid*.

[34] *Op. cit.*, see footnote 32.

[35] *Op. cit.*, see footnote 32.

[36] *The New York Times* editorial, August 21, 1965, "De-Sexing the Job Market."

[37] 29 U.S.C. §206 (d) (2) (1964).

[38] Leo Kanowitz, *Women and the Law*, Albuquerque, New Mexico: University of New Mexico Press, 1969, p. 135.

[39] 29 C.F.R. §800.106 (1968).

[40] *Murphy v. Miller Brewing Co.* [1965–1968 Transfer Binder]. CCH Empl. Pract. Guide ¶8069 (1966).

[41] Wisc. State Ann. §§111:31–.37 (1961).

[42] *Op. cit.*, see footnote 40.

[43] *Bowe v. Colgate-Palmolive Company*, 272 F. Supp. 332, 358 (S.D. Ind. 1967).

[44] Personal communication, October 5, 1971.

CHAPTER SIX: MONEY AND EMPLOYMENT (3)

[1] The Miami *Herald*, January 7, 1973.

[2] *Majority Report*, December 1972.

[3] *Ibid*.

[4] Mortgages article by Marilyn Goldstein, Newsday Service, January 7, 1973.

[5] *Ibid*.

6 *Op. cit.*, see footnote 4.

7 *In Matter of Carroll v. Flushing Federal Savings.*

8 The Miami *Herald*, January 7, 1973, by Eli Adams, *Herald* real estate editor.

9 *McCall's*, "The Credit Game—Unfair to Women?" September 1972.

10 *Reed v. Reed*, 40 USLW 19 (1971).

11 1963 Colo. Revised Statute 43–1–10.

12 Sec. 90–2–10.

13 Written in 1963.

14 Reported in the Denver *NOW newsletter*.

15 UCC, §3–305.

16 UCC, §3–302.

17 Uniform Laws Comment, §3–305, ¶ 7.

18 For the analysis of the tax code, I am grateful to Richard Abt, a New York tax attorney.

19 As a result of the Revenue Act of 1971.

20 *Moritz v. Commissioner*, 41 U.S.L.W. 2293 (10th Cir., November 22, 1972).

21 Internal Revenue Code, §152 (a).

22 Bonfield, *The Substance of American Fair Employment Practices* Legislation I: Employers, 61 Nw.U.L.Rev. 907 (1967).

23 The Illinois cases in this chapter were supplied to me by Charlotte Adelman, a Chicago attorney.
Alice Waterman v. Village of Northbrook, Charge no. 71NS–4, in the Fair Employment Practices Commission of the State of Illinois.

24 FEPC appeal was decided on December 11, 1972.

25 *Virginia Wisdom v. Rush Presbyterian St. Luke's Medical Center*, Charge no. 71NS–8, in the Fair Employment Practices Commission of the State of Illinois.

26 Ill. Rev. Stat. Ch. 48, Sec. 852 (d), Illinois Fair Employment Practices Act.

27 August 30, 1972.

28 *Pat Greenfield et al. v. Field Enterprises, Inc., et al.*; 71 C 2075, filed in the U.S. District Court for the Northern District of Illinois, Eastern Division. Suit filed on August 25, 1971.

29 February 1, 1972, Judge Frank McGarr.

30 *Civil Liberties,* December 1971.

[31] *Civil Liberties in New York*, December 1972–January 1973.

[32] *The New York Times*, December 20, 1972.

[33] *Lea v. Cone Mills Corp.*, 39 L.W. 2454.

[34] *Newman v. Piggie Park Enterprises, Inc.*, 390 U.S. 400 (1968).

[35] *Local Union No. 12, United Rubber, Cork, Linoleum & Plastic Workers of America v. National Labor Relations Board*, 368 F.2d 12 (5th Cir., 1966).

[36] *Ibid.*

[37] *Vaca v. Sipes*, 386 U.S. 171 (1967).

[38] *Local 189, United Papermakers and Paperworkers v. United States*, United States Court of Appeals, Fifth Circuit, 416 F.2d 980 (1969), *cert. denied*, 397 U.S. 919 (1970).

[39] *Griggs v. Duke Power Co.*, 420 F.2d 1225 (4th Cir.), 91 S. Ct. 849, 39 L.W. 4317 (1971).

[40] EEOC, Employee Selection Guidelines, August 1, 1970.

[41] *Ibid.*

[42] *General Motors Corp. v. United Automobile Workers*, Umpire Decision No. B-52 (1941).

[43] G. N. Alexander, "Seniority Provisions in Arbitration," Proceedings, 1950 University of Michigan Law School Summer Institute on "The Law and Labor Management Relations," pp. 240–42.

[44] *EEOC v. Woolco Dept.*, 39 L.W. 2417.

[45] Judicial Code Section 1337; the Civil Rights Act was enacted under the Commerce Clause.

[46] *Smith v. Hampton Training School for Nurses*, 360 F.2d 577 (4th Cir., 1966).

[47] *Bennett v. Gravelle*, 39 L.W. 2415.

[48] Universal Military Training and Service Act, 50 U.S.C. App. C.C. 459 (b) (g) (1964).

[49] The Miami *Herald*, January 7, 1973.

[50] Syracuse *Post-Standard*, January 19, 1973.

[51] *The New York Times*, January 21, 1973.

[52] Associated Press story, January 19, 1973.

CHAPTER SEVEN: ESTATE LAW

[1] *In re Strittmater's Estate*, 140 N.J. Eq. 94, 53 A.2d 205 (1947).

[2] *Greene v. Greene*, 145 Ill. 264, 33 N.E. 941.

[3] *Rice v. Rice*, 50 Mich. 448, 15 N.W. 545.

[4] §3–07.

[5] *Op. cit.*, see footnote 1.

[6] *In re Hoover's Estate*, 91 A.2d 155, 21 N.J. Super. 323.

[7] *In re Ruedy's Estate*, 66 N W 2d 387.

[8] *In re O'Neil's Estate*, 212 P.2d 823.

[9] Boyer, Gene, *Are Women Equal Under the Law?* Beaver Dam, Wisconsin, June 1971.

[10] Women's Bureau, U.S. Dept. of Labor.

[11] Cowan, Ronnie, "Doris Day: My Most Costly Mistake As a Wife," *Ladies' Home Journal*, January 1973.

[12] *Ibid*.

[13] Story, Ag. §2.

[14] Hunter, Rom. Law §49.

[15] *Black's Law Dictionary*, Revised Fourth Edition.

[16] Mackeld Rom. Law, §589.

[17] 5 Ir. Ch. Rep. 525.

[18] Deed of Rose, and Eliza Rose, Book 63, Page 301, August 20, 1836. Town of Salina (New York), School 12.

[19] The Miami *Herald*, December 3, 1971.

[20] II Blackstone, *Commentaries* (1765) 208 et seq.

[21] 32 Hen. VIII, c.1 (1540).

[22] The Bill Concerning the Explanation of Wills, 34 & 35 Hen. VIII, c. 5 (1542–43).

[23] 15 Geo. V, c.23 (1925).

[24] A uniform table of descent and distribution was contained in the Law of Property Act, 12 & 13 Geo. V, c. 16 (1922), but the operation of this statute was postponed.

[25] 15 & 16 Geo. VI & 1 Eliz. II, c.64 (1952).

[26] 14 & 15 Eliz. II, C. 35 (1966).

[27] Uniform Probate Code, §2–108.

[28] 13 Edw. I, c. 34 (1285).

[29] E.g., *Turner v. Cole*, 24 Ala. 364 (1854); *Mack v. Pairo*, 136 Md. 179, 110 A. 198 (1920).

[30] *Davis v. Davis' Estate*, 167 Wisc. 328, 167, N.W. 819 (1918).

[31] E.g., *In re Abila's Estate*, 32 Cal. 2d 559, 197 P.2d 10 (1948).

[32] *Underhill v. United States Trust Co.*, Court of Appeals of Kentucky, 1929, 227 Ky. 444, 13 S.W. 2d 502.

[33] Ritchie, Alford, and Effland, *Cases and Materials on Decedent's Estates and Trusts*, Mineola, New York: The Foundation Press, Inc., 1971, pp. 355 ff.

CHAPTER EIGHT: FAMILY LAW

[1] *U.S. v. Dege*, 364 U.S. 51 (1960).

[2] *Time-O-Matic, Inc. v. N.L.R.B.*, 264 F.2d 96 (7th Cir. 1959); *N.L.R.B. v. Ford*, 170 F.2d 735 (6th Cir. 1948); *Drennon Food Prod. Co.*, 122 N.L.R.B. 1353 (1959), *enforced in part*, 272 F.2d 23 (5th Cir. 1959).

[3] Gilman, Charlotte Perkins, *Women and Economics*, 1898.

[4] Rosenfarb, J., *The National Labor Policy and How It Works* 79 (1940).

[5] *N.L.R.B. v. Federbush Co.*, 121 F.2d 954, 957 (2nd Cir. 1941).

[6] *International Association of Machinists v. N.L.R.B.*, 311 U.S. 72, 78 (1940).

[7] *Op. cit.*, see footnote 3.

[8] *Ibid.*

[9] *Ibid.*

[10] Hawkins, *Pleas of the Crown*, 4th ed. 1792, Book I, Chapter xxii, Section 8, page 192.

[11] *Op. cit.*, see footnote 3.

[12] *Commonwealth v. Jones*, 1 Pa. D. & C. 2d 269, 274–75 (Leh. County Ct., 1954).

[13] *Time*, March 20, 1972.

[14] *McGuire v. McGuire*, 157 Neb. 226, 59 N.W.2d 336 (1953).

[15] Blackstone, *Commentaries* 433.

[16] *State v. Gardner*, 174 Iowa 748, 156 N.W. 747 (1916).

[17] Kanowitz, Leo, *Women and the Law: The Unfinished Revolution*, Albuquerque: University of New Mexico Press, 1969.

[18] Warren, "Husband's Rights to Wife's Services," 38 *Harv. L. Rev.* 421, 423 (1925).

[19] Tolchin, Martin, "Jewish Family Problems Are Settled out of Court," *The New York Times*, August 4, 1962, p. 28, col. 7.

[20] Ohio Rev. Code Ann. §3103.03, page 1060.

[21] Iowa Code Ann. 597.14 (1950).

[22] Many of these statistics come from a compilation by Gene Boyer, 218 Front Street, Beaver Dam, Wisconsin. They were gathered in May 1970, and revised in June 1971. Ms. Boyer's primary sources are publications of the Women's Bureau, U.S. Dept. of Labor.

[23] Seidenberg, Robert, *Corporative Wives, Corporate Casualties*, New York: American Management Association, 1973.

[24] "The Geography of Inequality—Women's Legal Rights in 50 States," *McCall's Magazine*, February 1971.

[25] *Op. cit.*, footnote 17.

[26] *Reimann v. Reimann*, 1942, 39 NYS2d 485.

[27] *Black's Law Dictionary*, Revised 4th edition, p. 299.

[28] *Wood v. State*, 48 Ga. 288, 15 Am. Rep. 664.

[29] *Domschke v. Domschke*, 1910, 138 App. Div. 454, 122 NYS 892.

[30] Reported in the Miami *Herald*, October 15, 1971.

[31] *People v. Gerow*, 1910, 136 App. Div. 824, 121 NYS 652.

[32] *People v. Lawson*, 1906, 111 App. Div. 473, 98 NYS 130.

[33] *Bunim v. Bunim*, 298, N.Y. 391, 83 N.E.2d 848 (1949).

[34] 24 *Notre Dame Law.* 597, 599 (1949).

[35] *Hild v. Hild*, 221 Md. 349, 157 A.2d 442 (1960).

[36] *Grimditch v. Grimditch*, 71 Arizona.

[37] *Shrout v. Shrout*, 224 Ore. 521, 356 P.2d 935 (1960).

[38] *People v. Snell*, 1912, 77 Misc. 538, 137, NYS 193.

[39] *Ullman v. Ullman*, 1912, 151 App. Div. 419, 135 N.Y.S. 1080.

[40] *Application of Kades*, 1960, 25 Misc.2d 246, 202 N.Y.S.2d 362.

[41] *Bowler v. Bowler*, 355 Mich. 686, 96 N.W.2d (1959).

[42] Complete text, as well as other information on changing the marriage and divorce laws, is available from Betty Berry, Chairwoman, NOW Task Force on Marriage and Divorce, 541 E. 20th Street, New York, New York 10010.

[43] New York Domestic Relations Law, Article 4, §50.

[44] *Marks v. Marks*, 1937, 250 App. Div. 289, 294, NYS 70.

[45] *Aaronson v. McCauley*, 1892, 19 NYS 690.

[46] See footnote 22.

[47] "Sicilian-Style Divorce Rough" by William Tuohy, the Miami *Herald*, May 7, 1972.

CHAPTER NINE: CRIMINAL LAW

[1] *The New York Times*, November 6, 1970.

[2] *Ibid.*

[3] *Ibid.*

[4] Verified by Lt. Col. L. Stephen Quatennens, Office of the Sec. of the Army.

[5] Henry Noble, in *Capital M*.

[6] Havelock Ellis.

[7] Shulman, Alix, "The Most Dangerous Woman in the World," New York: Times Change Press, 1970.

[8] Goldman, Emma, "The Traffic in Women," New York: Times Change Press, 1970. (Essay written in 1917.)

[9] *Ibid.*

[10] Goldman, Emma, "Marriage and Love," New York: Times Change Press, 1970. (Essay written in 1917.)

[11] John M. Murtagh and Sara Harris, *Cast the First Stone*, New York: McGraw-Hill Book Company, Inc., 1957.

[12] *Manley v. Manley*, 193 Pa. Super., 252, 264–65, 164 A.2d 113, 120 (1960).

[13] Pfaff, The Conciliation Court of Los Angeles County (litho., 1960), Exhibits No. II, Husband-Wife Agreement, p. 19.

[14] Prosser, *Torts* 896–98, 3rd ed., 1964.

[15] *Commonwealth v. Jones*, 1 Pa. D & C2d 269, 274–75 (Leh. County Ct., 1954).

[16] The Miami *Herald*, December 10, 1970.

[17] *Civil Liberties*, March 1971, p. 8.

[18] *Judicial Treatment of Negligent Invasion of Consortium*, 61 Colum. L. Rev. (1961). 1347–57.

[19] *Lockwoor v. Wilson H. Lee Co.*, 144 Conn. 155, 128 A2d 330 (1956).

[20] *Clark v. Southwestern Greyhound Lines*, 144 Kan. 344, 58 P.2d 1128 (1936).

[21] *Montgomery v. Stephen*, 359 Mich. 33, 101 N.W.2d 227 (1960); *Hitaffer v. Argonne Co.*, 183 F.2d 811 (D.C. Cir.), *cert. denied*, 340 U.S. 852 (1950); Annot., 28 A.L.R.2d 1378 (1952).

[22] da Costa, Mendes, "Criminal Law," *A Century of Family Law* 165, 181 (Graveson & Crane, eds., 1957).

[23] 1 Hale, Pleas of the Crown. 628 (1800).

[24] *Wyatt v. United States*, 362 U.S. 525, at 534.

[25] *In re Barbara Jean Cager et al.*, 248 At. Reporter2d 384 (1968).

[26] *Ibid.*

[27] Central Soviet, *On the Sentence in the "Judicial Proceedings Concerning a Prostitute,"* Rabochaya Gaesta (1925).

[28] *Carpenter v. People*, 8 Barb. N.Y., 610.

[29] *Com. v. Cook*, 12 Metc., Mass., 97.

[30] *People v. Rice*, 277 Ill. 521, 115 N.E. 631, 632.

[31] *State v. Stoyell*, 54 Me. 24, 89 Am. Dec. 716.

[32] *Wilson v. State*, 17 Ala. App. 307, 84, So. 783.

[33] *Trent v. Commonwealth*, 181 Va. 338, 25 S.E. 2d 350, 352.

[34] 18 USC, §2421–24.

[35] §230.00

[36] *Collette v. Morehead*, 1944, 50 N.Y.S.2d, 78.

[37] §230.05

[38] §230.10

[39] §70.15 (4).

[40] Flexner, *Prostitution in Europe*, App. iv, pp. 432–33.

[41] The Washington *Post*, February 17, 1973.

[42] *People v. Draper*, 169 App. Div. 479, 484, 154 N.Y.S. 1034, 1038 (1915).

[43] §230.30

[44] 1 N.Y. 2d 321, 152 N.Y.S.2d 479 (1956).

[45] *Ibid.*

[46] Antin, Eleanor, *ARTnews*, January 1971, p. 45.

[47] Lenin, V.I., "The Fifth International Congress for Combatting Prostitution," *Rabochaya Pravda*, July 26, 1913.

[48] Dickey, Anthony, "Soliciting for the Purpose of Prostitution," *Crim. L.R.* 1969: 538, October 1969.

[49] de Beauvoir, Simone, *The Second Sex*, New York: Bantam Books, translated and edited by H.M. Parshley, 1952.

[50] *Ibid.*, p. 578.

[51] Parl. Deb., Commons 1958–59, vol. 598, col. 1378 (January 29, 1959).

[52] Seidenberg, Robert, *Marriage in Life and Literature*, New York: Philosophical Library, 1970, p. 295; *Marriage Between Equals,* New York: Doubleday, Anchor, 1973.

[53] *The Times*, December 7, 1962, p. 6.

[54] Shakespeare, William, *The Taming of the Shrew*, Act III, Scene 2.

[55] 2 Pollack and Maitland 403.

[56] *Graham v. Graham*, 33 F. Supp. 936 (E. D. Mich. 1940).

[57] *Ms.*, December 1972, p. 128.

[58] *The Oswegonian*, December 7, 1972.

[59] "While moving to change the world, we must, on the way, live in it," Report by Jean Withers, Seattle NOW, May 1972.

[60] *The New York Times*, January 28, 1973.

[61] Uniform Crime Reports, 12–13, 1967, Department of Justice, FBI.

[62] Jo-Ann Evans Gardner, testifying for NOW. Recommendations to the Republican National Committee, Resolutions Committee, August 15, 1972.

[63] *The New York Times Magazine*, January 30, 1972.

[64] *The Vocal Majority*, December 1971.

[65] Uniform Crime Reports, 1970, Department of Justice, FBI.

[66] Essex County (N.J.) *NOW newsletter.*

[67] *The People of the State of New York v. Melvin Linzy also known as Melvin Linear*, 31 N.Y.2d 99, July 7, 1972.

[68] Penal Law, §130.15.

[69] *Op. cit.*, see footnote 67.

[70] *Ibid.*

[71] New York Family Court Act, §712 (b).

[72] *Ms.*, November 1972.

[73] Texas Penal Code 1220; Utah Code 76–30–10 (4).

[74] *United States ex. rel. Robinson v. York*, 281 F. Supp. (D. Conn. 1968).

[75] *Commonwealth v. Daniel*, 430 Pa. 642, 243, A2d 400 (1968).

[76] *Liberti v. York*, 246 A2d 106, 28 Conn. 9 (1968).

[77] Attorney is Aldridge and Pearlman, Albuquerque, New Mexico, for the NOW Legal Defense and Education Fund.

[78] *Congressional Record*, June 7, 1972.

[79] Central New Jersey *NOW newsletter*, September 1972.

[80] Jo-Ann Evans Gardner, testifying for NOW. Recommendations to the Republican National Committee, Resolutions Committee, August 15, 1972.

[81] The Miami *Herald*, May 28, 1972.

[82] *Time*, March 20, 1972.

[83] *Women's Rights Law Reporter*, Vol. I, No. 1.

CHAPTER TEN: MOTHERHOOD AND ABORTION

[1] *The Sunday Record*, August 27, 1972.

[2] Fred C. Shapiro, "Lost Women: The Transcending Margaret Fuller," *Ms.*, November 1972, pp. 36 ff.

[3] Margaret Fuller, "The Great Lawsuit—Men Versus Men, Women Versus Women," *Dial*, 1843.

[4] Kate Millett, *Sexual Politics*, New York: Doubleday, 1970, p. 35.

[5] Bronislaw Malinowski, *Sex, Culture and Myth*, New York: Harcourt, 1962.

[6] Bronislaw Malinowski, *Sex and Repression in Savage Society*, London: Humanities, 1927, p. 213.

[7] Aleta Wallach, "Comparative Legal Status of American and Soviet Women," *Valparaiso University Law Review*, Vol. 5, 1971, pp. 461–63.

[8] Gorkin, "Concern for the Soviet Family," *Soviet Law and Government*, Winter, 1968–69 at 32.

[9] M. Hindus, *House Without a Roof* 20, 1961.

[10] See Law of July 8, 1944, 31 (Supreme Soviet U.S.S.R.), as reported in G. Sverdlov, Sovetskoe Seminoe Pravo (Soviet Family Law) (1958), at 194.

[11] *Levy v. Louisiana*, 391 U.S. 68 (1968).

[12] *Glona v. American Guar. Co.*, 391 U.S. 73 (1968).

[13] 91 S. Ct. (1917) (upholding LA. Civ. Code Ann. 919) (West 1952).

[14] Law of July 8, 1944 (Supreme Soviet U.S.S.R.), 4 Embassy of the U.S.S.R.

[15] Law of July 8, 1944, art. 10 (Supreme Soviet U.S.S.R.).

[16] Law of July 8, 1944, art. 6 (Supreme Soviet U.S.S.R.).

[17] R.S.F.S.R. 161 (Criminal Code) art. 139.

[18] Fundamental Principles, art. 14.

[19] Fundamental Principles, art. 5,

[20] Schlesinger, "The Family in the U.S.S.R.," in *Changing Attitudes in Soviet Russia* 10 (1949).

[21] Quoted in "Comparative Legal Status of American and Soviet Women" by Aleta Wallach, *Valparaiso University Law Review*, Vol. 5, 1971, p. 464.

[22] World Congress of Women, Helsinki, Finland, June 1969.

[23] The Miami *Herald*, December 14, 1972.

[24] Chairone, Berkeley, California, NOW Chapter.

[25] Pat McCormick, "Rebuttal: State Social Welfare Board Position Statement on Illegitimacy."

[26] The Miami *Herald*, November 1971.

[27] *Civil Liberties in New York*, April 1972.

[28] *Ibid.*

[29] *Civil Liberties*, October 1972.

[30] *The New York Times*, October 29, 1972.

[31] Bureau of Labor Statistics, U.S. Department of Labor.

[32] *The New York Times*, January 28, 1973.

[33] *Ibid.*

[34] Syracuse *Post-Standard*, January 9, 1973.

[35] Boyer, Gene, *Are Women Equal Under the Law?* Beaver Dam, Wisconsin, June 1971.

[36] *Antonopoulou v. Beame*, reported in the newsletter of the American Arbitration Association.

[37] The Miami *Herald*, December 23, 1972.

[38] EEOC, Guidelines on Discrimination Because of Sex, Title 29, Labor, Chapter xiv, Part 1604, As Amended.

[39] *State v. Chamberlain*, 175 N.E.2d 539 (Ohio Com. Pl. 1961).

[40] Letter from Norman I. Klein, Member of the Secondary School pamphlet subcommittee, Academic Freedom Committee, American Civil Liberties Union, April 24, 1967.

[41] *Perry v. Grenada Separate School Dist.*, 300 F. Supp. 748 (D. Miss. 1969).

[42] *Ibid.*

[43] *Clydie Marie Perry, by her mother and next friend, Mrs. Rosie Bell Perry v. The Grenada Municipal Separate School District, et al.*, U.S. District Court for the Northern District of Mississippi, Western Division, No. Wc6736.

[44] *Ibid.*

[45] Reported in Chicago *NOW* newsletter, November 1971.

[46] *The New York Times*, October 29, 1972.

[47] *Civil Liberties in New York*, December 1972–January 1973.

[48] *New York Civil Liberties Union*, April 1972.

[49] *Roe v. Wade*, No. 70–18 (314 F. Supp. 1217 (1970)).

[50] *Doe v. Bolton*, No. 70–40 (319 F. Supp. 1048 (1970)); (40 LW 3300, 1971).

[51] *Op. cit.*, see footnote 49.

[52] *The New York Times*, January 28, 1973.

[53] *Ibid.*

[54] *Op. cit.*, see footnote 49.

[55] *Ibid.*

[56] New York *WONAAC Newsletter*, January 26, 1973.

[57] "Freedom for Women—The Supreme Court's Abortion Decisions," Washington, D.C.: Human Rights for Women, Inc.

CHAPTER ELEVEN: THE LAW OF NAMES

[1] William Shakespeare, *Hamlet*, Act I, Sc. 2, line 146.

[2] September 28, 1972.

[3] Boyer, Gene, *Are Women Equal Under the Law?* Beaver Dam, Wisconsin, June 1971.

[4] *In re Kayaloff*, 9 F. Supp. 176 (S.D.N.Y. 1934); *People ex rel. Rago v. Lipsky*, 327 Ill. App. 63, 63 N.E.2d 642 (1945); *Bacon v. Bacon Elec. Ry.*, 256 Mass. 30, 152 N.E. 35 (1926); *Chapman v. Phoenix Nat'l Bank*, 85 N.Y. 437 (1881).

[5] Aleta Wallach has called my attention to Iowa law, which allows a formal name change to be granted to "any person, under no civil disabilities, who has attained his or

her majority and is unmarried if a female." Iowa Code Ann. §671.1 (1947).

⁶ Colorado law allows "every person to change his or her name . . . if the judge is satisfied that the desired change would be proper, *and not detrimental to the interests of any other person*." Colo. Rev. Stat. Ann. 20–1–1 (1963) (emphasis added).

⁷ Washington *Post*, July 15, 1972.

⁸ *Ibid*.

⁹ The Miami *Herald*, November 6, 1971.

¹⁰ Hartford, Conn., September 29, 1972 (Associated Press).

¹¹ West's Louisiana Statutes Annotated, Code of Civil Procedure, Vol. 10, Form No. 208 c.

¹² Mary Meszaros French, "Names, Names, Names, or Who Are You Really?" *Nowletter*, Baton Rouge, La.

¹³ *Ibid*.

¹⁴ Washington *Post*, October 10, 1972.

¹⁵ *Glamour*, Letters to the Editor, December 1972.

¹⁶ Reported by KNOW, Pittsburgh, Pa., December 1972–73.

CHAPTER TWELVE: THE EQUAL RIGHTS AMENDMENT

¹ *Webber v. Webber*, 33 C.2d 153, 199 P.2d 943 (1948).

² John D. Johnston, Jr., and Charles L. Knapp, "Sex Discrimination by Law," *NYU Law Review*, October 1971.

³ *Reed v. Reed*, 92 S. Ct. 251 (1971).

⁴ *Ibid*.

⁵ 93 Idaho, at 514. 465 P.2d, at 638.

⁶ *Congressional Record*, November 20, 1971, Vol. 117, No. 80, S19424.

⁷ Idaho Code, §15–312.

⁸ Bird, Carolyn, Hearings on the Equal Rights Amendment Before Subcommittee on Constitutional Amendments of the Senate Committee of the Judiciary, 91st Congress, 2nd Session at 347 (May 1970).

⁹ *Higher Education Guidelines*, Office of Civil Rights, Department of Health, Education and Welfare, Executive Order 11246.

¹⁰ Gompers, Samuel, Editorial in *American Federation-*

ist, August 1913. Courtesy of Ann Scott and Aileen Hernandez, NOW.

[11] Jack M. Sable, Statement made on December 12, 1972, at Joint Legislative Hearings, Albany, New York.

[12] Women's Bureau, U.S. Dept. of Labor.

[13] Report No. 92–689, 92nd Congress, 2nd Session.

[14] *Yale Law Journal*, April 1971, Vol. 80, No. 5, pp. 871–985.

[15] *The liberated woman's appointment calendar and field manual*, New York: Universe Books, 1972.

[16] "The Equal Rights Amendment and Alimony and Child Support Laws," Citizens' Advisory Council on the Status of Women, U.S. Department of Labor, Washington, D.C., January 1972.

[17] "The Equal Rights Amendment: A Constitutional Basis for Equal Rights for Women," Brown, Emerson, Falk, and Freedman, 80 *Yale L.J.* 943, 1971.

[18] A California judge.

[19] 24 Am Jur 2d 633.

[20] *McEachnie v. McEachnie*, D.C. App. 216 A.2d 169 (1966).

[21] *Lamborn v. Lamborn*, 80 C.A. 494, 251 P. 943 (1926).

[22] Women's Bureau, U.S. Dept. of Labor.

[23] The Council of State Governments lists Arkansas, Idaho, Nevada, North Dakota, Oklahoma, South Dakota, and Utah as having such laws. Council of State Governments, Reciprocal State Legislation to Enforce the Support of Dependents 20 (1964). My thanks to Mary Eastwood for these sources.

[24] *Johnson v. State*, 476 P.2d 397 (Okla. Crim. App. 1970).

[25] Steele, "The Legal Status of Women," in *The Book of the States* 309, Council of State Governments, 1970.

[26] *Op. cit.*, see footnote 16.

[27] Nagel and Weitzman, "Women as Litigants," *Hastings Law Journal*, November 1971.

[28] *Op. cit.*, see footnote 26.

[29] U.S. Dept. of Commerce, Bureau of the Census, *Social and Economic Variations in Marriage, Divorce and Remarriage*, 1967; P–20, No. 223.

[30] Citizens' Advisory Council on the Status of Women,

Report of the Task Force on Social Insurance and Taxes
44–46 (1968).

[31] "The Equal Rights Amendment—What It Will and Won't Do," Citizens' Advisory Council on the Status of Women, U.S. Department of Labor, Washington, D.C.

[32] *Op. cit.*, see footnote 17.

[33] Alaska, Arkansas, Delaware, Hawaii, and Wisconsin.

[34] Women's Bureau, U.S. Dept. of Labor.

[35] *Ibid.* A District of Columbia law allowing women to be excused because of sex was repealed in 1968.

[36] *White v. Crook*, 351 F. Supp. 401 (M.D. Ala. 1966).

[37] List from Jean Witter, Equal Rights Amendment Commmittee, Pittsburgh, Pa.

[38] Senate Report no. 92–689.

[39] 50 U.S.C. App. §§451, 453 (1964).

[40] August 10, 1970. 116 *Congressional Record* H7953.

[41] Turner, "Women in Military Services," *Defense Management J.*, Winter 1970, at 12.

[42] Holm, "Women and Future Manpower Needs," *Defense Management J.*, Winter 1970, at 10.

[43] "Women and the Draft: What Does Equal Rights Mean?" Women United, Arlington, Va.

[44] Hearings before House Judiciary Committee Subcommittee no. 4, 1971.

[45] Public Law 625, 77th Congress.

[46] Senate Report no. 92–689.

[47] Washington *Post*, October 26, 1972.

[48] The Miami *Herald*, October 16, 1970.

CHAPTER THIRTEEN: SEXISM IN EDUCATION

[1] Claudia Dreifus, "Diary of a Traveling Feminist," *Social Policy*, November–December 1972/January–February 1973, p. 35.

[2] *Ibid.*

[3] The Miami *Herald*, December 17, 1972.

[4] U.S. Office of Education, Department of Health, Education and Welfare, *A Look at Women in Education*, 1972.

[5] Baldwinsville, New York, May 16, 1972.

[6] In the Matter of the Application of the Board of Education of the Syracuse School District, For a Judgment

Under Article 78 of the Civil Practice Law and Rules, v. The State Division of Human Rights and the members of the same: Robert J. Mangum as Commissioner of the State Division of Human Rights; Neal M. Hoffman, Regional Director of the State Division of Human Rights; and Marilyn J. Patrick and Carolyn S. Bratt, Supreme Court of the State of New York, Appellate Division: Fourth Department, November 22, 1971.

7 Gene Boyer, "There Ought To Be A Law! (Like the Equal Rights Amendment)," Wisconsin Psychiatric Institute *Forum*, No. 2, 1971.

About the Author

KAREN DeCROW, president of the National Organization for Women (NOW), is herself a lawyer. She holds a Bachelor of Science degree in journalism and received her law degree from Syracuse University. In 1969 she ran for mayor of Syracuse, New York. Ms. DeCrow lectures extensively throughout the country and frequently contributes articles to magazines and journals. She is the author of *The Young Woman's Guide to Liberation*.